Elizabeth Palmer Peabody
KINDERGARTEN PIONEER

Elizabeth Peabody of Salem. Portrait by Charles C. Burleigh, Jr., 1878.

Elizabeth Palmer Peabody

KINDERGARTEN PIONEER

by
Ruth M. Baylor

Philadelphia
University of Pennsylvania Press

7473

Printed in the United States of America

Preface

ALTHOUGH THE CHOICE OF THE TOPIC OF THIS BOOK WAS A natural consequence of the author's deep and continuous interest in early childhood education, yet the search for additional primary materials involved the enlightened assistance of scholars who had related interests. Thus, instead of a solitary and cloistered effort, the venture was made the more stimulating and enjoyable when aided by such knowledgeable guides. To these persons, engaged in varied literary and educational pursuits, the author wishes to express her indebtedness and gratitude.

Foremost is the late Robert Lincoln Straker. Over a period of many years, Mr. Straker collected and classified materials about Horace Mann. Because of Mann's marriage to Mary Peabody, many materials pertained to his sister-in-law, Elizabeth Peabody. The methodical and meticulous arrangement of these papers is as great a feat of scholarship as the research involved in gathering them from diverse sources. Mr. Straker's purpose was, as he explained to the author at one of many conferences in 1959, to make available to students a comprehensive body of accurate informa-

5

tion relating to Horace Mann. These papers now form part of the Antiochiana Collection in the Olive Kettering Library on the campus of Antioch College.

Mrs. Arthur C. Holden offered the generous hospitality of her extensive personal library. Through her unsolicited, and therefore the more appreciated, efforts, contact was made with authors of allied or related topics. The exchange of information thus brought about was stimualting and revealed many hitherto unknown techniques of research.

To Mr. Thomas H. de Valcourt, Curator of Longfellow House, thanks are due for assistance in determining dates of certain letters. Mrs. Gladys B. Jones, President of Garland Junior College, invited inspection of the holograph records of Miss Mary Garland. In Mrs. Jones's custody were also found early publications of the Eastern Kindergarten Association. For the undisturbed examination of these and other materials, appreciation is expressed. The Essex Institute of Salem, through its Director, Dean A. Fales, Jr., and its Curator, Miss Hulda Smith, gave permission for the reproduction of the portrait of Miss Peabody and of the Peabody family silhouette. Miss Marie Cotter, Librarian at Wheelock College, was most helpful in supplying the names and addresses of persons who knew of the whereabouts of materials concerning Miss Peabody. In this respect the suggestions of Mrs. Barbara Miller Solomon, Director of Women's Archives, Radcliffe College, proved of great value.

Gratitude for the courtesies extended by the staffs of the many museums and libraries noted in the bibliography is hereby expressed. Their gracious and intelligent cooperation greatly lightened the burden of research.

Mr. Paul Bisgaier, of the Board of Education of New York City, took time from his busy schedule to read the manuscript and to give helpful suggestions.

It remains to speak with appreciation of those Professors of Education whose assistance and patience have guided the study from its inception. Professor William W. Brickman of the University of Pennsylvania has given freely of his time and knowledge. To his prodigious memory for facts and events and to his painstaking editing may be attributed whatever degree of accuracy may be found in the study. Professor George Manolakes of New York University has by his example kept alive the image of the ideal teacher shared by Elizabeth Peabody and Friedrich Froebel. Dr. Robert S. Fleming of the Education Department of the State of New Jersey has provided the connecting link between past kindergarten history and that which is now in the making. Without his awareness and reminder of the value of both, the writer may have become so engrossed with the study of the past for its own sake as to have vitiated its interpretation. This would have been contrary to the spirit in which the study was conceived originally. To consider the present as a continuation of the past is a practice which Elizabeth Peabody would have approved.

If there were to be a dedication, then certainly that would be addressed to the writer's daughter, Joan Baylor Schilder. Without her encouragement and editorial criticism, this book must have suffered in the writing.

Never can a completed work entirely satisfy its maker. The pleasure of accomplishment is marred by the awareness of imperfections. The greatest satisfaction to be reached in retrospect is the realization that new areas of research may be suggested by this study.

Contents

Preface 5

Introduction 13

I The Origin of the Kindergarten 23

II Early Life of Elizabeth Palmer Peabody 41

III "Miss Thesaura" 64

IV The Kindergarten Experiment, 1860-1870 84

V Crusade For Kindergartens, 1870-1890 101

VI Kindergarten Training Schools 122

VII Elizabeth Peabody's Philosophy of Education 148

VIII Influence on American Education 163

Appendix A List of Books From Miss Peabody's Library and Bookshop 175

B Ruth M. Baylor Collection of Holograph Material on Miss Peabody 177

C Chronology of the Development of Kindergartens in America 179

Bibliography 191

Index 225

Illustrations

Elizabeth Peabody of Salem   Frontispiece
The following appear as a group after page 132:

Friedrich Froebel

Holograph letter from Friedrich Froebel to a German kindergartner

"Patche Kuchen," one of Froebel's Mother Plays

Silhouettes of the family of Dr. Nathaniel Peabody

Portrait of Elizabeth Palmer Peabody accompanying the sonnet in her honor

Kindergarten class of the West Newton English and Classical School

Froebel's Kindergarten Occupations

Holograph postcard from Elizabeth P. Peabody to Reverend Mr. Chaney

Replica of monument to Friedrich Froebel

Mrs. Eudora L. Hailmann's Training School for Kindergartners and Primary Teachers

Tombstone of Elizabeth Palmer Peabody

Introduction

WHEN INTEREST IN THE PAST IS WELDED TO CONCERN FOR THE present, both are benefited. The reactionary tendency of the first is alleviated and the comprehension of the second is increased. The recognition of the need for study of the past to supplement the experimentation of the present was the general motive for embarking upon a topic requiring historical research. "In the past we find the present reflected and the trend of tomorrow indicated."[1]

At successive times, the writer has been a kindergarten teacher, the mother of two children who attended kindergarten, an active proponent of state legislative support for kindergartens, an interested participant in kindergarten mothers' clubs and parent associations, an instructor in kindergarten methods for public school kindergarten and primary grade teachers, and a supervisor of student teachers in early childhood education. In these capacities, contact with parents, the lay community, politicians, teachers, and

[1] Myrtle M. Imhoff, *Early Elementary Education*, p. 22.

13

administrators has revealed an acceptance of the kindergarten, which is in accord with recent studies.[2] However,
also revealed from these contacts was the lack of understanding and knowledge of kindergarten's former sphere
of influence in community life, and the absence of realization of its possibilities in the solution of current social
problems. An awareness by lay and professional persons of
how the kindergarten has met community and child needs
in the past, and how it may do so in the future, is necessary
for the fulfilment of the potentialities of the kindergarten.[3]
To initiate, contribute to, and participate in this reawaken-
ing and reappraisal were motivations which inspired the
investigator to undertake this study.

How the kindergarten became an accepted and respected
institution in American education, why it flourished, and
who was responsible for the pioneer efforts are questions
relevant to a present-day appraisal. Even the most cursory
glance at the history of kindergarten education reveals
Elizabeth Palmer Peabody's unique position in its development.[4] Miss Peabody founded the first kindergarten conducted in the English language in the United States.[5]
Thenceforth, as pioneer and apostle, her name was forever
intertwined with its history. A study of the history of kin-

[2] Arch K. Steiner, "A Report on State Laws, Early Elementary Education," *School Life,* Vol. 39, No. 8, May 1957, pp. 7-9.

[3] Hazel F. Gabbard, *A Nation's Concern for Kindergartens,* Office of
Education, U. S. Department of Health, Education, and Welfare. Washington, D.C.: Superintendent of Documents, Government Printing Office,
1959. Chapter 2.

[4] George H. Martin, *Evolution of the Massachusetts Public School System,* p. 255. ". . . Apostle of the Kindergarten Movement in Massachusetts
and to her efforts with tongue and pen is due whatever success the movement has had."

Richard G. Boone, *Education in the United States,* p. 332. "Hers was
the first literature on the subject [kindergartens] . . . hers a pioneer labor."

[5] Stephen Duggan, *A Student's Textbook in the History of the United
States,* p. 265.

dergarten education in America involved, at the outset, the acknowledgment of her achievement.

If we accept the statement of William T. Harris that "the essential truth is not the present fact, but the entire process by which the present fact grew to be what it is,"[6] then to accept the existence of the kindergarten without knowledge of Miss Peabody's part in bringing it into being would be ignorance of the whole truth. Brubacher reminded us that if it were not for such pioneering persons, innovations like the kindergarten might not have become successful parts of the American public school system.[7] In consideration of these opinions, and in recognition of Elizabeth Peabody's connection with the establishment of kindergartens in the United States, this study proposes to investigate the role of Elizabeth Palmer Peabody (1804-1894) in the establishment and development of kindergarten education in the United States, with particular attention to the period of Miss Peabody's activities in its behalf.

Of the 4,101,000 five-year-old children in the United States, according to the latest figures available, 2,208,000, or 53.8 per cent, were enrolled in kindergartens, public and private.[8] Forty-six states have enacted some legislation authorizing localities to provide for kindergartens.[9] This dramatic increase from the one private kindergarten in the city of Boston in 1860 is evidence that kindergarten education has flourished in America, as its German founder, Friedrich Froebel, had foretold when he said:

Now, if they will not recognize and support my cause in my native country, I will go to America, where a new life is freely

[6] William T. Harris, "Editor's Preface," in Robert H. Quick, *Essays on Educational Reformers*, p. ix.

[7] John S. Brubacher, *A History of the Problems of Education*, p. 561.

[8] U. S. Office of Education, *Statistics of Kindergarten Enrollment in U. S. A.*, October, 1962. Washington, D.C. Bureau of the Census.

[9] Steiner, *op. cit.*, p. 7.

unfolding itself, and a new education of man will find a footing.[10]

The "footing" which the new education found is significant not only on the basis of quantitative growth but also because of its influence upon the program of elementary education. Parker noted that "the United States has adopted and developed the kindergarten more thoroughly than any European country."[11] Imhoff explained in more detail:

> Froebel contributed the kindergarten to the early elementary education field; the kindergarten, in turn influenced the whole of American education.[12]

An institution which affects so many young children directly, and which has influenced indirectly the methods and curriculum of the American educational program, deserves recurrent scrutiny. As Holmes has indicated, the task of adapting kindergarten education is not finished, for the organization of American education is "far from perfect."[13] In 1913, the International Kindergarten Union authorized a restatement of kindergarten principles "in the light of recent contributions of biology, sociology, and modern psychology."[14] Much research in the development of young children has taken place since that time. Miss Peabody's interpretation of Froebel's theories are not those

[10] Baroness B. Von Marenholtz-Bülow, *Reminiscences of Friedrich Froebel*, p. 200.

[11] Samuel C. Parker, *A Textbook in the History of Modern Elementary Education*, p. 454.

[12] Imhoff, *op. cit.*, p. 265.

[13] Henry Wyman Holmes, Committee of Nineteen, International Kindergarten Union (eds.), *The Kindergarten*, p. ix.

[14] Lucy Wheelock, "Preface," *Ibid.*, p. iii.

which today govern kindergarten education. Are there values in Miss Peabody's idealistic kindergarten philosophy which are pertinent to today's problems? To judge the significance of Elizabeth Peabody's efforts, a "doctrine of continuous criticism,"[15] must be applied to her philosophy and practices.

It has been recognized that the firmly established place of the kindergarten as an institution is due to the effort and devotion of its pioneers quite as much as it is due to the forces and circumstances of their time.[16] A tangible form of this debt of gratitude was the volume, *Pioneers of the Kindergarten in America,* authorized by the International Kindergarten Union in 1924. It was largely biographical, uncritical, and laudatory, as was consistent with its avowed purpose. It contained, as Professor Brickman noted, "popular, undocumented accounts" of early kindergarten educators.[17] An objective, detailed account of the early kindergarten movement appeared in 1908, *The Kindergarten in American Education,* by Nina C. Vandewalker. Of this Professor Brickman said that it was "useful but requires supplementation by more recent studies."[18] *Preschool Education* by Ilse Forest, an historical and critical study, was published in 1927. It contained a brief study of Froebelian theories and a description of the development of the kindergarten in America. It did not dwell at any length or in any depth upon Miss Peabody's activities. To enrich the literature of the pioneer kindergarten period

[15] Isaac B. Berkson, "Community Belief Versus Individual Experience as a Basis for Education," an address before the Middle Atlantic States Philosophy of Education Society at New York University, November 14, 1959.
[16] Holmes, *op. cit.,* p. ix.
[17] William W. Brickman, *Guide to Research in Educational History,* p. 54.
[18] *Ibid.,* p. 30.

by investigating the character, activities, and philosophy of Elizabeth Peabody is an aim of this dissertation.

Although this study is directed toward that period of Miss Peabody's life when she was involved in activities relating directly to the establishment of kindergartens, it cannot ignore the events, persons, and factors in her early life which may have had an impact upon her thought. Nor may it assume that Miss Peabody was untouched by the current dissatisfaction with the existing social conditions of her era. The intellectual relationship enjoyed by Elizabeth Peabody with leaders in religious, educational, and literary thought of nineteenth-century New England may not be dismissed summarily. A mere chronological description of her activities in behalf of kindergartens, however detailed, would fail to reveal the significance of these acts. As Professor Brickman has said:

> It is only when the historian shows the real meaning of his data, their interconnections and interrelationships, that he begins to approach the writings of history.[19]

Elizabeth Peabody was fifty-five years old when she heard of kindergartens for the first time. Her activities in their behalf may be judged to have begun in 1860, when she opened her own kindergarten on Pickney Street in Boston. Kindergartens were her main enthusiasm, despite such other interests as the education of the Indian, until her partial blindness and poor health incapacitated her. In a letter to Samuel Ward, in 1890, she acknowledged her failing powers when she spoke of herself as one "who without any acute pain am not so patient as I ought to be with the tediousness of this borderline between the two worlds."[20]

[19] *Ibid.*, p. 161.
[20] *Letter*, Elizabeth P. Peabody to Samuel Gray Ward, June 19-20, 1890. Elizabeth Peabody Collection, Houghton Library, Harvard University.

Miss Peabody's direct and active work was thenceforth nil. Her books, however, were reprinted, her friends continued to think of her, and her past efforts were acknowledged. These survivals of Miss Peabody's former efforts for kindergartens, which existed in her declining years, determined the inclusion of this period in the scope of the study, terminated by her death in 1894.

I

The Origin of the Kindergarten

THE INTERRELATION OF EDUCATION WITH POLITICS, PHILOS-
ophy, religion, and economics is exemplified in the efforts
expended in the establishment of kindergarten education.
Originally a German institution, conceived by Friedrich
Froebel for education of young children, it found its way
across the ocean to a country more appreciative of its value
than was its homeland.

Friedrich Froebel had spent a lonely and unhappy childhood.[1] This influenced his desire that a school for young
children be a happy place, where the children could learn
through occupations involving self-activity. He advocated
games, songs, finger plays, and contact with nature. He admired Johann Pestalozzi's philosophy of learning by doing. His realization of the significance of the best possible
education for young children brought him to seek further
insight from Pestalozzi. From 1808 to 1810 Froebel and
the three pupils in his care studied at Pestalozzi's school at
Yverdon, Switzerland. Of this period he said, "On the

[1] Friedrich Froebel, "Letter to the Duke of Meiningen," in Barnard
(ed.), *Kindergarten and Child Culture*, p. 21.

whole I spent in Yverdon an inspiring, grand, and for my life, decisive time."[2]

He left Yverdon to further his studies at the university at Göttingen. His idealism impelled him to join the army in 1813. As he explained:

I could not possibly think how a young man, capable of bearing arms, could become the teacher of children whose country he had not defended with his life-blood.[3]

It was while he was in service that Froebel met two fellow soldiers who were to become his lifelong associates in the propagation of his educational principles. Henry Langethal and William Middendorff were drawn by Froebel's enthusiasm to adopt education as a career.

For fourteen years, from 1817 to 1831, Froebel was the principal of a school in Keilhau. "Had he been successful as its principal," said Blake, "he would have been content with the place for the rest of his days, and consequently the world would never have heard of the kindergarten."[4] The reasons for his lack of success were largely political. Walz has commented upon the contradictory nature of political repression existing in Germany side by side with the effort toward intellectual progress in the nineteenth century.[5] In Froebel's Keilhau school, teachers and students wore German rather than Prussian-style clothing, and long hair in the German manner. The Prussian government, fearing socialistic influences, had the school investigated. The agitation surrounding this investigation caused many of the parents to withdraw their sons from

[2] *Ibid.*, p. 43.

[3] *Ibid.*, p. 44.

[4] Henry W. Blake, "Life of Friedrich Froebel," in Wiebe, *Paradise of Childhood*, p. 38.

[5] John A. Walz, *German Influence in American Education and Culture*, p. 14.

the school.[6] From 1831 to 1837, Froebel tried to establish schools in Switzerland, but opposition to him as a foreigner and a heretic came from the Catholic clergy.[7] Returning to Keilhau in 1837, Froebel was dissatisfied with the results of his educational program. He felt that one difficulty was that the children came to school with faculties undeveloped or misdirected.[8] Another weakness was, he thought, the use of men as teachers of young children. In the new school he proposed taking younger children and preparing them for school education through their mothers and through women teachers. This school at Blankenberg near Keilhau was at first without a name. Johannes Barop, Froebel's nephew by marriage, and a mainstay to him, related how he and William Middendorff walked to the summit of the mountain with Froebel, who exclaimed repeatedly, "If I could only find a name for my youngest child." Then he called, "Eureka! Kindergarten the institution shall be named."[9] Because of lack of financial support, this kindergarten at Blankenberg lasted only until 1844. During the next five years, Froebel and Middendorff traveled through Germany as missionaries for the propagation of kindergartens. He wrote to one of the women whom he had trained thanking her for her help in "raising the limited, defensive and negative action of a custodial institution to the enlarged, developing, educating, positive one of a 'kindergarten.' "[10] Froebel desired to interest young women in becoming kindergarten teach-

6 Blake, *op. cit.*, p. 36.
7 Wichard Lange, "Reminiscences of Froebel," in Barnard (ed.), *op. cit.*, p. 80.
8 Emily Shirreff, *A Short Sketch of the Life of Friedrich Froebel*, p. 26.
9 Johannes Barop, "Critical Moments in the Life of Froebel," in Barnard (ed.), *op. cit.*, p. 104.
10 *Letter*, Friedrich Froebel to Dear Madam [a kindergarten teacher], Keilhau, July 16, 1848. Ruth M. Baylor Collection.

ers. If the tuition for his training course was beyond their means, he reduced the amount requested. He wrote in regard to two girls who wanted to take his course:

However, the father must be willing to make some sacrifice, even if it would mean taking a loan. He ought to consider seriously that after his death this would mean a sufficiently assured future in such a wonderful sphere of action which insures them the esteem of all the well-disposed. Should you need to write me in this respect, I should like you to note whether the girls have a special love for children, inclination to play with them, and especially whether they have some singing ability and enjoy singing.[11]

It was in 1849, when Froebel had established a kindergarten in Liebenstein, that he met the Baroness Bertha Von Marenholtz-Bülow, who was vacationing there. The Baroness's acceptance of Froebel's theories of education and her dedication in expounding the kindergarten gospel were of the utmost significance in the establishment and development of the kindergarten. Said Blake:

But for the aid of Baroness B. Von Marenholtz-Bülow and her friends it is doubtful if the name of Friedrich Froebel would have come down to this generation as being of any importance.[12]

By January 1850, the Baroness had not only secured a building for Froebel's training school, but had also brought his ideas before the influential nobility and the educators of Germany. The Baroness's service was the more valuable because of Froebel's own "lack of literary expression" and "facility of speech denied to him," of

11 *Letter,* Friedrich Froebel, Bad Liebenstein, May 28, 1849, to Mrs. Pastor Winkler, Reichenbach. Ruth M. Baylor Collection.
12 Blake, *op. cit.,* p. 46.

which she was aware.[13] The Baroness brought Dr. Friedrich Diesterweg, Director of the Royal Seminary at Berlin, to observe the kindergarten at Liebenstein. Dr. Diesterweg was a respected and distinguished German educator. His good opinion meant much to Froebel. The impression the school made upon him may be judged by his words:

What Pestalozzi strove for his whole life long,—the restoration of the sanctity of family life, the training of mothers to their educational vocation, the guidance and culture of women in general that they may take the fitting point of view for the educators of the human race,—this is what he [Froebel] has accomplished, and for this he has found practical means . . .[14]

Because of Dr. Diesterweg's personal approval of Froebel's work, expressed in his publications, the new education began to penetrate pedagogical circles.

Despite the visits of important persons to the new kindergarten at Marienthal, and despite their many expressions of approval, the political unrest was such as to make the government wary of educational reforms which might hold seeds of national disorder. On the visit of Herr Von Wydenbrugh, the minister who superintended education in Weimar, the Baroness was reprimanded by Von Wydenbrugh for using the term "education for freedom" in describing Froebel's work because "it would always give rise to misapprehensions."[15] The Baroness's activity for the kindergarten cause in Berlin made her more aware of the political reaction than was Froebel in his small village. She tried to encourage a closer cooperation between the government and Froebel's cause by inviting Bormann, the

---

[13] Baroness B. Von Marenholtz-Bülow, *Reminiscences of Friedrich Froebel*, p. 20.
[14] *Ibid.*, p. 26.
[15] *Ibid.*, p. 127.

School-Counsellor of Berlin, to visit Marienthal. The Counsellor, who was also Director of the Berlin Seminary for the preparation of female teachers, wrote shortly thereafter, in July 1851, an article which ended: "There can be nothing more anti-revolutionary under the heavens nor upon the earth than Froebel's educational system."[16]

Therefore, it was with great shock that news was received of the Prussian decree of August 7, 1851, forbidding kindergartens. At first Froebel thought that this was an error which could be corrected, for the rescript referred to a pamphlet entitled, *High Schools and Kindergartens*, by Karl Froebel. These views of Froebel's nephew were termed "socialistic and atheistic."[17] Baroness Von Bülow presented a petition for Froebel to the king, to no avail. Minister Von Raumer, to whom the king gave the case for examination, refused to allow the re-establishment of Froebel's kindergartens. Froebel hoped that perhaps the publicity given kindergartens at the Teachers' Convention in September and the favorable judgments of pedagogues there might influence the decision, but this proved to be a false hope.[18]

During this discouraging time, Froebel considered emigrating to America. He had thought of doing this earlier in his career for he had a brother-in-law living in Philadelphia, who had sent him a plan for establishing a kindergarten training school there. It was the opinion of one of his biographers that Froebel would not have succeeded in establishing kindergartens, even if he had come to America.[19] His inability to speak English, his odd appearance, his advanced age, and his naive enthusiasm were all

16 *Ibid.*
17 *Ibid.*, p. 198.
18 *Ibid.*, p. 256.
19 Blake, *op. cit.*, p. 52.

more likely to invite him to ridicule rather than appreciation. Blake thought:

It was better by far that Froebel remained at home; that the Baroness became his biographer and representative in Europe and that on Elizabeth Peabody was laid the burden and the glory of transplanting the kindergarten to America.[20]

Froebel died on June 21, 1852, without hope for the reinstatement of kindergartens in his own country. The Baroness's query to Middendorff, "What will now become of the cause?" and his answer, "We will work with all our powers. Truth is not lost." proved prophetic for the Baroness.[21] She continued her missionary work for kindergartens in England, Belgium, Holland, France, Italy, and Switzerland. In her own country she was influential in having the prohibition against kindergartens removed in 1861. Translations of her publications, *The Child and Child Nature*, and *Reminiscences of Friedrich Froebel*, appeared in America. Although blindness and advanced age prevented her from teaching and preaching Froebel's philosophy, her interest in kindergartens was constant until her death in 1893.[22]

America in the nineteenth century was ripe for the acceptance of kindergarten education. As a modern educator commented, "the education of little children reflects the value system of the contemporary culture."[23] Froebel had realized this as far back as 1836 when he expressed his opinion that the United States of America was best fitted to receive his message because of its spirit of freedom, its

---

[20] *Ibid.*
[21] Marenholtz-Bülow, *op. cit.*, p. 303.
[22] Blake, *op. cit.*, p. 56.
[23] Elizabeth M. Fuller, "Early Childhood Education," in Harris (ed.), *Encyclopaedia of Educational Research*, Third Edition, p. 386.

true Christianity, and pure family life.[24] In 1896, Seeley, of the State Normal School in Trenton, New Jersey, agreed that there were certain qualities of American life that favored the acceptance of such new ideas. These were that

... we are not bound by unbending regulations, controlled by unprogressive conservatism, and loaded down with traditions which reach far back into the past.[25]

America's attention to German education was stimulated by various events. Among these were the emigration of educated political refugees to America, the establishment of private German-American schools, the interest in German culture brought back by American students at Göttingen University, the dissatisfaction with current educational conditions in America, and the desire of alert citizens for the reform and extension of the public school system. Among the famous scholars of the period who studied at Göttingen were Edward Everett, President of Harvard; George Ticknor, Professor of French and Spanish literature at Harvard; and George Bancroft, who held many important political and diplomatic posts. Elizabeth Peabody's West Street bookshop in 1840 catered to Boston's taste for foreign literature. Calvin E. Stowe of Lane Theological Seminary delivered an address at a teacher's convention in Ohio, in 1836, on the "Prussian System of Public Instruction and its Applicability to the United States."[26] Stowe was one of the first American educators who went to Europe to study and report on the Prussian system of education.[27] Horace Mann reported on his visit to Germany in 1843 in his *Seventh Annual Report to the*

24 William N. Hailmann, "Translator's Preface," in Froebel, *Education of Man*, p. xx.
25 Levi Seeley, *The Common-School System of Germany*, p. 11.
26 Walz, *op. cit.*, p. 17.
27 *Ibid.*, p. 20.

Massachusetts Legislature. Henry Barnard visited Germany in 1835 and again in 1854 and included in his *Connecticut Common School Journal* and in his later *American Journal of Education* reports on education in foreign countries. In May 1840, the *Connecticut Common School Journal* carried a lengthy article concerning the system of primary instruction and schools in Prussia.[28] In the journal were other items pertinent to the education of young children. There was an article on infant schools in England, describing specifically one in Quaker Street, Spitalfields,[29] and another on the Home and Colonial Infant School Society.[30] The establishment of an infant school in Rotterdam in 1828, and of two more in Holland in 1829, was also described.[31] Although reference was made to the use of Pestalozzi's methods in certain schools of Prussia, there was no mention of Froebel or of his institutions. The description of infant schools in Prussia stated:

They owe their establishment, in great measure, to private benevolence, and have not as yet become very general. There are already, however, twenty-one at Berlin, educating 1400 children.[32]

Williams noted that Barnard's *American Journal of Education*, established in 1855, had not "given either Froebel or the kindergarten more than one indexed reference before the twenty-eighth volume."[33] It would seem that

---

[28] Henry Barnard, *Connecticut Common School Journal*, Vol. II, No. 15, August, 1840, pp. 293–311.
[29] Barnard, *Connecticut Common School Journal*, Vol. II, No. 14, July, 1840, p. 267.
[30] *Ibid.*, p. 268.
[31] *Ibid.*, p. 288.
[32] Barnard, *Connecticut Common School Journal*, Vol. II, No. 15, August, 1840, p. 305.
[33] Talcott Williams, "The Kindergarten Movement," *The Century*, Vol. XLV, January, 1893, p. 377.

certain developments in America at that time were over-looked by the American pedagogical journals, for Froebel as early as 1838, in his publication *Ein Sonntagsblatt* (A Sunday Paper), mentioned a school in Columbus, Ohio, based on his principles.[34] In the paper, Froebel first stated the theory underlying the project:

As this paper is designed first of all to explain and introduce the proposed institution, it begins immediately with the foundation of the whole. In the germ of every human being lies embedded the form of its whole future life. On the proper comprehension and care of this beginning depends solely the happy unfolding of the man leading to perfection, and the ability to accomplish his destiny, and thus to win the true joy and peace of life.[35]

The name given to the project was *The Institution for the Culture of Occupational Inclinations of Children and Youth*. Listed on the cover were the locations of the schools that had been founded in accord with this theory. They were Blankenberg and Keilhau (in the Thuringian forest), Burgdorf (in the Canton of Berne, Switzerland), and Columbus (in the State of Ohio).[36]

The school in America thus referred to was established by Miss Caroline L. Frankenberg in 1838.[37] One of Miss Frankenberg's brothers, Adolf, was associated with Froebel at the school for girls at Willislau, in 1833.[38] Lange also noted that in 1839 Froebel, accompanied by Middendorff and Frankenberg, went to Dresden to estab-

---

[34] Edward W. Hocker, "The First American Kindergarten Teacher," in *The American-German Review*, Vol. VIII, No. III, February, 1942, p. 9.

[35] Ferdinand Winther, in Diesterweg's *Wegweiser*, 1876, as translated by Lucy Wheelock and reprinted in Barnard (ed.), *op. cit.*, p. 82.

[36] Hocker, *op. cit.*, p. 9. Contains a reproduction of the title page of *Ein Sonntagsblatt*.

[37] *Ibid.*, p. 9.

[38] Lange, *op. cit.*, p. 81.

lish a kindergarten.[39] Caroline Louise Frankenberg was born in 1806 in Eddigehausen near Göttingen. She came to Ohio, as did three of her brothers, and opened a German-speaking school on Rich Street in Columbus. The school was not a success, and Miss Frankenberg returned to Germany in 1840. After her return, Miss Frankenberg studied further with Froebel at Keilhau and taught kindergartens in Dresden and Bautzen.[40] In 1858, she returned to the same cottage in Rich Street and established a kindergarten. Since German was the language of the school, her method again had appeal only for the German population in Columbus, and she had difficulty in gathering a group. Later, in 1865, she introduced the kindergarten in the Lutheran Orphanage in Germantown, Pennsylvania. Elizabeth Peabody was aware of these later accomplishments, as was shown by the records of the Lutheran Home, connected with the orphanage, which chronicled her visit to Miss Frankenberg.[41]

The kindergarten in America received its next impetus from a young German refugee, John Kraus. While he was studying to be a teacher in Germany, John Kraus had been offered a position in Froebel's school. At that time, he declined because he did not wish to interrupt his studies for "what was partly unexplained."[42] However, his interest in the new method had been aroused by the offer and was furthered by a meeting with Froebel in 1844.[43] In 1851, Professor Kraus came to America. Here he continued to

[39] Lange, "Supplement to Letter to the Duke of Meiningen," in Barnard (ed.), *Kindergarten and Child Culture*, p. 47.

[40] Hocker, *op. cit.*, p. 10.

[41] Quoted from *Ohio State Journal*, March 31, 1901, by Elizabeth Jenkins, "How the Kindergarten Found Its Way to America," in *Wisconsin Magazine of History*, Vol. XIX, No. 1, September, 1930, p. 60.

[42] Rachel L. Rogers, "Professor John Kraus and Mrs. Marie Kraus-Boelte and Their United Work," in *Kindergarten News*, Vol. VII, No. 1, September, 1896, p. 2.

[43] Blake, *op. cit.*, p. 24.

teach and to contribute articles perpetuating the Pesta-lozzi-Froebel methods. His were the earliest articles and letters on the kindergarten published in American news-papers.[44] Unfortunately, these, together with his valuable library, were destroyed at Galveston, Texas, during the Civil War.[45] His writings were later recognized by Henry Barnard for whom he prepared in 1868 "an exhaustive history of the rise and progress of Kindergartens."[46]

Another refugee in search of political freedom, whose emigration to America affected the course of kindergarten education, was Mrs. Carl Schurz. Her husband achieved fame and honor through his political career in America, but Margarethe Meyer Schurz's place in history does not depend upon her husband's achievements, but upon her own contribution to kindergarten education. Before her marriage, Margarethe Meyer attended Froebel's course of lectures in Hamburg in 1849. Her sister, Bertha Meyer Ronge, her brother-in-law, Johannes Ronge, and her brother, Adolf Meyer, were all enthusiasts of Froebel's new education.

Bertha and Johannes Ronge founded "Children's Gar-dens" in Germany in 1849 and 1850. They introduced Froebel's system by forming an "Infant Garden" at Hamp-stead, England, in 1851. Since they spoke English fluently, they were able to adapt the schools, "to the character and habits of the English nation."[47] Madame Ronge was also responsible for the kindergarten exhibit, which so im-pressed Henry Barnard, at the Educational Exhibition in London in 1854. The Ronges published, in the English

44 Rogers, *op. cit.*, p. 3.
45 *Ibid.*
46 Maria Kraus-Boelte, "Reminiscences of Kindergarten Work," in Bar-nard (ed.), *op. cit.*, p. 550.
47 John and Bertha Ronge, *A Practical Guide to the English Kinder Garten*, p. iii.

language, a practical guide for kindergarten teachers. In the preface of their second edition, in 1858, they spoke of the difficulties involved in establishing a new idea:

There is perhaps no subject upon which *prejudice* and *sectarianism* exert a more withering influence than upon Education. Against these we have entered the lists, and successfully combatted. . . . We have not, however, been spared by Theological Journals. . . . Alas, what Christianity is this?—to tear open the wounds of those who suffer exile for their convictions and principles . . .[48]

They spoke with appreciation of Charles Dickens' favorable criticism of their publication.[49]

With this family background and her Froebelian training, it was not surprising for the younger sister, Margarethe, to continue her interest in kindergarten education and to put her knowledge to practical use after her marriage and her emigration to America. Although Carl Schurz and Margarethe were in America in 1852, Margarethe's delicate health took the family back to England in 1855.[50] It was in the summer of 1856 that they moved to the farm in Watertown, Wisconsin.[51] Here Mrs. Schurz amused her daughter Agathe and Agathe's four little cousins with Froebel's games, songs, and occupations. Since other relatives and friends wished their children to join the group, Mrs. Schurz held the class in a small building in the town.[52] Thus in November or December, 1856, Mrs. Schurz's kindergarten was established. A memorial tablet, erected on the site on May 2, 1929, reads:

In Memory of Mrs. Carl Schurz (Margarethe Meyer Schurz) August 27, 1833–March 15, 1876, who established on this site

[48] *Ibid.,* p. vii.
[49] *Ibid.*
[50] Jenkins, *op. cit.,* p. 51.
[51] Joseph Schafer, *Intimate Letters of Carl Schurz,* p. 169.
[52] Jenkins, *op. cit.,* p. 52.

the first kindergarten in America, 1856. Dedicated by the Saturday Club Women.[53]

Mrs. Schurz's contribution to the advancement of kindergarten education did not rest on the establishment of her private German-speaking kindergarten, for its influence was limited. More important was the influence she exerted on the kindergarten cause by convincing Elizabeth Peabody in 1859 of the value of Froebel's method of teaching. Or perhaps it was to young Agathe Schurz that the credit for Miss Peabody's interest belonged, for it was her remarkable behavior that so impressed Miss Peabody that she remarked to Mrs. Schurz:

That little child of yours is a miracle,—so child-like and unconscious, and yet so wise and able, attracting and ruling the children, who seem nothing short of enchanted.

Said Mrs. Schurz, "No miracle, but only brought up in a kindergarten." "A kindergarten," queried Miss Peabody, "what is that?" "A garden whose plants are human. Did you never hear of Froebel?" asked Mrs. Schurz. "No; who is he?"[54]

It was in this way, as related by Miss Peabody, that she first heard of Froebel and of the kindergarten. From the preface of Froebel's *Education of Man*, which Mrs. Schurz subsequently sent to her in pamphlet form, Miss Peabody was inspired to make her own first attempt at kindergartening in 1860. She was unaware that what she had read was merely the preface to a larger volume, nor did she know of Froebel's *Mutter und Kose-Lieder (Mother Play and Nursery Songs)*, published in 1839.[55] Judging from her query to Mrs. Schurz, she was ignorant of the men-

53 *Ibid.,* p. 48.
54 Elizabeth P. Peabody, "Origin and Growth of the Kindergarten," in *Education*, Vol. II, No. 5, May, 1882, p. 523.
55 *Ibid.*

tion of kindergarten by Henry Barnard in his *Journal* in July, 1856, after his visit to the exhibit in London in 1854. She knew nothing, her conversation with Mrs. Schurz indicated, of the review of *Le Jardin des Infants*, with its preface by Baroness Von Marenholtz-Bülow, by Miss Anna Q. T. Parsons and Mrs. Ednah D. Cheney in the *Christian Examiner* in 1859. There was also a German-speaking kindergarten in her own city, connected with the Boston German-English School, founded in 1859.[56]

Rebecca Moore, an English kindergartner, who had studied the system under Mme. Ronge's supervision, wrote to Miss Peabody in April, 1860:

You have probably heard of the Kinder Garten system of early training & education. It is a development of the Pestalozzian idea & was first propagated in Germany by F. Froebel, a pupil & assistant of Pestalozzi at Yverden. . . . You are probably already acquainted with the subject through German literature. I send you however two pamphlets by this mail which will give you in outline the idea & plan of the system.[57]

In the same letter Mrs. Moore asked for Miss Peabody's aid in finding a position in America. She continued:

. . . if it is found desirable to add a Kinder Garten Department to the beautiful educational establishment at Eagleswood, I should like, if compatible with other things, & agreeable to the wishes of Mr. & Mrs. Weld & Mr. Spring, to take charge of that Kinder Garten & to introduce the subject to mothers & young girls for home use & co-operation.

Elizabeth Peabody had taught at Eagleswood, Theodore Weld's progressive school at Perth Amboy, New Jersey, and knew Mr. and Mrs. Marcus Spring, "the pecuniary

[56] Adolf Douai, "German Schools in the United States," in Barnard, (ed.), *Special Report of the Commissioner of Education*, 1868, p. 583.

[57] *Letter*, Rebecca Moore to Miss Elizabeth P. Peabody, April 2, 1860. Robert Lincoln Straker Collection, Antioch College Library. The original spelling is used in the quotations from this letter.

founders."[58] Whether or not she complied with Mrs. Moore's request to give Mr. Spring and Mr. Weld "important help in the consideration of the question,"[59] at least here was more information given to her concerning kindergartens.

With such information, and her many years of experience as a teacher, Miss Peabody began her class. Despite its financial success and the approval of the young pupils and their parents, Elizabeth Peabody felt that the class was founded "without such study into the practical details of the method as to do any justice to Froebel's idea; and, on the whole, the premature attempt was unfortunate."[60] In this judgment history has proven Miss Peabody's statement to be wrong. On the whole, the attempt was most fortunate indeed. It was the first practical attempt to establish an English-speaking kindergarten in America and from it, reinforced by Miss Peabody's other activities in behalf of kindergartens, and by the efforts of others, has grown the kindergarten system in America.

The term, "first kindergarten in America," would seem to need further clarification. Miss Caroline Frankenberg's kindergarten was the first class for young children established in America on Froebelian principles. Since the word, "kindergarten," had not yet been coined by Froebel in 1838, and since the work was conducted in the German language, its claim as "first"[61] was limited. Mrs. Schurz's class in 1856 was a kindergarten in name as well as in method, although German-speaking and limited to the

[58] Moncure D. Conway, *Autobiography, Memories and Experiences,* Vol. I, p. 332.

[59] Moore, *op. cit.*

[60] Peabody, "Brief Notice of the Kindergarten in America," in Barnard (ed.), *op. cit.,* p. 10.

[61] Hocker, *op. cit.,* p. 9.

children of relatives and friends. Elizabeth Peabody repudiated any claim to the honor of establishing the first kindergarten in America. She did not consider that her "premature attempt"[62] was a true kindergarten. She wrote in March, 1869:

The so-called kindergarten which I had established, was gladly given up to make room for this [Miss Kriege's] genuine one . . .[63]

She gave as her opinion that

The first kindergarten strictly according to Froebel's idea, that was begun in America, was Miss Alma Kriege's, in Boston, October, 1868 . . .[64]

September, 1960, marks the one-hundredth anniversary of Miss Peabody's pioneer effort. Boston in 1928 seemed confused about this entire question of firsts, for the *Boston Evening Transcript* proclaimed on January 18, 1928, in a page-wide spread, "Boston Kindergartens to Celebrate Their Fiftieth Anniversary."[65] The article added a further note of confusion by stating that it was the "fortieth and fiftieth anniversary of this phase of education in Boston"[66] that was being celebrated. Even if the *Boston Evening Transcript* had chosen Miss Kriege's kindergarten, established in 1868, as the object of its celebration, the anniversary year was in error.

Elizabeth Peabody House, the settlement house established in Boston in 1896, in Miss Peabody's memory,

---

62 Peabody, "Brief Notice of the Kindergarten in America," *op. cit.*, p. 10.
63 Peabody, *Kindergarten Guide*, p. iii.
64 Peabody, "The Kindergarten,—Attempts in America," in *The Michigan Teacher*, Vol. VII, No. 10, October, 1872, p. 338.
65 Karl Schriftgiesser, *Boston Evening Transcript*, Wednesday, January 18, 1928, Part 3, p. 12.
66 *Ibid.*

stated in 1960 that they "would not be taking special notice of her this year."[67]

Despite Miss Peabody's self-critical and modest disclaimer, and despite Boston's confusion and indifference, the Association for Childhood Education International, in a leaflet *This Is What Happened*, recognized the year 1860 as the date of the first English-speaking kindergarten in the United States.[68] The year 1868 was noted as significant because "the first kindergarten training school in America was established in Boston by Mme. Matilde Kriege and her daughter . . ."[69] In answer to a query, the Association replied, "We have heard of no plans celebrating Miss Peabody's kindergarten."[70] The Association celebrated the kindergarten centennial in 1937, recognizing Froebel's school for young children at Blankenberg as the first kindergarten although it had not been so named.[71] The United States Office of Education concurred in recognizing this centenary.[72]

Though her efforts in establishing the kindergarten in the United States have been recognized, the date of the founding of Miss Peabody's first kindergarten class has become obscured. The kindergarten started on Pinckney Street was significant because it established the pattern of Froebelian kindergartens followed for many years by other neophyte kindergarten teachers in the United States.

[67] *Letter*, Janet Dale, Head Worker, Elizabeth Peabody House, to Ruth M. Baylor, n.d. [1960].

[68] ACEI, *This Is What Happened*, n.d., not paginated.

[69] *Ibid.*

[70] *Letter*, Epsie Young, Staff Associate, ACEI, to Ruth M. Baylor, January 4, 1960.

[71] Edna Dean Baker, Association for Childhood Education Kindergarten Centennial Committee, *The Kindergarten Centennial*, p. 5.

[72] Mary Dabney Davis, "A Century of the Kindergarten," p. 1, reprint from *School Life*, November, 1936, by United States Government Printing Office, Washington, D.C., 1936.

II

Early Life of
Elizabeth Palmer Peabody

ELIZABETH PALMER PEABODY WAS BORN ON MAY 16, 1804, IN
Billerica, Massachusetts, the first child of Elizabeth Palmer
and Nathaniel Peabody. Her father, Nathaniel Peabody,
was a teacher at Phillips Andover Academy when he
met, in North Andover, Miss Palmer, the first "Preceptress
of Franklin Academy."[1] It was not a mere coincidence that
from the union of two teachers should stem one whose interest in teaching was such as to lead to a life of unselfish
dedication to education. Miss Peabody commented on the
influence of her mother's career upon her own life:

My mother began her teaching at the North Andover Academy
about the year 1800 . . . In 1803–4–5, she had a boarding school
of her own in Billerica, while my father was studying his
profession. There I was born in 1804—Being as it were pre-
natally educated for the profession which has been the passionate pursuit of my life.[2]

[1] Sarah L. Bailey, *Historical Sketches of Andover*, pp. 552–3.
[2] Elizabeth P. Peabody, *Female Education in Massachusetts*, p. 308.

According to *A Genealogy of the Peabody Family*,[3] the name "Peabody" had its origin in the year 61, when the ancient Britons were vassals of the Roman Emperor Nero. Boadicea, Queen of the Britons, courageously opposed the Roman tyrant. Unsuccessful in the revolt, the Queen took poison rather than submit. Her kinsman Boadie and remnants of the tribe then fled to the hills to escape the Roman foe. "Pea," meaning mountain, and "Boadie," meaning man, ultimately became "Peabody." The Peabody coat of arms was assured to the descendants by King Arthur when a "Peabody" again proved his fidelity and valor. The registered coat of arms "borne by the name of Peabodie" bears the inscription, "Murus aereus conscientia sana." Could Miss Peabody disdain to live up to such a motto? "A sound conscience is a wall of brass."

Although Mrs. Peabody could not boast of such ancient lineage, yet she was descended "from the two Joseph Palmers, one of whom was President and the other secretary of the first Provincial Congress that assembled in Massachusetts to consider British wrongs."[4] Brigadier-General Palmer, with his son as his aide, had engaged in the Battle of Lexington. The inspiration Mrs. Peabody derived from the heroes of the two families, and which she transmitted to the next generation, is thus expressed by her eldest daughter:

Born and brought up in the midst of a family all of whom devoted all their means to their country, she [Mrs. Peabody] looked upon national life as God's education of mankind, and it was the pattern on which she modeled the education of every citizen.

I therefore breathed in, from my mother's arms, the idea

3 C. M. Endicott, *A Genealogy of the Peabody Family*, pp. 1–3.
4 Sarah Josepha Hale, *Woman's Record*, p. 835.

which Frobel [sic] has at this date embodied in a system which is at once the high school for mothers, and the primary education of humanity.[5]

After the Revolution, Joseph Pearse Palmer, Mrs. Peabody's father, became a farmer, but without success. He then opened a school in Framingham, Massachusetts.[6] Thus, the pattern of teaching as a means of livelihood was not unfamiliar to the children of Nathaniel and Elizabeth Peabody.

If we pay heed to the eulogistic comments of Miss Peabody's friends and acquaintances, we may conclude that the phrase descriptive of Queen Boadicea, "a woman of great abilities and valor,"[7] may be applied just as aptly to Miss Peabody. Awareness of her illustrious ancestry may have served as an inspiration to the idealistic Miss Peabody. It may also have served the more mundane purposes of securing pupils and opening doors to many Boston homes for which neither the Peabody talents nor purse would have been sufficient to gain recognition. For it was true, unfortunately, that the Peabodys were very poor.

The ambitious and energetic young Mrs. Peabody encouraged her husband to study medicine. This he did, as was the common practice of his day, by accompanying the local doctor on his daily visits to his patients, by assisting him in the office, and by reading available medical literature. Appreciative as she was of the best in education, Mrs. Peabody moved the family to Cambridgeport so that her husband could attend the medical lectures at Harvard University. Here he became interested in dentistry, and although he was, at various times, a physician of an alms-

[5] Peabody, *op. cit.*, p. 310.
[6] Mary Hunt Tyler, *Grandmother Tyler's Book*, p. 144.
[7] Endicott, *op. cit.*, p. 2.

house, and a dispenser of homeopathic medicines, yet dentistry was the profession which he pursued most assiduously.[8]

Even after Mr. Peabody, the teacher, had become Dr. Peabody, the dentist, the financial affairs of the family were precarious. Soon after the birth of a second daughter, Mary Tyler Peabody, in 1806, Mrs. Peabody supplemented the family income by a position at the Lynn Academy in Cambridgeport.[9] In 1809, Sophia was born, then Nathaniel in 1811, George in 1813, and Wellington in 1815. In 1819, another girl was born, but she died in infancy.[10] It hardly seemed possible, in view of her increased family responsibilities, that in 1809 the indefatigable Mrs. Peabody opened a school in Salem, "where she kept school with one short interval until 1818."[11] It was here that Elizabeth received her early education, and from this source that she acquired the interest in history and the historical sense of linking the present with the past which she showed so aptly in her later teaching career. Her mornings at school included the study of arithmetic, geography, English composition, and elements of physics and natural sciences. She described the afternoons as follows:

We read Goldsmith's Histories of England, Greece, and Rome on two afternoons in the week; and on two others, the great works of literary art, the Iliad and Odyssey, Tasso's Jerusalem, etc. . . . There was a good deal of conversation about what was read; and part of the time was taken up in reading papers that she [Mrs. Peabody] selected for their beauty or interest, from the *Spectator, Rambler,* and sometimes from the

8 Dr. Nathaniel Peabody, "Advertisement," *Salem Gazette,* September 10, 1830.
9 Peabody, *op. cit.,* p. 309.
10 Endicott, *op. cit.,* p. 43.
11 Peabody, *op. cit.,* p. 309.

Edinburgh and *Quarterly Reviews*; and accounts of books from the old *Monthly Review*.[12]

In addition to her multifarious duties as teacher and mother, Mrs. Peabody published *Sabbath Lessons* in 1810. She also translated Spenser's *Faerie Queene* from its obsolete English, so that it could be understood more easily by her pupils. It first appeared in print as *Holiness: or The Legend of St. George: A Tale from Spencer's* [sic] *Faerie Queene,* by a Mother, published in Boston by E. R. Broaders in 1836.[13] Miss Peabody's later acceptance of Friedrich Froebel's emphasis on the importance of the mother in education may have been grounded in her early familiarity with mothers who taught or superintended the education of their own children. Thus had her mother and her aunts, Mrs. Curtis and Mrs. Putnam, educated their families and been educated themselves.[14] Her eager appreciation of Froebel's idea of self-activity was also rooted in this early period. "It seems to me," she explained, "that the self-activity of the mind was cultivated by my mother's method in her school. If not so much was poured in—or rather on—more was brought out."[15] This idea of bringing out that which was within the child was also expressed by Froebel:

The Mother's [and teacher's] influence thus resembles that of the spring sun, which by warmth awakens the life (the impulse, the power, the self-activity, and the self-determination) in each seed kernel, arouses in it the impulse to unfold according to its natural capacities that which lies in it by its own activity and all-sided union with Nature.[16]

[12] *Ibid.,* p. 308.
[13] Ruth M. Baylor Collection.
[14] Peabody, *op. cit.,* p. 307.
[15] *Ibid.,* p. 309.
[16] Friedrich Froebel, *Education by Development,* p. 16.

Mrs. Peabody did not believe in leaving her children with "ignorant hirelings." As Miss Peabody explained:

In every instance she invited into the family some refined lady, who was desirous of more literary education, that she might herself keep school. This lady was to have the care of the child during the six school hours, and the rest of her time to study and read and recite to my father or mother, and share all the life and society of the house, which was always much frequented by the cultivated people among whom we lived.[17]

Mrs. Peabody also trained, in her day-school, poor young women who wished to learn to be teachers. In the afternoon session, while listening to the reading and discussion in the class, these young neophytes occupied their fingers in sewing for the Peabody family.

As a means of instructing her own girls, this closely-knit family-type school was completely in accord, all unbeknownst to Mrs. Peabody, with Froebel's expression of his thoughts:

In the family the child grows up to boyhood and pupilage; therefore the school must link itself to the family. The union of the school and of life, of domestic and scholastic life, is the first and indispensable requisite of a perfect human education of this period.[18]

Mrs. Peabody's awareness of the necessity of educating young women to be teachers was a counterpart of Froebel's which he developed in his seminaries for kindergartners. The activities in Elizabeth's later years in behalf of the establishment of training schools for kindergartners seemed but an extension of the ideas and practices which she had observed and participated in during her childhood at her mother's school.

---

17 Peabody, *op. cit.,* p. 310.
18 Friedrich Froebel, *Education of Man,* p. 230.

Certain basic tenets which formed the foundation for Froebel's philosophy had been accepted by Miss Peabody before she heard of Froebel's work. She admitted that many of the characteristics and methods of teaching employed by her when she taught "were implicitly suggested" by her mother's example.[19] Froebel's idea that man does not work and create only in order to preserve his body and secure food, clothing, and shelter, but to recognize his own spiritual nature,[20] was similar to Mrs. Peabody's idea of education as predominantly moral and high-principled.[21] The eagerness with which Miss Peabody later gave of her services to so many philanthropic, charitable, and unpaid literary endeavors was not due solely to the fact that she lived in Boston in an era of reform, but was also the ultimate expression of those early ideals of character development as the aim of education, which she had imbibed from the teaching and example of her mother. Not only her ability to comprehend and absorb Froebel's philosophy, but the self-sacrifice with which she labored to put it into practice in the United States, was grounded in her early training. Later reading and experiences, and the impact of other personalities, may have had their influence upon her, and later pages of this study will show how and to what extent this was true, but the seeds had already been sown by Mrs. Peabody before Elizabeth was fourteen years old.

The young Elizabeth was taught Latin by her father for one or two hours daily. Since the school committee of Salem met in her father's study, she learned much about the reformation of the school system. When she accompanied her father, who was at that time physician of the

---

19 Peabody, *op. cit.*, p. 289.
20 Froebel, *op. cit.*, p. 32.
21 Peabody, *op. cit.*, p. 289.

almshouse, on his daily visits, she was impressed with "educating the [pauper] children in shoemaking and other trades."[22] In speaking of this period of her life, Miss Peabody avowed that "the idea that women were less capable of the highest education in literature and science, and of authorship on any subject, truly never entered my mind."[23] This trust in women's capabilities in many fields was substantiated by the actualities of her own family life. Dr. Peabody, though an able scholar, was an inadequate provider for his family. This unfortunate characteristic resulted in the assumption of family financial responsibilities by the women of the family. The avenues to financial gain open to women at the time were not many. Keeping boarders, teaching school, taking in sewing, and, if so gifted, writing, were some of the more common means by which women earned a livelihood. As early as 1798, Mother Peabody had published her poetry and articles in *The Haverhill Gazette.*

At an early age, Mary followed Mother Peabody's and Sister Lizzie's example and became teacher and author. By these means, the Peabody women contributed to the support of the family. Elizabeth was just sixteen when she "kept a school" in the family's home in Lancaster. Mary and Sophia were among her scholars; neither sister ever went to any other school.[24] Sophia, although invalided by severe headaches from 1823 until her marriage to Nathaniel Hawthorne in 1842, was encouraged by Elizabeth in her career as an artist. The education of the three Peabody boys was not so fortunate. They attended the Salem Latin School and, says Elizabeth, "had terrible hard les-

22 Peabody, *Reminiscences of Rev. William Ellery Channing, D.D.,* p. 37.

23 Peabody, *Female Education in Massachusetts,* p. 21.

24 Norman Holmes Pearson, *Elizabeth Peabody on Hawthorne,* Essex Institute (Mass.) Historical Collections, Vol. XCIV, No. 3, July, 1958, p. 270.

sons under old Eames—who was a most severe master, flogging for mistakes in recitation,"[25] the usual teaching procedure of the day.

Considering the nature of Elizabeth Peabody's earliest education and family life, it was unfortunate that Mr. Sanborn, her neighbor when she later lived in Concord, ignored her childhood and credited her noble educational ideals to the period of her youth when she had left her home and was teaching in Boston. He claimed that:

Like Mr. Alcott's, Miss Peabody's life-work was originally education,—now in this form, now in that, but always with the noblest ideal of what education is. She had derived this ideal from the spiritual surroundings of her youth in Boston, at that fortunate period when Dr. Channing, Alcott, the Emersons, Dr. Howe, Horace Mann, the Everetts, Eliots, Quincys, Charles Sumner and so many more, citizens or public teachers, were all in their own way seeking to promote a broader, more profound culture.[26]

The facts of Miss Peabody's early training and family life, as herein mentioned, refute the contention that her lofty ideals of, and her lifetime interest in, education stemmed alone from her later contact with Channing, Emerson, Alcott, and others. Not many young ladies in the America of Miss Peabody's era were so well educated, so independent in their thinking, so courageous, as was Elizabeth Palmer Peabody when, at the age of eighteen, she came alone to Boston. She arrived, said she, "in a high heroic mood, intending to get money to educate at college my brothers."[27]

Miss Harriet Martineau, an English visitor to America in 1834, in her critical account of her travels in America, portrayed the difficulty with which intelligent American

25 *Ibid.*, p. 271.
26 Frank B. Sanborn, *Recollections of Seventy Years*, p. 562.
27 Pearson, *op. cit.*, p. 271.

women pursued any career but marriage. In speaking of their education she said:

The intellect of woman is confined by an unjustifiable restriction of both methods of education,—by express teaching, and by the discipline of circumstance . . . As women have none of the objects in life for which an enlarged education is considered requisite, the education is not given . . . But what is given is, for the most part passively received; and what is obtained is, chiefly, by means of the memory. There is rarely or never a careful ordering of influences for the promotion of clear intellectual activity.[28]

As a comment on their courage, she bemoaned, "How fearfully the morals of women are crushed, appears from the prevalent persuasion that there are virtues which are peculiarly feminine."[29] It may be assumed, if the above generalizations about women are accepted, that Elizabeth at eighteen was indeed an unusual woman. Sarah Josepha Hale, in her sketches of distinguished women, emphasized Elizabeth's stature among the women of her era:

Miss Peabody's writings are of a class unusual to her sex. They evince great learning and research, a mind free from the trammels of prejudice, and capable of judging for itself on whatever subject its attention may be turned, one whose aim is high—no less than the progressive improvement of her race, and who presses forward to the end she has in view, with an earnestness and energy proportioned to its importance.[30]

"Miss Peabody had the most remarkable woman's mind that has been known in America," said Maria Porter, who attended Miss Peabody's history lectures.[31]

28 Harriet Martineau, *Society in America*, Vol. II, p. 228.
29 *Ibid.*, p. 233.
30 Hale, *op. cit.*, p. 835.
31 Marie S. Porter, "Elizabeth Palmer Peabody," in *The Bostonian*, January, 1896, Vol. 3, No. 4, p. 340.

The Boston upon which the young teacher descended, fortified by her exalted resolves, her Boadicean courage, and her family connections, was the center of many great literary, religious, and social endeavors. Into this mélange, Miss Peabody willingly plunged, contributing to and being influenced by the new enlightenment. At this time, the Unitarian protest against the ecclesiasticism of the Congregational Church was at its height. William Ellery Channing was its genius and acknowledged leader. According to Miss Peabody, he found himself in the Unitarian movement "because he had a temperament of that great moral sensibility which prophesies the future developments of spiritual truth; and he had the genius for expressing that which his contemporaries felt."[32] The Unitarian protest against the doctrine of a universal inherited depravity found a place in Miss Peabody's philosophy of education and made for her ready acceptance of the theories of Pestalozzi and Froebel, which also were founded in opposition to the Calvinistic doctrine of inherited sin. The young Miss Peabody was tremendously impressed by Channing's sermons. Her comment upon them was that they

. . . seemed to me more profoundly spiritual than any I had ever heard, because I was just on the eve of entering upon the vocation for which I had been educated from childhood,—I will not say the vocation of teaching a school, but of educating children morally and spiritually as well as intellectually from the first; which my mother had taught me was the most sacred of the duties of the children of the Pilgrims who founded the Republic to bless all the *nations* of the earth.[33]

When Elizabeth Peabody heard Dr. Channing in 1820, he was preaching upon people's responsibilities for each

[32] Peabody, *Reminiscences of Rev. William Ellery Channing, D.D.*, p. 28.
[33] *Ibid.*, p. 40.

other's happiness, which was the essential duty of each individual to promote.[34] That many of Dr. Channing's par-
ishioners followed his exhortations was attested to by the
Reverend Charles Graves, a more recent Unitarian minister:

Unitarians have been most conspicuous in all enterprises
which aim to improve the general well-being, morally, intellectually and even materially. Thus it happens that in an
unusually large number of instances Unitarians have been
pioneers in philanthropic and educational enterprises and
have been pre-eminent in literature.[35]

The instances quoted by the Reverend Graves included
Dr. Samuel G. Howe, the founder of the Perkins Institute
for the Blind; Dorothea Dix, who initiated the movement
which resulted in a more humane treatment of the in-
mates of prisons, almshouses, and hospitals for the insane;
Margaret Fuller, advocate of "rights of women" in the
United States; Horace Mann, pioneer in educational reform; and Reverend Henry W. Bellows, minister of the
Unitarian Church of All Souls in New York City, who
originated the United States Sanitary Commission, which
served during the Civil War. Dr. Graves claimed that
their devotion to humanitarian work was not accidental,
but was, in large part, the result of the emphasis of the
Unitarian church upon the religion of service to mankind.[36]

All these recognized leaders in social and educational
reforms were known personally to Elizabeth Peabody. Indeed, to the list of famous Unitarians may be added her
name as the founder of the kindergarten movement in

34 *Ibid.*
35 Rev. Charles Graves, *What Unitarians Believe*, Pamphlet, not paginated, n.d.
36 *Ibid.*

America. Nurtured from infancy on the ideals of translating Christ's teachings into acts of daily life, she welcomed such a sermon as the "Intimacy of Human Relations," wherein was preached the mutual dependence of the members of a family, and where the good mother of a poor family was extolled as "the most interesting object in the world."[37] The Swiss educational reformer, Pestalozzi, also exalted the teaching role of the mother and the family, and there is no doubt that Elizabeth was readied for his educational doctrines by the preceding events of her life.

The first time Elizabeth had heard Dr. Channing preach was in Salem when she was but eight or nine years old. At that time, her mother, recognizing that "it takes genius to reach children,"[38] took her to hear the famous visitor. Said Elizabeth of her mother's pronouncement, "Mysterious words! which I pondered many years, and never quite understood, till I learned their meaning from Frederick [sic] Froebel, in my old age."[39] For the duration of his life, Channing was not only her revered friend and her spiritual leader, but her financial advisor, literary critic, and confidant. When she informed him in 1840 of her intention to open a bookshop, he wrote to her on June seventh, "I see nothing in the business inconsistent with your sex,"[40] but questioned her capacity for business. He explained, in another letter, that:

My fear on this subject came from the impression which was quite common in your school-keeping days, that you want order, method, arrangement. If I mistake not, you had a notion that in regard to order, as in everything else, what we need is the spirit rather than the letter; that rules and machinery

---

[37] Peabody, *Reminiscences of Rev. William Ellery Channing, D.D.*, p. 162.
[38] *Ibid.*, p. 12.
[39] *Ibid.*, p. 13.
[40] *Ibid.*, p. 408.

are worth little; that the principle within us will meet intuitively the wants of the moment.[41]

Later, Miss Peabody was to find in Froebel's systematic procedures in the use of the kindergarten gifts and occupations just the amount of order acceptable to her philosophy of teaching young children. Miss Peabody enjoyed many conversations with Dr. Channing. In her journal of 1825, she recorded their discussions on education. In 1875, she was to find them to be equally true. In looking back fifty years she recalled:

. . . I am struck with the fact that, sure enough, we were dwelling then in the dawning light of those truths which make up the character-forming portion of Froebel's system,—truths which both Dr. Channing and F. Froebel consciously made use of, like Jesus Christ, to counteract the despair inherited from the old Pagan doctrine lurking in Judaism, and in the Orthodoxy of this day, of *naked sovereignty* as the essence of God. They both affirmed that the true human life is a constant growth . . .[42]

Dr. Channing's confidence in Miss Peabody's teaching abilities may be assumed from the presence of his little daughter, Mary, among the thirty pupils in her school in Brookline. In turn, Elizabeth's admiration and respect was shown by her generous offer to serve as Channing's unpaid secretary in order to copy for posterity those sermons which so delighted her. In her own words:

My intimacy with him came in large measure from the circumstance that I had his only daughter as a pupil in my school for seven years; and he was one of those rare parents who knew what the relation ought to be of persons engaged in the greatest duty of one human being to another,—that of educating the free spirit, from the unconsciousness of infancy into self-

41 *Ibid.*
42 *Ibid.*, p. 93.

direction and self culture. After school-hours were over, it was a great recreation to me to go and read to him in the afternoons or evenings.[43]

The years from 1830 to 1840 were extraordinarily lean and difficult years for the Peabody family. The family correspondence revealed the worry caused by Wellington's departure from Harvard and the unsuccessful attempts of George and Nat to establish themselves profitably in a profession or business. Wellington entered Harvard College in August, 1831, and "took up connexions" the 4th of April, 1832. This would indicate that he left voluntarily. Sometimes, however, the Faculty asked a student's parents to take up his connections.[44] That the family was worried about Wellington was confided by Elizabeth to Lydia Haven:

Will you ask your husband to tell me if he received from *Mr. Weld* any intimation, direct or indirect, that Wellington had better not go to college. Tell him if he will tell me—I will promise that it shall not go any farther—& Mr. Weld shall never know. But I want *to know* for the most important reasons.

You will be sorry to hear that we are quite worried about Wellington. The stimulus of doing well at college is not great enough to send that vital energy into his soul—which is wanting and we are thinking about his going a whaling voyage! However, that is as yet a secret—even from him—but my father has made enquiries at N. Bedford and Mother *has consented!* Mary and I think it will be his salvation.[45]

The family's courage, energy, and optimism were sorely tested. It would give a distorted picture of Elizabeth Pea-

---

[43] *Ibid.*, p. 10.

[44] *Letter*, Clifford K. Shipton, Custodian of the Harvard University Archives to Ruth M. Baylor, June 13, 1960.

[45] *Letter*, Elizabeth P. Peabody to Lydia Haven, Friday, [1832]. Berg Collection, New York Public Library.

body to distinguish between the private and the public person. So interwined was her life with those of the members of her family that what she did professionally was often affected by the private demands upon her time and generosity.

Nat married early and tried, successively, storekeeping, teaching, and dispensing homeopathic drugs. Wellington, after an unprofitable whaling voyage to the west coast of South America, joined George in New Orleans and studied medicine. Just as hope for his future was inspired in his family, he contracted yellow fever and died in 1837. George had gone South earlier, seeking to benefit his health. He had suffered from a disease of the spine contracted when he was fifteen years old. While clerking in New Orleans, his illness became progressively worse. In 1838, he returned home to be nursed by his loyal and loving family until his death in 1839.

In 1833, Mary accepted a position as governess in Cuba so that Sophia could come with her, in the hope that the warm climate would relieve Sophia's constant headaches.

There was one bright gleam in those depressing days. The Peabody sisters, Mary and Elizabeth, met Horace Mann at the boardinghouse at which they lived in 1832, before Mary sailed for Cuba. He, too, was melancholy, for his wife, Charlotte, only twenty-three years old, had died the previous year. The sympathy Elizabeth felt for the troubles of others was shown by her many letters of consolation over a period of years. In one such letter she wrote:

I have wished that I was in Boston tonight, not that I could be sure that you would come, and tell the tale of sorrow to my aching ear and heart, but that I should feel that if you *did not,* it was from *your choice,* from your feeling that it was better to be alone. . . . That note of yours, which closed with speaking of yourself as buried in a living grave (an image containing much truth and some consolation to such a heart as yours, as it implies the conception of the loved one, *in life*) had in it a sweet assurance.[46]

Elizabeth's admiration for Mr. Mann could be judged from her comparison of him with the revered William Ellery Channing. She said that they were identical in their conviction that the purpose of human life on earth was all for education.[47]

In 1836, when Elizabeth was endeavoring to launch an educational magazine, *The Family School,* he advised her as an "older brother." Having seen the prospectus in the morning paper, he urged her to refrain from discussing "the processes of nature and parts of the anatomy," as she had done in the preface of *Record of a School.* He knew that Miss Peabody's mind was "pure," but he was also aware of Boston's prudery.[48] He was the practical idealist, working unceasingly for education. He respected her advice and opinion, and often sought it:

My dear Miss Peabody

If you have any time this morning, you may look over the enclosed sheets, which is my Report on School Houses. I want your wise suggestions about it.

Yours affectionately
Horace Mann[49]

Such requests for her opinions, together with suggestions for reading certain books pertaining to school laws, and copies of his lectures, must have claimed much of her at-

[46] *Letter,* Elizabeth P. Peabody to Horace Mann, [August 1, 1836]. Horace Mann Collection, Massachusetts Historical Society.

[47] Peabody, *Reminiscences of William Ellery Channing, D.D.,* p. 382.

[48] *Letter,* Horace Mann to Elizabeth Peabody, September, 1836. Horace Mann Collection, Massachusetts Historical Society.

[49] *Letter,* Horace Mann to Elizabeth Peabody, n.d., Robert Lincoln Straker Collection, Antioch College Library.

tention. They served also to make her aware of the effort necessary to reform education. In later years, she, too, was ready to travel, to lecture, to write articles, pamphlets, and countless letters in behalf of kindergarten education. Horace Mann exemplified the sacrifice and labor needed to make an idea a reality.

In the *Journals* of Amos Bronson Alcott rests ample evidence of the interaction of two devotees of education for young children, Alcott and Miss Peabody. The entry for September 22, 1834, reads:

I open school today with 30 children between the ages of three and twelve; and am assisted in their instruction by Miss Elizabeth P. Peabody whose reputation is of the highest character; both as regards original and acquired ability, uniting intellectual and practical qualities of no common order. The proposition to aid me in instruction comes from the deep interest which she feels in human culture, and from the friendly desire to establish me, as an educator of youth, in this city, where I am to receive more encouragement both as regards intellectual appreciation, and pecuniary reward, than I can expect [from the people of any other city] elsewhere.[50]

The school referred to is the famous—infamous to some Bostonians of that era—Temple School. A judgment of the extent of Alcott's influence upon Miss Peabody must be tempered by the realization that by this time, "Elizabeth Palmer Peabody was one of the ablest and most thoughtful teachers in America, and she had, moreover, one of the most alert and well-stored minds in Boston."[51] However, she was impressed by and sympathetic to Alcott's theories, as was shown in the help she gave him in gathering children for his school and by her acceptance of the position

50 A. Bronson Alcott, *Journals*, September 22, 1834. Concord Free Public Library.
51 Odell Shepard, *Pedlar's Progress*, p. 128.

of assistant to teach Latin and Arithmetic. She did more; when there were no funds, she served without remuneration, boarding with the Alcotts in lieu of salary.

Bronson Alcott and Elizabeth Peabody shared certain religious convictions which influenced their methods of teaching. They believed in the innate goodness of the child, were indifferent to creeds, held a completely unmaterialistic approach to life, and considered Jesus an exemplary man and teacher. Mr. Alcott favored the Socratic question and answer method, the keeping of journals of their thoughts by the children, and "Epistolatory Correspondence." He wrote:

February 21 and 27—Correspondence—to two of my pupils from whom I also receive letters, on subjects connected with their studies and the means of their improvement—this Correspondence, together with the *Journals* which they keep constitutes an important part of the exercises intended to develop and discipline their minds. I have great reason to hope for *much* from its continuance.[52]

"Much" more that was unpleasant was to result from this procedure than Mr. Alcott anticipated. "The theory of education," said Mr. Alcott, "is Self-Realization."[53] His efforts to lead the children to self-analysis were recorded by Miss Peabody in the *Record of A School*. Odell Shepard commented that on every page of the book, which he considered one of the most interesting descriptions of the forgotten doctrines of transcendentalism,

there is evidence of the writer's highly intelligent and always independent admiration. One sees that a skillful practitioner of the art of teaching is watching a master of that art at work, setting down without extenuation both hearty praise and polite

[52] Alcott, *op. cit.*, February 21 and 27, 1834.
[53] *Ibid.*, April 22, 1834.

disagreement. Merely as an example of what may be called intellectual good manners and of the complete conquest of professional jealousy, the little book speaks well of the two persons chiefly concerned.[54]

Miss Peabody agreed that "contemplation of Spirit is the first principle of Human Culture; the foundation of self-education." She continued: "Considering early education as a leading of the young mind to self-education, he, Mr. Alcott, would have it proceed on the same principles. And few will disagree with him, in drawing this inference from the premises."[55] However, Miss Peabody made certain objections to this forcing of strictly personal sentiments:

It would be as wise to tear the rosebud open, or invade the solitude of the chrysalis, with the hope of obtaining insight into the process of bloom or metamorphosis, as to expect to gain any knowledge of the soul, by drawing forth, by the personal power which an instructor may possess over the heart, conscience, or imagination, that confidence, which it is the precious prerogative of an individual to bestow spontaneously, when old enough to choose its depository.[56]

This was the issue which led to the ultimate disagreement between Mr. Alcott and Miss Peabody, and to her departure from the Temple School. The issue was intensified when Alcott in 1835 began his *Conversations on the Gospels* with the pupils in his school. When the teacher's inquiries concerned the mystery of birth, not only the "best families," but also Dr. Channing and Miss Peabody became concerned. Since Miss Peabody had recorded many of these *Conversations*, she wished to be relieved of the re-

54 Shepard, *op. cit.*, pp. 166–7.
55 Peabody, "Explanatory Preface to Second Edition," *Record of a School*, p. iii.
56 *Ibid.*, p. viii.

sponsibility of having them considered as her own, and she wrote to Alcott as follows:

The very day after my letter to you I received a communication from a friend; by which I learn that much more extensive than either you or I were aware of is the discussion of such subjects as it is known were discussed in connection with the birth of Christ censured even by friends of your system and of yourself, and that something of an impression was gratuitously taken up that I left the School on that account—an impression for which I can in no ways account, except it was thought I ought to leave it.[57]

She reassured Alcott that she agreed with him that it was impossible to keep children ignorant of the facts of life and therefore that it was better to lead their imagination than to leave them to be directed by idle curiosity. However, she admitted that she would never have dared to venture "so far" nor to have asked so many "superfluous" questions which were not worth the risk of having repeated and misunderstood.[58]

Harriet Martineau, after her visit to America, voiced her criticism of Alcott's methods:

There is a school in Boston, (a large one, when I left the city) conducted on this principle. The master presupposes his little pupils possessed of all truth, in philosophy and morals, and that his business is to bring it out into expression; to help the outward life to conform to the inner light; and, especially, to learn of these enlightened babes with all humility. Large exposures might be made of the mischief this gentleman is doing to his pupils by relaxing their bodies, pampering their imaginations, over-stimulating the consciences of some, and hardening those of others; and by his extraordinary manage-

[57] *Letter,* Elizabeth Peabody to Bronson Alcott, August 6, 1836. Alcott *Journals,* Concord Free Public Library.
[58] *Ibid.*

ment offering them every inducement to falsehood and hypocrisy.[59]

Miss Martineau's prophesy that, "a few weeks are enough to convince sensible parents of the destructiveness of such a system,"[60] proved true. The stigma upon Miss Peabody, as well as upon Alcott, was sufficient to make the success of opening a new school by either one extremely doubtful. In 1859, when Miss Peabody became acquainted with Froebel's method, she welcomed the objectivity of his approach in contrast to the introspective, subjective method used by Alcott.

Miss Peabody recognized and courted genius. She yearned to help each child or adult fulfill his capabilities. In this spirit, she sought out and befriended Nathaniel Hawthorne, Jones Very, Margaret Fuller, and many others. Her acquaintance with Ralph Waldo Emerson began in 1822 when she took a few private lessons in Greek from him. When next they met in 1833, it was to discuss the theme, the Eternal Relations of God. So impressed was she with Emerson's thoughts that she not only attended his sermons, but, on her frequent visits to his home, read the sermons he had in manuscript. They remained fresh in her memory forty years later, when she said:

Mr. Emerson understood and believed with Froebel—the cosmopolite prophet of the nineteenth century—what Jesus meant when he said that "whoever receiveth a little child in my name receiveth me, and whoever receiveth me receiveth Him that sent me."[61]

59 Harriet Martineau, *op. cit.*, pp. 277–8.
60 *Ibid.*, p. 278.
61 Peabody, "Emerson as Preacher," in F. B. Sanborn (ed.), *The Genius and Character of Emerson*, p. 155.

In her admiration for Washington Allston, the painter and poet, Miss Peabody was moved not only by his art, but by the deep religious nature of the man. In a lecture to kindergarten teachers in 1886, Miss Peabody quoted at great length from Allston's lectures on art. She pointed to his idea of "those intuitive powers, which are above and beyond both the understanding and the senses . . ."[62] She elucidated to the kindergartners:

The object of the lecturer Allston was what the kindergartner's first object should be,—to awaken the self-respect of the eternal soul within us all, making the life of our individuality—our personality . . . It is no part of the kindergartner's duty to give—she can only awaken the feelings of harmony, beauty, and conscience.[63]

If the thought and the language seem involved, it is to be remembered that to Miss Peabody, the Transcendentalist, the words of the poets were just a prelude to the mystical thought of Froebel.

From the foregoing may be seen the importance of inherited and environmental influences in shaping Miss Peabody's character. She drew her impulses to live "the higher life" from the strong characters and the great minds of the reform era in which she lived. All the friends mentioned had certain traits in common: a belief in the goodness of man, a deeply religious nature, a respect for the beauty and wonder of nature, an acceptance of Jesus as a great teacher, and a willingness to sacrifice, or rather an obliviousness of the sacrifice involved in putting ideals into practice. Friedrich Froebel not only expressed these qualities in his writings, but evolved a system whereby they could be practiced with little children. To Miss Peabody, of such was the Kingdom of Heaven.

[62] Peabody, "Lectures in the Training School for Kindergartners," p. 190.
[63] *Ibid.*, p. 194.

III

"Miss Thesaura"

ELIZABETH PEABODY'S PHILOSOPHY AND PRACTICE OF EDUCA-
tion were influenced not only by the circumstances of her
life and by the enlightened minds with which she came
into contact, but also by the books she read. Miss Peabody sought knowledge for its own sake, not as did Bronson Alcott, "for confirmation of what in some sense he
already knew."[1] In comparing her to Alcott, Odell Shepard said, "So far as what is ordinarily called knowledge is
concerned, she knew far more than Alcott did."[2] Like
Alcott, however, she was largely self-educated, since after
her childhood lessons at home, she never attended any
other school. She practiced in her daily life the gospel of
self-improvement preached by William Ellery Channing
and set forth in Degerando's *Self-Education*.[3] Her purpose
in studying was revealed in a letter written when she was
only eighteen years old, but already living alone and
teaching in Boston:

1 Odell Shepard, *Pedlar's Progress*, p. 152.
2 *Ibid.*, p. 128.
3 Van Wyck Brooks, *The Flowering of New England*, p. 2.

. . . you do not study for the sake of being admired, for the sake of attracting attention, nay *even* so much for the pleasure it will afford you as for the good effect it has upon yr mind, considered in its influence upon yr own moral character, and upon society as it is around you.[4]

The seriousness of her purpose may be judged by her aforementioned statement as well by her warning to fourteen-year-old Sophia:

I think . . . *no considerations* should hinder us from cultivating to the highest degree *circumstances* will *possibly* allow of, our *intellectual faculties.*[5]

Elizabeth not only was a student of theology through her discussions with Dr. William Ellery Channing, but she read many theological tomes. From those she had read, she selected some for young Sophia's reading, but cautioned her: "Wait till you have time and feel like it for it should absorb your whole soul as it did *mine* when I pursued it."[6]

The books on theology that Elizabeth claimed to have found most rewarding were Paley's *Natural Theology and Evidences of Christianity*, Dr. Priestley's *Institutes of Natural and Revealed Religion*, Middleton's *Letter from Rome*, Stewart and Norton's *Controversy*, Wood and Ware's *Controversy*, Dr. Priestley's *History of the Corruptions of Christianity*, Tucker's *Light of Nature*, and Brown's *Philosophy*. She concluded her recommendations by saying:

There are many—very many more books which I have pursued in relation to this controversy that I know would be instruc-

[4] *Letter*, Elizabeth P. Peabody to Sophia A. Peabody, June 23, 1822. Berg Collection, New York Public Library.
[5] *Ibid.*
[6] *Letter*, Elizabeth P. Peabody to Sophia A. Peabody, March 31, 1823. Berg Collection, New York Public Library.

tive but I must limit my advice to a few. A long string of books would frighten you from beginning the course.[7]

That Elizabeth had some interest in science may be assumed from her attendance at Mr. Hale's lectures on metals, in 1824, and by the copious notes she took of the lectures. For example, her summary of the lecture on the history and properties of potassium filled four closely written pages.[8] Her explanation of the atomistic theory of light, in 1859, showed the serious thought she still gave to science.[9]

Phrenology, an empirical system of psychology formulated by F. J. Gall about 1800, was of interest to some nineteenth-century educators. Horace Mann recommended the study of phrenology to teachers.[10] His son, George Combe Mann, was named after the Scottish phrenologist, George Combe. The Baroness Von Marenholtz-Bülow had received instruction in phrenology.[11] Her teacher, Dr. Schewe, examined Friedrich Froebel's head. The Baroness reported:

Froebel had never given any attention to phrenology, but was nevertheless of the opinion that it could not but be true that the organs of the human brain should show the stamp of the mind, which they served as an instrument.[12]
. . . Froebel was very eager to know the results of the examination of his head, which Dr. Schewe made in my presence, and assented to most of his conclusions.[13]

---

7 *Ibid.*

8 *Letter,* Elizabeth P. Peabody to Sophia A. Peabody, February 15, 1824. Berg Collection, New York Public Library.

9 Elizabeth P. Peabody, *Memorial to Dr. William Wesselhöft,* p. 46.

10 Richard E. Thursfield, *Henry Barnard's American Journal of Education,* p. 185.

11 Marenholtz-Bülow, *Reminiscences of Friedrich Froebel,* p. 310.

12 *Loc. cit.*

13 *Ibid.,* p. 311.

No evidence has been found that would reveal the extent of Elizabeth Peabody's knowledge of or interest in phrenology. Her acquaintanceship with the subject and her admiration for the phrenologist, Johann Gasper Spurzheim, were expressed in the original poem she wrote, entitled *Welcome of Angels and Farewell of Men to the Beloved Spurzheim.* The third verse of the poem expressed her sentiments:

Hail to heaven! pious spirit
Humbly searching Nature's plan—
Hail to heaven! and inherit
Power the universe to scan
Let it not—the earthly power
Finite ear and bounded eye—
Well then worked Time's little hour—
Gaining what can never die—[14]

It was in 1850 that Froebel said that he agreed with Dr. Schewe that education might derive great gain from this branch of knowledge, if its results were completely and scientifically established.[15] The Baroness's *Reminiscences of Friedrich Froebel,* in which she related Froebel's experience, was translated by Elizabeth's sister, Mary, and so it may be assumed that Elizabeth was familiar with Froebel's opinion expressed therein.

Elizabeth had begun the study of languages in her childhood. She recalled that by her father she was "taught and well-grounded in Latin and Greek."[16] She was studying French in 1824 for she wrote to Sophia, "I am writing exercises on the reflective verbs in French."[17] Her knowledge

[14] Elizabeth P. Peabody, *Ms.,* n.d., Manuscript Room, New York Public Library.

[15] Marenholtz-Bülow, *op. cit.,* p. 310.

[16] Maria S. Porter, "Elizabeth Palmer Peabody," *The Bostonian,* Vol. 3, No. 4, January, 1896, p. 340.

[17] *Letter,* Elizabeth P. Peabody to Sophia A. Peabody, February 15, 1824. Berg Collection, New York Public Library.

of Greek, French, Italian, and German can be judged
from her translations. George Ripley commended her ability as a translator in his criticism in the *Christian Examiner*. In a review of *Self-Education*, translated from the
French of M. le Baron Degerando, he said:

We ought not to close our remarks, without expressing our
thanks to the translator for presenting us this work in English
dress. We cheerfully give our testimony to the good judgment
and pure taste, with which the task has been executed. It
bears marks of a faithful study of the original, a sufficient
knowledge of the author's language, a ready perception of his
style of thought and illustration, and a deep sympathy with
the beautiful and elevated spirit of his philosophy.[18]

Miss Peabody's translations included *Phaedo and Crito*,
from the Greek of Plato; and *Angela Sleeps*, from the
Italian. In *The Family School*, in 1836, Elizabeth published an excerpt from the German of J. P. Richter which
was entitled "Recollections of the Most Beautiful Hours
in Life for the Last Hour."[19]

Miss Harriet Martineau was impressed by the prevalent
accomplishment in languages of the intellectual women
of America:

All American ladies are more or less literary: and some are
so to excellent purpose: to the saving of their minds from
vacuity. Readers are plentiful: thinkers are rare. Minds are of
a very passive character: and it follows that languages are
much cultivated. If ever a woman was pointed out to me as
distinguished for information, I might be sure beforehand
that she was a linguist. I met with a great number of ladies
who read Latin; some Greek; some Hebrew; some German.

18 George Ripley, "Degerando on Self-Education," *Christian Examiner*,
Vol. IX, September, 1930, p. 105.
19 Elizabeth P. Peabody, *The Family School*, Vol. 1, No. 2, November
1, 1836, p. 11.

With the exception of the last, the learning did not seem to be of much use to them, except as a harmless exercise.[20]

Since Miss Martineau's talents were in the area of social commentary, rather than linguistic fluency, her criticism lacked authority. However, there was some truth in her observation, for certain of Miss Peabody's acquaintances studied foreign languages. In a letter to Anna Hazard Ward, Elizabeth extended an invitation to join in such study:

Next Friday a class begins with Dr. Kraitsir in German. I wish you were to join it. It only comes once a week and when you do come I hope you may be able to come into it a few times at least. We also begin next week a class once a week to read Italian. And a lady and I are reading Plautus once a week with him—so you see I am a little busy with study.[21]

Evidence that Elizabeth was interested in, if not proficient in, other languages was found in her correspondence. In a letter to Charles Folsom she indicated her desire to borrow books on chronology from the Athenaeum. In return she proposed to present her Polish library to this institution. No list of the books which constituted her library was enclosed.[22] Later in the month, she asked for permission to borrow Wilson's *Sanskrit Grammar* and a first book in that language.[23] The depth or extent of her study of Sanskrit was not indicated by her correspondence. She informed Mr. Folsom, in this same letter, that she had procured all "the means and appliances for studying Icelandic

[20] Harriet Martineau, *Society in America*, Vol. II, p. 256.
[21] *Letter*, Eilzabeth P. Peabody to Anna Hazard Ward, [1848]. Elizabeth Peabody Collection, Houghton Library.
[22] *Letter*, Elizabeth P. Peabody to Charles Folsom, November [1858]. Manuscript Room, Boston Public Library.
[23] *Letter*, Elizabeth P. Peabody to Charles Folsom, November 27, 1858. Manuscript Room, Boston Public Library. The book referred to is Horace Hayman Wilson, *An Introduction to the Grammar of the Sanskrit Language*.

for eighteen dollars."[24] In 1835, she sought books for learning the Basque language, naming the books she wanted her friend to send her from Europe. Said she, "There was a New Testament printed in Basque at Rochelle in 1571 —I should like to have that."[25] No evidences were found to indicate that Elizabeth Peabody ever conversed in or translated from any of these languages or the others, such as Chinese and Hebrew, which other persons have said she studied. It may be that her interest in language was more historical and philosophical rather than a desire to speak the foreign tongue. In a lecture on language she explained:

Language is the element in which the intellectual nature makes a sphere wherein to live and move and have its being. What breath is to the material body, making man alive in nature, language is to the social body, making it alive in history.[26]

Although she may never have spoken Chinese, she described the technique of pronouncing it in a lecture before kindergarten teachers in order to demonstrate its relation to musical sounds.[27]

Elizabeth Peabody was, according to her nephew Julian Hawthorne, "a thesaurus of all knowledge." To him,

She was probably the most learned person in the world—certainly the most learned woman, in an era of feminine pundits . . . Greek, Latin, Sanskrit, and Hebrew were household tongues with Aunt Lizzie. And not content with knowing things, she wanted everybody else to know them, and had invented ingenious ways of instructing them.[28]

24 *Ibid.*
25 *Letter*, Elizabeth P. Peabody to Mr. Capon, September 9, 1835. Peabody Correspondence, Essex Institute.
26 Peabody, *Lectures in the Training Schools for Kindergartners*, p. 89.
27 *Ibid.*, p. 90.
28 Julian Hawthorne, *The Memoirs of Julian Hawthorne*, pp. 45–7.

This was, of course, an exaggerated statement by an admiring nephew. Aunt Lizzie seemed to a young boy to be "the most learned person," and this was the picture Julian carried with him to manhood. The quotation showed by its effusive admiration and use of a nickname, Aunt Lizzie, that the young man had affection for this "pundit." Her great knowledge was not a barrier between herself and others such as himself. Julian Hawthorne may be forgiven for his accolade. His statement, however, need not be dismissed summarily as having no truth at all. There were many persons, more experienced and objective than he was, who uttered similar words of praise and who sought her advice, opinion, and assistance. Horace Mann, also referred to her as "Miss Thesaura" when he was preparing a lecture and sought materials about ancient history. He asked:

If you have them copied off, please send them, as it will save my busy fingers some labor,—if not, tell me book and page where I can find them. This is my modest request of you, *Miss Thesaura*.[29]

Dr. William Ellery Channing asked how Elizabeth thought the congregation would like Mr. Hedge's sermons. "On this point," said he, "I would like your judgment."[30] Henry James, Sr. wrote to her:

I left word with Mr. Osgood at Mr. Ticknor's to put aside one of my books for you when it comes out. . . . I hope you will let me know your opinion of it.[31]

[29] *Letter*, Horace Mann to Elizabeth P. Peabody, January 8, 1838. Robert Lincoln Straker Collection, Antioch College Library.

[30] Peabody, *Reminiscences of Rev. William Ellery Channing, D.D.*, p. 393.

[31] *Letter*, Henry James, Sr. to Elizabeth P. Peabody, June 10, [1863]. Horace Mann Collection, Massachusetts Historical Society. The book referred to was *Substance and Show*.

After an evening in her company, Moses Coit Tyler wrote to his wife:

I spent last evening with Mr. ———. It was a brilliant assemblage. I had a long talk with Miss Peabody, who was there, and found her conversation very interesting. She is a scholar and it is a rare treat to hear her.[32]

Theodore Parker was also impressed by her. He said:

She is a woman of most astounding powers; has a many-sidedness and a largeness of soul quite unusual; rare qualities of head and heart.[33]

Harriet H. Robinson, in 1882, placed her "among the Massachusetts women whose literary reputations are almost cosmopolitan."[34]

Another subject of interest to Elizabeth was nature. She believed that the keen observation of natural phenomena would lead from its physical beauty to the sense of the moral beauty in life.[35] From this it may be seen that Elizabeth was more interested in the symbolic than the scientific aspect of nature. She found that nature could be studied to advantage "with the association of poetry, such as Thompson and Cowper."[36] In the same letter to Sophia, she made these recommendations:

Moore's has an enervating effect if too intimately known from the looseness of its morality. . . . *Byron* cannot be relished without a mind is more fully stored than yours is, with classical recollections . . . his Childe Harold can only be relished

32 Jessica Tyler Austen (ed.), *Moses Coit Tyler,* p. 17.

33 F. B. Sanborn, *Recollections of Seventy Years,* Vol. II, p. 548.

34 Harriet H. Robinson, *Massachusetts in the Woman Suffrage Movement,* p. 154.

35 *Letter,* Elizabeth P. Peabody to Sophia A. Peabody, June 23, 1822. Berg Collection, New York Public Library.

36 *Loc. cit.*

by a scholar . . . Scott, his poetry is not of the sentimental type and therefore less dangerous.[37]

Although Miss Peabody was an indifferent poet, she was an ardent reader of Milton, Wordsworth, Longfellow, Lowell, and Tennyson. Quotations from their works illuminate her own writings. It was, however, Washington Allston, the poet and painter, from whom she drew her deepest inspiration. She, in fact, quoted Milton in order to describe Allston adequately. " 'He who makes a true poet,' said Milton, 'must be in himself an heroic poem.' Allston verifies this sentence."[38] Considering Miss Peabody's high ethical and moral standards, it would seem doubtful that she could or would approve of any poetry, however gracefully phrased, that did not reflect these inclinations.

The symbolism which is often present in poetry appealed to her just as Froebel's efforts at symbolism in verse were to be accepted by her wholeheartedly. Froebel's sometimes awkward rhymes and labored symbols were translated and used literally by Miss Peabody. William Torrey Harris was more critical of Froebel as a poet, noting that:

He [Froebel] was able to see symbols; but poetry is something more than symbolism. He lacked the true poetic sense which can find appropriate forms of personification for ideas. . . . It has happened that most of the literal imitations of Froebel's poetry have contributed in a greater or less degree to ruin the poetic sense of teachers and pupils.[39]

---

[37] *Loc. cit.*

[38] Elizabeth P. Peabody, "Life and Genius of Allston," *Last Evening with Allston,* p. 21.

[39] William T. Harris, "Editor's Preface," in *Mottoes and Commentaries of Froebel's Mother Play,* translated by Susan E. Blow and Henrietta R. Eliot, p. ix.

Another measure of the extent and nature of Elizabeth Peabody's reading may be taken from the reviews and critical notices which she wrote. In her short-lived periodical, *The Family School*, a review by her of a current book was a regular feature. She brought to the attention of her readers Heine's *Letters on German Literature*, as translated by G. W. Haven. The book, she declared, offended her religious nature. She was shocked by Heine's "moral enmity with the spiritual religion of Jesus." She compared him, to his disadvantage, with other philosophers. Continued Miss Peabody, "We see no benevolence in him. In this respect, he makes a poor figure beside Godwin, Rousseau, and even Voltaire."[40] Her reactions to Harriet Martineau's *Five Years of Youth; or Sense and Sensibility* were more favorable. She thought that:

Miss Martineau has never been appreciated, simply as a first rate artist in the Story [sic] telling line. And yet here lies her only indisputable claim to Genius. . . . This book is not a new publication. We notice it, because it has not been spoken of, that we have seen; and yet nothing we have, of this voluminous author, seems to us more beautiful.[41]

Excerpts from German authors were published in translation, if the "thought" was considered worthy by the editor, publisher, and translator, who was none other than Miss Peabody. Such an example was "Speech and Writing," from the German of Herder. Its flowery and poetic language gave it a place in the "Poetical Department." It began:

Hail to thee! invisible offspring of the breath of man—angel—sister, sweet speech! without whose true service the full heart would sink under the weight of feeling; no song of olden time

40 Peabody, *The Family School*, Vol. 1, No. 1, September 1, 1836, p. 10.
41 Peabody, *The Family School*, Vol. 1, No. 2, November 1, 1836, p. 21.

would visit a human ear; antiquity would be dumb; and the heart of the sage, be the grave of his songs.[42]

Because Miss Peabody's reading influenced her career to so great an extent, and since as teacher and lecturer she put her knowledge to work, she may be exempted from Miss Martineau's condemnation of her as possessing a mind of "a very passive character." Elizabeth Peabody was quick to recognize the marks of genius in literature, and was of such generous heart as to give full acknowledgment and encouragement to such authors. It was she who discovered the writings of Nathaniel Hawthorne in a current magazine under a nom-de-plume and who endeavored to further his writing career so that he would enrich literature for the young. In her friendliness, Nathaniel Hawthorne "at last found a person who expressed a genuine and heartfelt appreciation of his work, and it was like the return of the sun to the Arctic explorer after his long winter night."[43] In a letter to Horace Mann, she referred to Hawthorne as a "man of first rate genius," and, since "he has not thriven with the booksellers," she beseeched Mann to read *Twice-Told Tales* and then suggested that Capon, a bookseller, would attend to any recommendation Mann would make in Hawthorne's behalf.[44]

Elizabeth Peabody's passion for learning was explained by Frank Preston Stearns:

The Graces had not been bountiful to the Peabody family so, to compensate for this, they all cultivated the Muses, in whose society they ascended no little distance on the way to Parnassus.[45]

[42] Peabody, *The Family School,* Vol. 1, No. 1, September 1, 1836, p. 2.

[43] Frank P. Stearns, *The Life and Genius of Nathaniel Hawthorne,* p. 119.

[44] *Letter,* Elizabeth Peabody to Horace Mann, March 3, 1838. Horace Mann Collection, Massachusetts Historical Society.

[45] Stearns, *op. cit.,* p. 117.

During her first experience as a governess in the home of Benjamin Vaughan in Hallowell, Maine, in 1823, Elizabeth experienced the delight of being literally surrounded by books, which she lost no time in reading. Her employer possessed a ten thousand volume library in an era when the library of Harvard College held only twelve thousand books on its shelves. No one could have taken better advantage of the opportunities it offered during the severe Maine winter than did Elizabeth.[46]

Her love of books was in part gratified by her circulating library and foreign bookshop venture in 1840. Her brother Nathaniel described its beginnings:

My sister Elizabeth did then, partly through the assistance of wealthy friends, open a Room which went by the name of "Book Room" for the sale of foreign books and artists' materials. A library of English, German, French, and of a few other books in Swedish, Spanish and other languages was added.[47]

The quality of Miss Peabody's stock of books may be judged by her determined purpose as expressed in a letter to Samuel Ward:

This was the original plan of my store—that I should keep one in which were to be found no *worthless books*—shadows of shadows—and nothing of any kind—of a secondary quality.[48]

To judge the influence of books upon her educational career, one must first appreciate her sensitivity to beautiful human relationships in literature, as well as her desire to practice in her daily life the high aspirations of which

---

46 Louise H. Tharp, *The Peabody Sisters of Salem,* p. 31.

47 Notes compiled by Nathaniel Cranch Peabody, dated about 1870. Robert Lincoln Straker Collection, Antioch College Library.

48 *Letter,* Elizabeth Peabody to Samuel Ward, September 13, 1841. Elizabeth Peabody Correspondence, Houghton Library.

she read. She expressed this thought in the preface to her translation of *Gunderode* in March, 1842:

To those who have eyes to see, and hearts to understand the deep leadings of the two characters, these leaves present a treasury of sweetest satisfactions, of lively suggestions;—to the obtuse, the vulgar, and the frivolous, they will seem sheer folly, the cobweb tissues of a misled fancy, the bubbles on waters yet undrained. They will be much or nothing to the reader, according to the degree in which he has sought, felt, and lived a pure, a private, and aspiring life.[49]

The range of the subject matter in her personal library, as well as the number of languages in which the books are written, revealed the cosmopolitan nature of Miss Peabody's literary interests and the breadth of her sources of information.[50] Here was found the popular contemporary weekly journal, *Household Words,* conducted by Charles Dickens. Miss Peabody was always aware of the interests of women and of the importance of reaching the mother in the home. Among her books of German literature were *Lieder und Romanzen* by August Graf v. Platen, and *Die Krieger,* a novel by Heinrich Laube.

From her parents, Miss Peabody derived much of her interest in literature. Her sister, Mrs. Horace Mann, related that when they were children, a friend of Dr. Peabody's, a retired actor, would come to their home to read Shakespeare to the family. Continued Mrs. Mann, "This early Shakespearian education was a great thing for myself and my sister and I always had access to the books which lay on the table."[51]

[49] E. P. Peabody, translator and publisher, *Gunderode,* "Preface," p. vii.
[50] Consult Appendix A, *infra,* for list of books from Miss Peabody's library.
[51] Peabody, *Female Education in Massachusetts,* p. 304.

Elizabeth Peabody early evidenced a great interest in history. In her history book written for children, she informed her pupils in the dedication:

Scripture history being the most important subject that can engage our attention, as evolving both temporal and eternal interests, I am induced affectionate [sic] to dedicate the annexed lessons particularly to you.[52]

This interest persisted even after she had stopped "keeping school." She had come to the conclusion "that in women's education history should take the place that law, medicine, or theology takes in the liberal education of men."[53] Her advocation of such a practice may have developed from her awareness of the applicability of the solutions of past problems to current problems. Because her interest in the social problems of the day was continuous with, and not unrelated to, the problems of the past, she had faith that a knowledge of history was the most important source of moral influence for Americans. It was characteristic of Miss Peabody's zeal that she would assume a study, which she had found valuable, to be of equal enlightenment to other women. Her idealism was such as to lead her to believe that mankind could be recreated by a proper knowledge and use of the past and that women, as mothers and potential educators of a new generation, were just the persons to use this knowledge. She, therefore, taught history to a group of women who met twice a week for a six-month term of fifty sessions. Her teaching methods were similar to those of Bronson Alcott and Margaret Fuller. She did not lecture to her adult students, but employed a conversational method. Her students did

[52] Peabody, *First Steps to the Study of History,* "Dedication," not paginated.
[53] Peabody, *Female Education in Massachusetts,* p. 304.

much reading and preparation outside of the classroom.
These "Historical Conferences" were so successful that
Miss Peabody was able to go to Europe on the fees she received. She returned enriched with the knowledge of Froebel's method and ready to conquer new fields.

Miss Peabody was able to see the figures of history as
real people and to apply their learnings to the problems of
her own times. This vivid sense of participation she was
able to impart to her scholars, as was shown by the popularity of her lectures. Her fundamental curiosity about
places and people led her to read American history, European history, and the history of ancient times.[54] Her
reading, extensive as it was, was of secondary materials.
She used Layard's *Nineveh*, Landseer's *Cylinders of Baby-
lon*, and Karl Otfried Muller's *History of the Dorians*.[55]
In preparing a lecture series on the eight centuries immediately before Christ, Miss Peabody used as texts Herodotus, Thucydides, Xenophon, Plutarch, and Livy. Her
lecture series on Greek literature and Greek theatre were
so well prepared, and Miss Peabody was considered so
erudite, that some of the Harvard students came to her
sub rosa while this conference was in progress, and asked
her advice as to their historical reading. She related that
they "followed out this course and read the tragedies, and
I advised them to read the Greek historians and Livy in
the original."[56]

From this well-stocked mind came history books for the
young[57] as well as "Conferences," "Conversations," and
such treatises as *The Dorian Measure* for adults. That the
past could be used to interpret the present was shown in

[54] *Ibid.*, p. 306.
[55] *Ibid.*, p. 305.
[56] *Ibid.*, p. 304.
[57] See Bibliography, *infra*.

this latter volume, which she wrote in 1848. For Miss Peabody, people were similar and recognizable in whatever century they happened to live. She found no difficulty in applying a solution used by the Greeks to a modern problem:

But the question for us is, whether, on the new platform upon which Christendom finds itself, now that the spiritual future has descended as it were into human life, there may not be found a harmony corresponding to the Dorian measure;— whether there may not be a social organization which does as much justice to the Christian religion and philosophy, as the Dorian state did to Apollo.[58]

This search for perfection in practical living was Miss Peabody's constant vision. If she found in her study of history some practice of ancient time which she considered educationally valuable, she immediately planned for its transference to current wants. An example again was found in *The Dorian Measure*. In this paper, which was based upon her study of Greek history, she described the gymnastic exercises of the Dorian youth, their dancing, and music. So impressed was she with their value in the educative process that she proposed the introduction of these arts into general education of the nineteenth century.[59] Today, the presence of these subjects in school curricula is accepted without surprise, if not without question. In Miss Peabody's era, such subjects were not common. Only such "progressive" and dauntless souls as Bronson Alcott were aware of the need of the child for any activity. As Dorothy McCuskey pointed out, "He introduced physical exercises at a time when knitting and sewing were the only such activities permitted in most

[58] Peabody, "The Dorian Measure," *Aesthetic Papers*, p. 86.
[59] Peabody, *Female Education in Massachusetts*, pp. 102–3.

schools."[60] In Froebel's conception of education for young children was to be found the singing, the rhythmic movements, the physical activity, and the drawing which seemed so right and proper to Miss Peabody when she read of their use by the Greeks, before she found them advocated by Froebel.

Although Miss Peabody was well versed in the transcendental literature of her day, she was unable to accept its ultra-egoism and extreme individualism. She preferred to emphasize "the culture which is alike in all men."[61] Being cognizant of the philosophies of Kant and Hegel and of the socialism of Fourier, she yet rejected them as not being "true reform."[62] Said John B. Wilson of Miss Peabody:

What Elizabeth Peabody learned from Dr. Channing, Washington Allston, and from her omnivorous readings in theology, history, and philosophy she made peculiarly her own. It was precisely this eclectic combination of modified individualism, the aesthetic ideal, and a positive philosophy of history that enabled her to effect a reconciliation between transcendentalism and humanism and to integrate all her interests around a dynamic concept of culture that combined the best features of both Hebraism and Hellenism.[63]

To Miss Peabody's aforementioned love of books may be added her desire to share them with other kindred spirits as another motivating force in the opening of her West Street bookshop. Thomas Wentworth Higginson, one of the bright young men who patronized the shop, noted this aspect of her character:

[60] Dorothy McCuskey, *Bronson Alcott, Teacher,* p. 164.
[61] Peabody, *Reminiscences of Channing,* p. 365.
[62] Peabody, *Last Evening with Allston,* p. 248.
[63] John B. Wilson, "A Transcendental Minority Report," *The New England Quarterly,* Vol. 29, No. 2, June, 1956, p. 151.

The Brook Farm people were also to be met occasionally at Mrs. Harrington's confectionary shop in School Street, where they took economical refreshments; and still oftener at Miss Elizabeth Peabody's foreign bookstore in West Street, which was a part of the educational influence of the period . . . There was also Miss Peabody herself, desultory, dreamy, but insatiable in her life for knowledge and for helping others to it.[64]

The Brook Farm people referred to by Higginson included Ripley, Alcott, Emerson, and Russell. Miss Peabody had visited the farm, but was not a member. Her approval of certain of its practices, despite their derivation from Fourier's *The Social Destiny of Man,* was expressed in the transcendental magazine, *The Dial,* wherein she wrote that Brook Farm realized Christ's idea of society by identifying living with learning.[65] Later, she was to grasp eagerly at Froebel's idea of learning through doing, having been prepared by the reading of the German literature which was then in such vogue in New England. John Wilson explained:

Goethe had stressed "learning by doing" in his *William Meister,* which in Carlyle's translation of 1824, was one of the early Bibles of Transcendentalism. Carlyle's "work" doctrine was presented as a social cure-all in *Sartor Resartus.*[66]

There was no doubt that Miss Peabody was familiar with these and many other books, for her correspondence abounded in references to books she was reading or had read. Miss Maria Porter, who met Miss Peabody at the West Street bookstore and who attended her history

[64] Thomas Wentworth Higginson, *Cheerful Yesterdays,* p. 85.

[65] Peabody, "Christ's Idea of Society," *The Dial,* Vol. 2, 1841, p. 227.

[66] Wilson, "The Antecedents of Brook Farm," *The New England Quarterly,* Vol. 15, No. 2, June, 1942, p. 330.

classes, said that Miss Peabody often wrote long letters of twelve or fourteen pages about new books. "Even after she had passed her eightieth year she wrote to tell me what she thought of Mrs. Burnett's *Little Lord Fauntleroy*."[67]

Thus, through her appreciation and love of knowledge, and through her constant use of books to attain it, Elizabeth Peabody achieved an enviable education in an era that was not fully awakened to the need of education for women. Despite the heavy burdens of her family life, and her lack of leisure, she found the precious time necessary to free her intellect from petty concerns. Where opportunities were presented to enjoy good books and intelligent discussions, she seized them. When no opportunities were offered, such was her zest for knowledge, that she made her own opportunities. By her reading in philosophy, history, literature, poetry, and theology, she achieved the great purpose of life advocated by Degerando—moral progress accomplished by self-education. And as Degerando had pointed out, "The character of great men is always partly their own work. Self-education alone raises us above the vulgar."[68] Elizabeth Peabody believed in and acted upon Degerando's pronouncement that "moral progress is a career open to all."[69]

[67] Maria S. Porter, "Elizabeth Palmer Peabody," *The Bostonian*, Vol. 3, No. 4, January, 1896, p. 345.

[68] Degerando, *Self-Education*, p. 6.

[69] *Ibid.*, p. 7.

IV

The Kindergarten Experiment, 1860-1870

AS HAS BEEN NOTED, BY 1860 THERE HAD BEEN SEVERAL AT-
tempts in America to put Froebel's theories into practice.
Because these were in German-speaking kindergartens, the
attempts had little effect upon American educators or upon
the American public. How then was the word spread and
the kindergarten gospel preached? Talcott Williams declared that it was done "by the simplest of all paths—experiment. By the best of all leadership—devoted women."[1]
Elizabeth Peabody was the first of these devoted women
to try the experiment in her own English-speaking school.
She was especially well-adapted to give the kindergarten
wide publicity for "she knew everyone worth knowing in
the neighborhood of Boston."[2] The twenty years of Elizabeth's life, from 1860 to 1880, were devoted to establishing
the kindergarten as an American educational institution.

[1] Talcott Williams, "The Kindergarten Movement," *The Century,* Vol.
XLV, January, 1893, p. 369.
[2] Norman Holmes Pearson, "Elizabeth Peabody on Hawthorne," *Essex
Institute Historical Collections,* Vol. XCIV, July, 1958, No. 3, p. 258.

Alerted by her understanding of young children, and by her years of experience as a teacher in her own school, as well as by her observation in Alcott's Temple School, she welcomed the opportunity to propagate Froebel's ideas of education as the most suitable and effective method of instruction for young children.[3] She always was considered *"avant garde* both in the theory and the practise [sic] of children's education, as her *First Steps to the Study of History* (1832) showed and her later influential role in the introduction of the kindergarten was to prove."[4]

After Miss Peabody's first kindergarten experiment at 15 Pinckney Street in Boston, she found that "accommodations for growing plants or keeping animals,"[5] which the program called for, required that she take larger quarters. Hence, she moved to 24½ Winter Street and on October 28, 1861, opened the new school with thirty children in attendance and with two assistant teachers. A special French teacher, Madame Destre, came three times a week to converse "with all the children who can sit still, for twenty minutes."[6] All of the class learned to print and draw and more than half had learned to read by the term's end. A special teacher came weekly to instruct in gymnastics. The expense of maintaining such a program was beyond the receipts from tuition. Miss Peabody found that she needed even more rooms and more funds. She pleaded:

If I can advance my price twenty-five per cent, I can do all I wish, and have something for my own labor, *which is life-*

---

[3] Elizabeth P. Peabody, "Preface to 1874 Edition," *Record of Mr. Alcott's School,* p. 4.

[4] Pearson, *op. cit.,* p. 268.

[5] Peabody, *Report and New Prospectus of Kindergarten,* April, 1862, p. 1. Robert Lincoln Straker Collection, Antioch College Library.

[6] *Ibid.*

absorbing. I will therefore resume the Kindergarten on the 22nd of September, 1862, for forty weeks, to July 4, exclusive of half a week at Christmas and Thanksgiving times, if I can be paid fifty dollars a year for each pupil, in advance, as I call for it.[7]

While at the Winter Street School, Miss Peabody published an article "Kindergarten—What is It?" in the *Atlantic Monthly.* The following year, she, with her sister Mary Mann, then widowed, published their *Moral Culture of Infancy and Kindergarten Guide.* The scarcity of literature in English about the kindergarten made these works doubly important. Miss Peabody continued her experiments and modifications of Froebel's plan with great appreciation of Froebel's philosophy, but with growing dissatisfaction and acute realization of her inadequacy because of lack of preparation for the undertaking. Endeavoring to enlist the interest and aid of many people in Froebel's principles of education, she mailed her circular concerning the kindergarten to educators, ministers, parents, and to her famous and influential acquaintances. To be sure, not all of the replies were favorable. The idea of play as a means of learning was not always accepted, as was evidenced by one response:

. . . I think children must learn soon that play is not the end of life, but that nothing really worth having is got without work, and little by little they will learn to take their share, and I don't think it hurts them. . . . What I mean to say is, that the Kindergarten plan as long as it lasts is *play,* it puts off the time of *work.* This must come some time or other or the child will never be good for much.[8]

[7] *Ibid.,* p. 7.
[8] *Letter,* L. P. Hale to Elizabeth P. Peabody, September 27, 1861. Robert Lincoln Straker Collection, Antioch College Library.

Miss Peabody must have been cheered, however, by a letter from Dr. E. A. Sheldon, for, as the founder of the Oswego Normal School in New York, his opinion carried great weight. Dr. Sheldon wrote:

It affords me no ordinary pleasure to find one so capable of exerting a good influence in an educational way, interested in what I regard as an important reformation in our methods of teaching. Hitherto our teaching has been done in a haphazard way, with no system, with no proper understanding of the character of the infant mind, or the proper appliances, or the natural order of succession in the development of the mind. This reformation will prove a rich blessing to the children. I call it an *emancipation*.[9]

Such recognition of the value of her efforts coupled with his invitation to her to join the educators, who were to assemble in Oswego later in the year to examine the principles of the new system, were bright events in the difficult days of securing acceptance of the new idea.

Strangers to Miss Peabody were informed of the "kindergarten system" through current newspapers. The type of requests Miss Peabody received, after mention of her activities by the press, was exemplified by this note from a stranger:

I read, with some interest, in last Saturday's *Christian Register,* some account of a conversation at the Warren St. Chapel on what is called the "Kindergarten" system of instruction, in which conversation you took a conspicuous part. One of my grand daughters [sic], Miss Elizabeth Gordon, has just commenced, in this city, a school in which she is endeavoring to pursue, so far as I can judge, a similar plan of instruction. She has received no aid in this undertaking, except from the

9 *Letter,* E. A. Sheldon to Elizabeth P. Peabody, November 25, 1861. Robert Lincoln Straker Collection, Antioch College Library.

promptings of her own heart and the suggestions of her own mind. Will your leisure and inclination permit you to communicate an outline or sketch of the system and the mode of its practical application for her benefit?[10]

No doubt prompted by the grandfather's interest in his granddaughter's "laudable undertaking," Miss Peabody rejoiced in another convert and referred them to "some publication in our vernacular" as they requested. The Reverend John Weiss did promise to "magnify" her excellent plan to those he thought likely to be interested.[11] Miss Peabody also wrote to Henry Wadsworth Longfellow to seek aid for Mrs. C. M. Rollins in establishing a "Sanitarium and Kindergarten for the promotion of physical education."[12] Mrs. Longfellow had been a pupil in Miss Peabody's school in 1827. Elizabeth could expect sympathetic attention from the husband of the former Fanny Appleton.

In 1864, the Boston Directory listed Miss Peabody as a kindergartner, a strange word to most citizens, at 15 Pinckney Street, again. In September of the same year, Mrs. Louise Pollock ventured to open a kindergarten in Professor N. T. Allen's English and Classical School at West Newton, Massachusetts, where she was then residing. Born in Prussia, Mrs. Pollock had become interested in Froebel's ideas from the article in the *Christian Examiner* and from interviews with Miss Peabody. Under Miss Peabody's personal promptings, and using the newly published *Moral Culture of Infancy and Kindergarten Guide*

10 *Letter,* John H. Williams to Elizabeth P. Peabody, December 9, 1861. Robert Lincoln Straker Collection, Antioch College Library.

11 *Letter,* Rev. John Weiss to Elizabeth P. Peabody, October 8, 1861. Robert Lincoln Straker Collection, Antioch College Library.

12 *Letter,* Elizabeth P. Peabody to Henry W. Longfellow, October [1860]. Elizabeth Peabody Correspondence, Houghton Library.

as well as Madame Ronge's *Kindergarten Guide*, she carried on her class in the true spirit of Froebel.[13] Professor Allen had learned of the kindergarten from his brother James, who was in Germany in 1859, and was eager to see the class established.[14]

Her desire to bring more young women into the new field of education led Miss Peabody to urge Louisa May Alcott to open a kindergarten. Although the kind of education Louisa had received gave her the ability to understand and influence children, she did not like the routine of teaching, nor the poor pay.[15] Since she was the only breadwinner of the family, and not as altruistic as Bronson Alcott or Elizabeth Peabody, the entries in her journal for 1862 revealed the sacrifices demanded of kindergarten pioneers. In January she wrote:

E. P. wanted me to open a Kindergarten, and Mr. Barnard gave me a room at the Warren Street Chapel. Don't like to teach, but take what comes; so when Mr. F. offered $40 to fit up with, twelve pupils, and his patronage, I began.[16]

In February she was obliged to "visit about" as her school did not bring enough to pay for her own board and for the salary of the assistant who Miss Peabody felt was necessary, although Louisa "didn't want her."[17] In April, Louisa's kindergartening came to an end as she recorded:

The school having no real foundation (as the people who sent didn't care for Kindergartens, and Miss P. wanted me to take pupils for nothing, to try the new system), I gave it up, as I could do much better at something else.[18]

[13] Henry Barnard, *Kindergarten and Child Culture*, p. 650.
[14] *Ibid.*
[15] Ednah D. Cheney, *Louisa May Alcott*, p. 71.
[16] *Ibid.*, p. 130.
[17] *Ibid.*
[18] *Ibid.*

This was hardly the attitude Miss Peabody expected of kindergarten teachers and especially of Bronson Alcott's daughter. It was ironic that, as early as 1835, in her preface to the *Record of a School*, Elizabeth Peabody should have decried that teaching had been "too often assumed, on the part of teachers, with avowedly mercenary ends."[19] Here was Alcott's daughter, in 1862, as an example of the "poor-spirited" teacher.

Miss Peabody's own dedication to the kindergarten cause was of such intense caliber that neither financial hardships, the Civil War, nor the problem of the emancipation of the Negro swerved her from her chosen work. Sympathetic as she was to every call for freedom, whether German, Hungarian, Polish, or Negro, she was keenly aware of the factors involved in the American crisis. The plight of the colored orphan children was her special concern and she gave active aid in establishing and sustaining the Orphan's Home for Colored Children in Georgetown, D. C.[20] She held a fair at her home in Boston for the benefit of the colored regiment, for which she solicited autographed original verses from her literary friends. These were sold to provide needed funds.[21] She spoke of this period of her life in later years as a time at which she was

so thoroughly buried in my school, that I had neither time nor opportunity to go to Antislavery meetings—though my heart and judgment were always on the Antislavery side from my earliest infancy when my mother induced us children all to refuse to eat sugar because it was the fruit of slave labor.[22] She was deeply saddened when Foster Haven, the son of

19 Peabody, "Preface," *Record of a School*, First Edition, p. v.

20 *Letter*, Elizabeth P. Peabody to Mr. [William C.] Bryant, October, 1864. Berg Collection, New York Public Library.

21 *Letter*, Elizabeth P. Peabody to Mr. Longfellow, October 15, 1864. Elizabeth Peabody Correspondence, Houghton Library.

22 *Letter*, Elizabeth P. Peabody to Theodore Dwight Weld, November 11, 1886. Robert Lincoln Straker Collection, Antioch College Library.

her former pupil, was killed in the battle of Fredericks-
burg. As a little boy, he had been especially dear to Miss
Peabody, for he had lived with the Peabody family during the prolonged illness of his mother and for a long time
after her death.[23] The story of the supervision of his early
education was the theme of a lecture Miss Peabody later
published called "A Psychological Observation."[24]

There were some educators sufficiently sympathetic and
interested in the new education to offer constructive suggestions. Among these was Charles Hoffman, in England,
who had assisted Mme. Ronge in setting up the London
kindergarten exhibit in 1854. He wondered why Miss
Peabody had not established a normal school for preparing kindergarten teachers, rather than just a kindergarten
class. In his opinion, that would have been a more efficient
method of furthering the cause.[25]

By 1864, Elizabeth Peabody must have agreed that her
efforts could be more effective if otherwise applied, because her sister, Mary, wrote to Horace Mann, Jr. that
"Aunt Lizzie is gradually slipping out of her school."[26]
Another reason may have been the realization that she
must seek more enlightenment on kindergarten procedures. To her knowledge of the system obtained by books,
she determined to add careful observations of kindergartens as taught by persons who had been trained by Froebel. She explained her predicament:

But seven years of experience with my so-called Kindergarten,
though it had a pecuniary success and a very considerable

23 *Letter,* Elizabeth P. Peabody to Miss Rawlins Pickman, undated
[1863]. Horace Mann Collection, Massachusetts Historical Society.

24 Elizabeth P. Peabody, *Lectures in the Training Schools for Kindergartners,* pp. 108–56.

25 *Letter,* F. Macdaniel to Elizabeth P. Peabody, October 13, 1863. Robert Lincoln Straker Collection, Antioch College Library.

26 *Letter,* Mary Mann to Horace Mann, Jr., November 3, 1864. Robert
Lincoln Straker Collection, Antioch College Library.

popularity,—stimulating to other attempts,—convinced me that we were not practicing Froebel's Fine Art, inasmuch as the quiet, certain, unexcited growth of self-activity into artistic self-relying ability which he promised, did not come of our efforts; but there was on the contrary, precocious knowledge, and the consequent morbid intellectual excitement quite out of harmonious relation with moral and aesthetic growth.[27]

Other motives may have unconsciously intensified her resolve. Many acquaintances of her intellectual circle had been abroad. Mary, her sister, had gone immediately following her marriage to Horace Mann in 1843. Then in 1853 her brother-in-law Nathaniel Hawthorne, as American consul, with Sophia and the children, went to Liverpool to live until 1860. If Julian Hawthorne could say that this egress to Europe was for both Hawthorne and his wife "the unlooked-for realization of the dreams of a lifetime,"[28] then how much more must have Elizabeth desired such a departure. She, who had been the support and mainstay of her brothers, of Sophia, of father and mother for so many years, was now free of responsibility. As early as 1858 the thought had been in her mind. At that date she had written to Parke Godwin of the *New York Evening Post*:

I am exceedingly desirous to go and spend the winter in Paris —for I have heard that my sister—Mrs. Hawthorne—who is so badly acted on by the climate of England that she is ordered out of it—and who only changed for the worse to Lisbon and Madeira last year—is ordered to Paris to spend the winter.[29]

Emerson, Alcott, Longfellow, and the ill-fated Margaret Fuller had been abroad. Elizabeth's correspondence with

[27] Elizabeth P. Peabody, "Our Reason for Being," *Kindergarten Messenger,* Vol. 1, No. 1, May, 1873, p. 1.

[28] Julian Hawthorne, *Nathaniel Hawthorne and His Wife,* Vol. II, p. 3.

[29] *Letter,* Elizabeth P. Peabody to Parke Godwin, August 19, 1858. Manuscript Room, New York Public Library.

foreign authors and publishers during her West Street venture had multiplied her foreign acquaintanceship.

To secure funds for the journey, since none would be forthcoming from her school, despite its relative "pecuniary success," Elizabeth gave a course of lectures on history in Boston, Concord, and Jamaica Plain.[30] Her audiences of friends, sympathetic to her desire to travel, and appreciative of her erudition, contributed the eleven hundred dollars she needed. On the eighth of June, 1867, she sailed from New York on the *Bellone* for London, attired in "a wardrobe judiciously selected" by her pupil-friends and looking "like a Duchess."[31] One of her pupil-friends judged this trip to be one of the most "commemorative experiences" of Miss Peabody's life, beginning as it did with the admission of an error and the effort "to retrieve it."[32]

Miss Peabody traveled for fifteen months, visiting all the kindergartens of any standing in Europe and becoming acquainted with the most eminent teachers. Her friends thought that no woman of America ever went abroad better prepared to appreciate and understand the old world than Miss Peabody. Knowing its history, its philosophy, the symbolism of its art, its pedagogics, she could assimilate all she saw. Said her pupil-friend:

Her meeting with Madame Marenholtz was then from the very nature of her preparation a pre-destined one. Madame Marenholtz had for years been awaiting the coming of the woman from the New World that she might transmit her message and so vitalize the system of which she was the Apostle.[33]

[30] *Letter*, Elizabeth P. Peabody to Mrs. Whieldon, May 24, [1867]. Elizabeth Peabody Correspondence, Houghton Library.

[31] *Mss.*, F.L.M., "Impressions and Recollections of Elizabeth Palmer Peabody," written for the Memorial Meeting, March 3, 1894. Miscellaneous Manuscripts, Boston Public Library.

[32] *Ibid.*

[33] *Ibid.*

Thus did Elizabeth Peabody fulfill her historic mission, uniting the old world and the new for the education of little children. In September, Miss Peabody visited Mme. Louise Froebel and Mme. Marquart in Dresden.[34] She wrote home of her exciting visit to Hamburg where she met "the Transcendental Jews and their sympathizers— the friends of Carl Schurz."[35] In February of 1868, Miss Peabody journeyed to Rome to meet Guiseppe Mazzini. Miss Peabody's experiences were duly chronicled for her American admirers in a series of articles for the *Herald of Health and Journal of Physical Culture.*

Fully enlightened, she returned home enthusiastic for the truths embodied in Froebel's system, and was the center of an educational movement in this country. She repudiated her former *Kindergarten Guide* and replaced it with a second edition, whose preface explained the errors in the first edition, and revised about thirty pages of text.[36] Finding a training school for kindergartners and a kindergarten already satisfactorily established in Boston by Mme. Kriege and her daughter, Miss Peabody determined to devote herself to enlightening the lay public and educators by writing and lecturing about the "true" kindergarten. By their practical work, these well-qualified teachers, the Krieges, would illustrate the Froebelian principles preached by Miss Peabody. This they faithfully did for four years.[37]

In 1868, a young music teacher of Springfield, Massachusetts, Edward Wiebe, tried to interest his neighbor,

---

[34] Elizabeth P. Peabody, "Our Reason for Being," *Kindergarten Messenger*, Vol. 1, No. 1, May, 1873, p. 2.

[35] *Letter*, Elizabeth P. Peabody to Mrs. Godwin, September 12, [1867]. Manuscript Room, New York Public Library.

[36] Peabody, "Preface," *Moral Culture of Infancy and Kindergarten Guide*, Fourth Edition, p. v.

[37] Mary J. Garland, "Madame Matilda H. Kriege," *The Kindergarten News*, Vol. 4, No. 10, December, 1894, p. 344.

Milton Bradley, in the kindergarten system. Mr. Wiebe had become acquainted with kindergarten principles and practices through his association with Mme. Louise Froebel in Germany. To no avail, he urged Mr. Bradley to publish his explanation of Froebel's system, "The Paradise of Childhood," and to manufacture some of the kindergarten material needed. Milton Bradley, as head of a factory which made children's games and toys, had never heard of the kindergarten and was unmoved by the plea. A year later, Elizabeth Peabody, at a meeting held in a public-school in Springfield, stirred her audience by her detailed and sincere presentation of the aims and methods of Froebel's kindergarten. Miss Peabody made an important convert to the cause. By Mr. Bradley's admission at a later date:

To that single evening talk, given in a school-house near his home, the editor [Milton Bradley] attributes what ever he has done in the name of kindergarten during the last twenty-five years, and as an immediate result he yielded to Mr. Wiebe's entreaties to publish the manuscript of *The Paradise of Childhood* . . . [38]

This was the book that in 1870 Miss Peabody recommended to William Torrey Harris of St. Louis in an effort to effect his conversion to the kindergarten philosophy.[39] Elizabeth Peabody encouraged Mr. Bradley to persevere in his commercial undertaking in behalf of kindergartens despite the small demand at that time for the material. She imbued him with her optimistic opinion that his cooperation would hasten the acceptance of kindergartens and stimulate their rapid growth. Said Mr.

[38] Milton Bradley, "Editor's Preface," in Wiebe, *Paradise of Childhood,* Quarter Century Edition, p. 5.
[39] *Letter,* Elizabeth P. Peabody to Mr. Harris, August 25, [1870]. The Harris Papers, Missouri Historical Society.

Bradley, "Ever after this, Miss Peabody was my faithful guide and critic in every move made in the preparation of the material. . . ."[40]

In 1869, Miss Peabody's *A Plea for Froebel's Kindergarten* gained new friends for the kindergarten when published with a lecture by Cardinal Wiseman on *The Identification of the Artisan and Artist.* It was recommended as "an admirable condensed statement of this mode of instruction"[41] by the Boston School Committee which prepared the school report for the year ending September 6, 1869. This committee on receipt of a petition asking for the establishment of an experimental "Kindergarten school" took favorable action.[42] Thus, Boston became the first city in which a public-school kindergarten was established. The kindergarten was carried on successfully for seven years but was given up because the city was not ready to appropriate the needed funds. A second public kindergarten, under the direction of Miss Susan Pollock, who had studied in Germany, was opened in Brighton in January, 1873, but abolished when Brighton was annexed to Boston in 1874.[43]

Many papers and periodicals accepted Miss Peabody's articles on the kindergarten for publication during 1870. *The Boston Daily Advertiser, The Cambridge Chronicle, The Illinois Teacher, The Massachusetts Teacher,* and *The Herald of Health* brought the new kindergarten message from Miss Peabody's pen to their readers and subscribers. Dr. M. L. Holbrook, editor of *The Herald of*

40 Milton Bradley, "A Reminiscence of Miss Peabody," *The Kindergarten News,* Vol. 4, No. 2, February, 1894, p. 39.

41 *Annual Report of the School Committee of the City of Boston,* 1870, not paginated. Boston City Documents.

42 *Loc. cit.*

43 Susan E. Blow, "The History of the Kindergarten in the United States," *Outlook,* Vol. 55, April 3, 1897, p. 932.

Health, gave sufficient publicity to news of the kinder-garten to be termed its "first journalistic friend."[44]

The Woman's Club of Boston celebrated Miss Pea-body's sixty-sixth birthday with her on May 16, 1870. Not at all daunted by her age, Elizabeth Peabody was planning a midwestern lecture tour. *The Illinois Teacher* carried this notice:

Kindergartens. The approaching meeting of the Principals' Association at Chicago will attract the attention of the teach-ers of the West especially to the Kindergarten system of instruction. Miss Peabody, the first to introduce the subject to the considerations of American educators, will present its methods, and it may be expected, from its importance as well as from the preparations made for its discussion, that the occasion will be of unusual interest.[45]

Miss Peabody gladly accepted the invitation to speak on "Genuine Kindergartens Versus Ignorant Attempts at It" at the convention of The Society of Superintendents and Principals of Chicago. She spoke at a teachers' convention in Watertown, Wisconsin, and in private parlors to in-vited audiences. Miss Peabody's tour was a great stimulus to kindergarten activity in the midwestern states.[46] How-ever, she was disappointed at not meeting William Torrey Harris, Superintendent of Schools in St. Louis, at the con-ventions. She wrote to him, hoping to make another friend to Froebel's system.[47] Some of her ambitious plans for the extension of the kindergarten never materialized. She wrote:

[44] Nina C. Vandewalker, *The Kindergarten in American Education,* p. 28.

[45] "Notices of Books and Periodicals," *The Illinois Teacher,* Vol. 16, No. 7, July, 1870, p. 249.

[46] Peabody, "Our Reason for Being," *Kindergarten Messenger,* Vol. 1, No. 1, May, 1873, p. 4.

[47] *Letter,* Elizabeth P. Peabody to Mr. Harris, August 25, [1870]. The Harris Papers, Missouri Historical Society.

But I am in hopes to get an endowment for another [normal school] to be set up, in the District of Columbia perhaps, to educate teachers for Kindergartens there and in the territories. The Chairman of the Congressional Committee, if he can secure by private endowment a salary of $2000 for three years, will be able to call from Lubec that teacher [Maria Boelte] of whom I speak in my Plea appended to Cardinal Wiseman's lecture, and open a free normal school to those *qualified* to enter on the study.[48]

Miss Peabody also failed in her attempt to become a trustee for a fund of $10,000 to set up a free normal school in Boston and one in the Middle States because "death mocked her hopes."[49] However, she was not disconcerted but tried other avenues to her goal. She was elated by the enthusiastic response which she had received when lecturing in private parlors as well as at the conventions in the midwest where there was not such apathy as in Boston. She continued to solicit funds to establish kindergartens and to train young women as kindergartners. Her friend Anna C. Lowell offered:

If you are getting up subscriptions for a Kindergarten class you may put us down for 20 dollars—that is a small sum, but just now, we are engaged in so many various objects that we cannot promise more.[50]

Other exciting happenings in 1870 made Elizabeth Peabody optimistic for the future of the kindergarten. In the village of College Point, New York, a charity kindergarten, the first of its kind, was opened.[51] A kindergarten association was formed in Milwaukee. Professor John Kraus

48 Peabody, "Kindergarten," *The Illinois Teacher*, Vol. 16, No. 11, November, 1870, p. 365.

49 *Ibid.*

50 *Letter*, Anna C. Lowell to Miss Elizabeth P. Peabody, November 22, 1870. Robert Lincoln Straker Collection, Antioch College Library.

51 Nina C. Vandewalker, *The Kindergarten in American Education*, p. 19.

translated a pamphlet by Baroness Marenholtz-Bülow and reported on the kindergarten for the Commissioner of Education.[52] An article by Professor Kraus on "Froebel's Method of Education in America" based on this report appeared in Germany in a magazine for home education, *Cornelia*.[53] The trend in the flow of publications across the ocean was now reversed. America was sending news of its kindergartens to Germany. Dr. Adolph Douai of Newark wrote *The Kindergarten; A Manual for the Introduction of Froebel's System of Primary Education into the Public Schools*. It was Professor Douai who went to the home of Dr. Thomas Hunter, founder and president of Hunter College, to teach him Froebel's kindergarten system. Dr. Hunter was so charmed by what he learned that he invited Elizabeth Peabody to lecture on the kindergarten at Hunter College.[54]

One other person claims mention as one of the kindergarten pioneers during the decade after Elizabeth Peabody had set up her experimental kindergarten in America. When Miss Peabody visited Hamburg in 1867, it was Emma Marwedel who introduced her to the genuine kindergarten at Hamburg and inspired her with the desire to extend the work to America.[55] Miss Peabody, in turn, induced Emma Marwedel to come to America. Part of Miss Peabody's plan for developing the kindergarten in America consisted in importing German teachers who had been trained in Froebel's methods. Miss Marwedel was also interested in the problem of industrial education and traveled through Europe studying this with its special application to women. Early in 1870, Miss Marwedel arrived

[52] Barnard (ed.), *op. cit.*, p. 550.
[53] *Ibid.*
[54] Anna M. and Jenny Hunter (eds.), *The Autobiography of Dr. Thomas Hunter*, pp. 294–95.
[55] Fletcher Harper Swift, "Emma Marwedel," *University of California Publications in Education*, Vol. 6, No. 3, 1931, p. 139.

in America and established near Brentwood, Long Island, a cooperative, self-supporting school to train women as florists and fruit growers and preservers.[56] The school was a failure, but even that did not seem too bad to Miss Peabody for now there was in America another trained kindergartner with the ideal of improving the human race through education.

William Hailmann had become interested in kindergarten on his visits to his old home in Switzerland. In 1865, the German-American Academy at Louisville, Kentucky, of which he was principal, included a kindergarten. He also established relations with the parents similar to those in a modern parent association.[57]

In the fall of 1870, Elizabeth Peabody evaluated what had been accomplished in the ten-year period since the inception of the kindergarten at 15 Pinckney Street. She was encouraged by the kindergarten in the Boston Public School System and by the promise of one in the New York Normal School for the following year. Rutger's Institute, at 5th Avenue and 42nd Street in New York, was to start a kindergarten immediately, despite the lateness of the season. The fact that eminent Catholics did not consider the kindergarten anti-Catholic boded well for its universality. "But," concluded she, "it is the general and not a private interest which is the main thing—the regeneration of humanity by the second coming of the Christchild."[58] After sowing the seed, she was ready now to nurture it patiently until it flowered in the true spirit of Froebel.

[56] Will S. Monroe, "Emma Marwedel and the Kindergarten," *Education,* Vol. 14, February, 1894, p. 338.

[57] Barbara Greenwood, "William Nicholas Hailmann," Committee of Nineteen, International Kindergarten Union (eds.), *Pioneers of the Kindergarten in America,* p. 245.

[58] *Letter,* Elizabeth P. Peabody to Anna Hazard Ward, Monday, [fall, 1870]. Elizabeth Peabody Correspondence, Houghton Library.

V

Crusade for Kindergartens, 1870-1890

IN THE YEARS FOLLOWING 1870, ELIZABETH PEABODY'S EF-
forts and influence in the dissemination of knowledge of
kindergartens and in assuring their public acceptance
were unique. Although during these years she neither
taught a kindergarten class, nor established her own kindergarten training school, her effort was unceasing, determined, and widespread. At sixty-six years of age she had
lost nothing of her crusading spirit, her love of children,
nor her faith in the kindergarten as a means of regenerat-
ing humanity. Having pioneered in its establishment in
one small area, Boston, she henceforth engaged in bringing the kindergarten to every spot in the United States
that could be reached by her voice, by her pen, and by her
disciples. Elizabeth Peabody's thoughts and plans were not
confined narrowly to one locality but were universal. The
agnostic and materialistic tendencies of thought in America were alien to her nature. She was prepared to battle
them by means of education of the very young; in effect,

by Froebel's kindergarten system. In later years, at a lecture on Goethe at the Concord School of Philosophy, Mrs. Caroline M. Sherman made this comment:

Goethe has clearly shown that, where women are denied the marriage which the heart prompts, their resort is not, as has been hinted, in marriage with another. According to Goethe, their happiness is then found in useful service, especially to children.[1]

Whether or not Miss Peabody agreed with this statement, her life had the purpose of unselfish, useful service noted by Goethe. Edward Wiebe quoted her as saying:

It [my purpose] is . . . that I may work for Kindergarten *without price*—which is necessary in order that people should realize that it is the living water, a true gospel.[2]

It was a tribute to her eloquence and sincerity that she was able to inspire others with a like idealistic aim. The kindergarten cause was served by many young women who were impressed by her example. Kate Douglas Wiggin spoke of her as the one who had been more instrumental in inspiring a greater number of mothers and educators than any other woman of her day.[3] Miss Peabody established the pattern that evoked the comment about the early kindergartners that:

They brought to their calling a consecration which no money, no salary, no fame could possibly procure or pay for—but might destroy.[4]

[1] Caroline K. Sherman, "Child Life as Portrayed by Goethe," in Sanborn (ed.), *The Life and Genius of Goethe*, p. 311.

[2] Edward Wiebe, "Froebel," Barnard (ed.), *American Journal of Education*, November, 1871, p. 11.

[3] Kate D. Wiggin, *My Garden of Memory*, p. 154.

[4] Harriet Niel, "William Torrey Harris," in Committee of Nineteen, International Kindergarten Union (eds.), *Pioneers of the Kindergarten in America*, p. 178.

The practical methods by which she put into action her idealistic principles were effective because of their variety and because of her persistence. One of the most important means of disseminating information in the late nineteenth century was by the printed word. Nina Vandewalker noted that:

It is astonishing but true that more books were translated and written concerning the kindgarten during the decade between 1870 and 1880 than were translated or written on the whole of general education besides.[5]

Williams said that in the five years between 1871 and 1876, seventeen works on the kindergarten appeared "with Miss Elizabeth P. Peabody leading in the vigorous polemic."[6] Her "Kindergarten Culture" was reprinted from the *Annual Report for 1870* of the National Commissioner of Education and so not only received wider distribution but also greater stature from government approval. Miss Peabody spent ten weeks in the Bureau of Education, Washington, D. C., from January to March, 1871. A direct result was her essay, *The Kindergarten*, published by the Bureau of Education the following year.[7]

The death of Sophia Hawthorne, in London, occurred while Elizabeth was in Washington. Mrs. Hawthorne and her three children, Julian, Rose, and Una had gone to Dresden to live after Nathaniel Hawthorne's death in 1868. When the Franco-Prussian War broke out they moved to London.[8] Although Miss Peabody was again at

---

[5] Nina C. Vandewalker, *The Kindergarten in American Education*, p. 162.

[6] Talcott Williams, "The Kindergarten Movement," *The Century*, Vol. XLV, January, 1893, p. 377.

[7] Elizabeth P. Peabody, *The Kindergarten*, U.S. Bureau of Education, July, 1872.

[8] Julian Hawthorne, *Nathaniel Hawthorne and His Wife*, Vol. II, p. 353.

work in the Bureau of Education in June,[9] she departed for London to nurse Una Hawthorne. After Una's recovery, Miss Peabody seized this unexpected opportunity of being in Europe to renew her acquaintance with the leading European proponents of kindergarten. Of great significance was her meeting with Maria Boelte in London. Miss Peabody was a friend of Amèly Boelte, Maria's aunt, and had corresponded with Maria about kindergartens since 1869. During her stay in London, they saw one another almost daily.[10] Maria Boelte had been trained in the kindergarten method by Froebel's widow in Hamburg. When she had finished this course of studies, she went to England where she learned to speak English while assisting at Mme. Ronge's kindergarten in London.[11] Maria later had great success with a kindergarten at Lübeck, Germany. Mme. Froebel was so impressed with Maria's work that she called her "Froebel's spiritual daughter."[12] It was due in part to Miss Peabody's persuasion that Maria came to teach in Miss Henrietta Haine's well-known private school in New York.

Miss Peabody's friends valued her valiant spirit. This was shown by their willingness to gratify her desires and to support her plans. Her trip to Rome, after leaving Una in London, to see Baroness Marenholtz-Bülow once again, was financed by two American friends, Mrs. Cole and Susan Cabot.[13] However, her cherished trip was curtailed by her own poor health and she regretfully returned to

9 *Letter,* Elizabeth P. Peabody to William T. Harris, June 28, 1871. The Harris Papers, Missouri Historical Society.

10 Maria Kraus-Boelte, "A Tribute to My Old Friend, Elizabeth P. Peabody," *Kindergarten Review,* Vol. 14, May, 1904, p. 549.

11 Maria Kraus-Boelte, "Reminiscences of Kindergarten Work," in Barnard (ed.), *Kindergarten and Child Culture,* p. 543.

12 *Ibid.,* p. 548.

13 *Letter,* Elizabeth P. Peabody to Mrs. Cole, July 10, 1872. Elizabeth Peabody Correspondence, Essex Institute.

America with her nephew, George Mann. In the interim, she had tried to revive interest in kindergartens in England by assisting in the organization of a Froebel Union there.

Before her trip to Europe, Miss Peabody had persisted in her correspondence with William Torrey Harris of St. Louis, so anxious was she to gain his support for the kindergarten. Her patience was almost as long as her letters. She informed him of the latest Froebelian writings and begged him to print some in his "Speculative Journal."[14] When he did not reply, she wrote again to give him news of a new kindergarten to be opened in Washington by Susan Pollock. She presumed from his silence that he did not "wish to enter into relations with so voluminous a correspondent."[15] She wrote three months later telling him of the attention given to her paper in General Eaton's report and of her hope of making "a revolution in this citadel of stupidity," Washington.[16] Mr. Harris finally succumbed to her importunings and sent her some copies of his *Journal of Speculative Philosophy*, which she acknowledged by writing, "for though I am a woman and terribly driven by practical work, I find my heaven on earth in Speculative Philosophy."[17] She added that if his schools were so "deficient for *room*," she supposed that there was no hope for kindergartens in St. Louis and Chicago public systems. In that case, she urged that a private kindergarten be initiated.[18] No event pertaining to kindergartens

14 *Letter*, Elizabeth P. Peabody to William T. Harris, January 30, [1871]. The Harris Papers, Missouri Historical Society. The actual name of the magazine was *The Journal of Speculative Philosophy*.

15 *Letter*, Elizabeth P. Peabody to William T. Harris, March 20, 1871. The Harris Papers, Missouri Historical Society.

16 *Letter*, Elizabeth P. Peabody to William T. Harris, June 28, 1871. The Harris Papers, Missouri Historical Society.

17 *Letter*, Elizabeth P. Peabody to William T. Harris, November 26, [1872]. The Harris Papers, Missouri Historical Society.

18 *Ibid*.

occurred but that Miss Peabody informed Superintendent Harris. Her letters to him were lengthy and detailed reports of kindergarten history in the making. Mr. Harris was eventually won to the cause by a combination of Miss Peabody's perseverance and Susan Blow's financial aid. He established, under Miss Blow's supervision, a public-school kindergarten in St. Louis, in 1873. These two women, both ardent supporters of kindergarten, were rather critical of one another, as their respective letters to Mr. Harris show. Miss Blow wrote:

I received this afternoon a letter from Miss Peabody requesting details with regard to our Kindergarten and giving as her reason for so doing that she has new requests to write a report on the genuine Kindergartens now established in the United States. Recognizing that our Kindergarten is an *experiment* and knowing something of Miss Peabody's character I feel a great disinclination to write her anything more than the simple facts of number of pupils—hours employed per day, etc.[19]

That this distrust was reciprocated may be judged from Miss Peabody's remark:

From something Miss Blow once said to me, I was inclined to think that her Presbyterian creed clouded her perception of Froebel's benignant religion.[20]

Miss Peabody's conquests for the kindergarten cause were sometimes more easily made. Charlotte Cushman, who was known as America's greatest tragic actress and the only Boston woman to attain international fame on the stage, was greatly attracted by Miss Peabody's generous

19 *Letter*, Susan E. Blow to William T. Harris, November 10, 1873. The Harris Papers, Missouri Historical Society.
20 *Letter*, Elizabeth P. Peabody to William T. Harris, February 6, [1873]. The Harris Papers, Missouri Historical Society.

and dynamic spirit. She, too, had been a poor but courageous girl, and at thirteen years of age had supported her
mother and four siblings.[21] During Elizabeth Peabody's
trip to Europe in 1871, Miss Cushman contributed $1000
to carry on the Krieges' kindergarten and normal class,
"knowing of my enforced absence whose *begging* had supported it the three previous years,"[22] explained Miss Peabody to her friends. When Madame Kriege returned to
Europe for rest and recreation, the school was left in the
hands of her ablest pupil, Miss Mary J. Garland. Miss Peabody continued to sponsor the school and to supply the
financial support needed. She explained to Mr. Harris:

This year I had planned to give the lectures on the philosophy
and theory and by making them public and selling tickets.
I have myself raised the money to keep Miss Garland and give
her better conditions of room than has been before.[23]

The importance of the kindergarten training school as
a means of entrenching the kindergarten system in the
United States was evident to Miss Peabody. (Its full significance will be analyzed in a later chapter.) Without
properly trained teachers, the system could not be perpet-
uated. Emma Marwedel, after the failure of her industrial
school, went to Washington to establish a "School for
Practical and Physical Culture."[24] The new school contained a kindergarten, a training course and a primary
school. Miss Peabody was delighted to have a person of
Emma Marwedel's vision and experience in Washington,
for she had thought it "preposterous and injurious" for

21 Mary C. Crawford, *Romantic Days in Old Boston*, p. 243.
22 *Letter*, Elizabeth P. Peabody to William T. Harris, November 11,
[1872]. The Harris Papers, Missouri Historical Society.
23 *Ibid.*
24 Fletcher H. Swift, "Emma Marwedel," *University of California Publications in Education*, Vol. 6, No. 3, 1931, p. 154.

young Susie Pollock to advertise to train Southern ladies.[25] Miss Marwedel made many contributions to kindergarten literature. Her best known work, *Conscious Motherhood*, was highly endorsed by Elizabeth Peabody, Henry Barnard, and other important educators when it was published in Boston by D. C. Heath and Company in 1889. This volume also contained an advertisement of Miss Marwedel's "system of materials" for kindergartens. In her dedication and devotion to the idea of helping humanity by education, Miss Marwedel was in full accord with Elizabeth Peabody's views.

Just as the dissemination of kindergarten information led gradually to the establishment of more kindergartens, so their existence and the aroused interest led to a greater demand for information and advice, which Miss Peabody and her cohorts were ever anxious to fill. Mrs. Pauline Agassiz Shaw, the beautiful, wealthy daughter of Louis Agassiz, came under Miss Peabody's influence. It has been estimated that Mrs. Shaw spent from $30,000 to $50,000 a year[26] to maintain kindergartens in thirty-one schools in Boston.[27] The publication of Matilda Kriege's lectures and Miss Peabody's many magazine articles only partially supplied the demand of the new kindergarten teachers. Miss Peabody recognized the call for a monthly periodical whose object would be to speak of the reform of earliest education, known as Froebel's Kindergarten. With her accustomed alacrity in supplying such a worthwhile need, Elizabeth Peabody established the magazine *Kindergarten Messenger*. The first issue of this monthly periodical of

25 *Letter,* Elizabeth P. Peabody to William T. Harris, February 6, [1873]. The Harris Papers, Missouri Historical Society.

26 Richard Boone, *Education in the United States,* p. 336.

27 Laura Fisher, "Mrs. Shaw's Service to the Kindergarten," Committee of Nineteen, International Kindergarten Union (eds.), *Pioneers of the Kindergarten in America.* p. 104.

twenty-four pages appeared in May, 1873. The terms were $1.00 a year, payable in advance. One thousand subscribers were needed to keep the enterprise solvent. By the December, 1874, issue, Miss Peabody woefully informed her readers that:

The present number . . . must be the last issue unless the subscription list be doubled for 1875. I find I have but 500 subscribers reliable for payment, which does not pay my printer. But so many of these protest against my giving up, that I am encouraged to say that I WILL RESUME as soon as my subscription list shall have grown to a thousand names.[28]

Unable to continue its financial support, Miss Peabody permitted her *Kindergarten Messenger* to be issued as a department of the *New England Journal of Education*. She regretted this hasty action for she realized that had she held it over the summer while the Centennial Kindergarten was on exhibit in Philadelphia, she could have gotten her thousand subscribers easily. The kindergartner in charge of the kindergarten demonstration had distributed thousands of Steiger's *Kindergarten Tracts*. Miss Peabody left the *New England Journal of Education* within a year primarily because Mr. Bicknell, the editor, took "into his advertising column Miss Coe's boastful and deceptive advertisement."[29] Miss Coe had professed to use other and better materials and called hers an American kindergarten. Miss Peabody held the opinion that:

to be trained for a kindergartner—that is trained to educate children as organisms—by exercises in synthesis and analysis . . . cannot be a different thing in Germany and America.[30]

[28] Peabody, *Kindergarten Messenger*, Vol. 2, No. 12, December, 1874, p. 1.

[29] *Letter*, Elizabeth P. Peabody to William T. Harris, January 10, 1876. The Harris Papers, Missouri Historical Society.

[30] *Letter*, Elizabeth P. Peabody to William T. Harris, January 19, [1877]. The Harris Papers, Missouri Historical Society.

In 1878, Miss Peabody united with Professor Hailmann to form *Kindergarten Messenger and the New Education*. It was because of her unpleasant experience with Mr. Bicknell's *Journal* that she wrote in the first issue of the new venture:

> I am now getting old [she was seventy-three at the time], and my ten years of propaganda, five years having been given to the "Kindergarten Messenger" at my own cost, and without being able to afford myself any assistance in the mechanical drudgery, have exhausted me, and I think, if I give up editorial responsibility and send contributions to you only when I naturally overflow, what I write will be of more worth.[31]

She stressed the need for high standards when she continued:

> I would not give up, even though I have not got the thousand subscribers, without which I did not promise to go on even through the year, was I not entirely satisfied that you are as sound in the doctrine of Froebel as myself, with intellectual insight more profound, and superior executive ability, and that you will never compromise the truth through fear or favor or for mere *business success*.[32]

Despite the trouble it caused her, Miss Peabody realized the value of a kindergarten magazine in uniting widely scattered kindergarten teachers and in keeping before them the loftiest ideals. As Miss Peabody said:

> If I did not think kindergarten education touched the springs of *moral life*—I should not work and suffer for it *as I do* and shall do as long as I live.[33]

---

[31] *Letter,* Elizabeth P. Peabody to William N. Hailmann, December 10, 1877. Printed in *Kindergarten Messenger and the New Education,* Vol. 1, No. 1, January, 1878, p. 4.

[32] *Ibid.*

[33] *Letter,* Elizabeth P. Peabody to William T. Harris, January 19, [1877]. The Harris Papers, Missouri Historical Society.

William Hailmann, at this time, was the principal of a German-American Academy in Milwaukee, which boasted both a kindergarten and a training school. With the financial assistance of Mr. Carl H. Doerflinger, *The New Education* was sent free of charge to the leading educators of Wisconsin.[34]

Ernst Steiger, a New York publisher, also gave his special abilities as well as his personal funds to promulgate kindergarten ideals. He was a staunch ally in Miss Peabody's struggle to reach a large public. An especially wide distribution of kindergarten information was achieved through the *Kindergarten Tracts,* small pamphlets from two to four pages in length. They were often reprints of addresses, reports, or articles of importance to kindergartens. These small pamphlets were sold in bulk for distribution at meetings or often given gratis by the publisher. Included in the issues were Tract No. 20, Miss Peabody's *The Kindergarten Commencement*; Tract No. 23, Mrs. Mann's *The Kindergarten or the New Education*; Tract No. 14, *Friedrich Froebel's Developing System of Education* by Karl Froebel; and Tract No. 10 by A. N. Bell, M. D., entitled *The Medical Profession Recommend* [sic] *the Kindergarten*. In a tract in the German language, distributed gratis by the publisher in 1872 for the purpose of encouraging German-Americans to support kindergartens and send their children to them, Mr. Steiger asserted that it was "more necessary" to give children an early education in America than in Europe. He reasoned that the kindergarten was important because America was more crowded and had many different kinds of people. Children, he felt, learned no more than their ABC's in school.[35] An unusual argument presented by him was that

34 Vandewalker, *op. cit.,* p. 33.
35 Ernst Steiger, *Der Kindergarten in Amerika,* p. 1.

no more fat children would enter the primary grades if they attended kindergarten first.[36] The logic behind this statement was that the games, garden work, and physical exercises were all strengthening for the body.

In addition to the tracts, Mr. Steiger published many of the early manuals, guides, and translations by the leading kindergarten exponents. Of great practical value then, as well as of historical interest now, was *Steiger's Kindergarten Catalogue*. It was advertised as a "list of the Most Complete Assortment of Material, Gifts and Occupations carefully manufactured in accordance with the directions of Mrs. Maria Kraus-Boelte and other Authorities on the Genuine Froebel System . . ."[37] Profusely illustrated and painstakingly explained, the catalogue must have been of inestimable value in the setting-up of new kindergartens. In 1877, Elizabeth Peabody informed William Torrey Harris that:

A half dozen ladies of Cambridge and Boston including the widow and daughter of Agassiz, have concluded to start a Froebel Society like that of London for the express purpose of keeping the standard of the kindergarten up to the mark of Froebel.[38]

These members subscribed $100 apiece to begin a fund which ultimately was to be used to enable gifted persons of limited means to get training as kindergartners. Miss Peabody was aware from experience that:

Most of our best kindergartners have had to borrow money to get trained—and were burdened by the debt in their first years of work when they require all their spirits.[39]

[36] *Ibid.*, p. 3.
[37] *Steiger's Kindergarten Catalogue*, No. 30, 1892.
[38] *Letter*, Elizabeth P. Peabody to William T. Harris, n.d., [February 19, 1877]. The Harris Papers, Missouri Historical Society.
[39] *Ibid.*

Other provisions of the society were that the *Kindergarten Messenger* would be the organ of the Society and that there would be examiners in various sections of the country to inspect and report upon the kindergartens in their sections. Mrs. Kraus-Boelte was inspector for New York, Miss Garland for Boston, Mr. Harris for St. Louis, Mr. Hailmann for Milwaukee, and so forth. The society also expected to encourage publishers to put forth more and better kindergarten publications. The organization was incorporated in 1878. At the meeting of the newly named American Froebel Union, in Boston on April 27, 1878, Miss Peabody was elected acting president, representing Baroness Marenholtz-Bülow, the honorary president.[40] At the meeting it was reported that the Union had given a loan to Lee and Shepard, Boston publishers, to publish Baroness Marenholtz-Bülow's *Reminiscences of Froebel* as well as Froebel's *Mother Play and Nursery Songs*. A member had loaned extra funds to establish charity kindergartens in and around Boston.[41]

This was not the only national organization working for the benefit of kindergartens. As far back as 1872, the National Education Association had been formed and had held its meeting in Boston on August 7th. The membership list included, of course, Miss Elizabeth P. Peabody.[42] Mr. Hailmann, who was then head of a school in Louisville, Kentucky, read his paper entitled *The Adaptation of Froebel's System of Education to American Institutions.* He proposed a resolution that a committee of seven be appointed to inquire into the form in which Froebel's prin-

[40] *Kindergarten Messenger and New Education,* Vol. 2, No. 8, August, 1878, p. 1.
[41] *Ibid.*
[42] *The Addresses and Journal of Proceedings* of the National Education Association, 1872, p. 123.

ciples of education might be applied most efficiently to the educational wants of the United States, and to report at the next meeting. Professor Douai, Elizabeth Peabody, Henry Barnard, and Bronson Alcott contributed to the discussion that followed.[43] The favorable committee report, signed by John Kraus, was made at the Elmira meeting in 1873. Here again, kindergarten education was brought to the forefront by a paper read by Maria Kraus-Boelte.[44] At the Centennial Convention of the National Education Association in 1876, Mme. Kraus-Boelte lectured on and exhibited kindergarten children's work. Later in the same year, this material was sent to the Centennial Exhibition in Philadelphia.

Miss Peabody was very active in making arrangements for the exhibit for she had great hopes that it would stimulate interest in kindergartens. Upon the recommendation of the Froebel Society of Boston, Miss Ruth Burritt was the kindergartner chosen to give the demonstration, using children from the orphan asylum in Philadelphia.[45] She was so successful that she was engaged by a group of Quakers to organize a kindergarten and training program in Philadelphia. Many other cities were encouraged to start kindergartens and many individuals were inspired to become kindergartners. All seemed to turn to Miss Peabody for advice, and her correspondence became so heavy that her sister Mary was pressed into service in answering letters.[46]

All during these years of ceaseless activity in behalf of kindergarten education, Miss Peabody had continued her

[43] *Ibid.,* p. 147.
[44] Vandewalker, *op. cit.,* p. 22.
[45] Emma Lou Thornbrough, *Eliza A. Baker,* p. 10.
[46] *Letter,* Mary Mann to Henry Barnard, December, 1876. Will S. Monroe Collection, New York University Library.

regular courses of lectures at training schools in various cities. Those classes at Miss Burritt's, Mrs. Van Kirk's, and Miss Garland's and others were her regular assignment. In addition, she spoke at commencement exercises, signed diplomas, raised large sums of money to finance kindergartens, wrote articles on kindergarten education for magazines in many parts of the country, and went on lecture tours to the South and Midwest, speaking before teachers' groups or parlor groups. Her sister said of her, "Elizabeth holds out like the widow's cruse."[47]

Yet despite her own constant strivings, she was deeply moved by the dedication of others to human welfare. After a visit to the Perkins' Institute for the Blind, she wrote:

[There] . . . in the simplest surroundings we found Dr. Howe with the half dozen first pupils . . . I shall not in all time and eternity, forget the impressions made on me, by seeing the hero of the Greek Revolution . . . wholly absorbed and applying all the energies of his genius to this—. . . and doing it—as Christ did—without money and without price . . .[48]

It was in 1878 that Miss Peabody advanced her theory of teaching reading simultaneously with writing, the writing to begin with the copying of the small printed letters. With her sister Mary, she published the book *After Kindergarten—What?* as a primer of reading and writing for primary schools. Elizabeth's kindergarten interests overflowed into her sister's life to a great extent.

At this time, Miss Peabody's health began to fail. Her niece, Rose Hawthorne Lathrop, was

very much disturbed by your [Mary Mann's] account of Aunt Lizzie, it is as sad news as you could have sent me. I hope you

[47] *Letter*, Mary Mann to Henry Barnard, April 20, 1876. Will S. Monroe Collection, New York University Library.
[48] *Letter*, Elizabeth P. Peabody to Julia Ward Howe, February 9, 1876. Elizabeth Peabody Correspondence, Houghton Library.

have, or will have at my petition, Dr. Wesselhoeft's advice as to her diet and medicines.[49]

Miss Peabody was seventy-four years of age and suffering from cataracts, which partially blinded her. Nonetheless, her correspondence was not less animated and her interests were unabated. Her letters were less legible than usual, but just as long. Maria R. Mann, Mary's niece and a kindergartner in California, thanked her "for her good long letter, with its answers to my inquiries and additional matter of interest to me."[50] Maria, in turn, related all the intrigue and gossip in regard to Miss Marwedel, the California Froebel Union, the sale of kindergarten books, and all the people she had met who knew Elizabeth Peabody.[51]

Miss Peabody, though she could write only a little at a time, finished her *Reminiscences of William Ellery Channing* in 1879. She made arrangements for speakers at the August meeting of the American Froebel Union and tried to ignore the signs of advancing age. Two activities, in addition to her kindergarten chores, made life very interesting and worthwhile to her. One was her endeavor in raising funds to help Henry Barnard finance the publication of thirty-one volumes of the *American Journal of Education*. The other was her participation in the lectures and discussion at the Concord School of Philosophy, whose first session began on July 15, 1879. Just in case she was asked to lecture, she had prepared a paper, "Milton's Paradise Lost." However, she was not a lecturer that first season, but did deliver a paper on "Childhood" in 1882, and

---

[49] *Letter,* Rose Hawthorne Lathrop to Mary Mann, April 14, [1878]. Robert Lincoln Straker Collection, Antioch College Library.

[50] *Letter,* Maria R. Mann to Elizabeth P. Peabody, January 8, [1879]. Robert Lincoln Straker Collection, Antioch College Library.

[51] *Letter,* Maria Mann to Mary Mann, n.d., [March, 1879]. Robert Lincoln Straker Collection, Antioch College Library.

the one on "Milton" in 1883. She was described by a younger member as follows:

Miss Peabody, who always spoke well in debate, usually slept in her chair on the Faculty platform until the lecturer concluded, when she took up the thread of debate with singular closeness in joining in. She rambled a little but was ever entertaining in her ramble.[52]

Elizabeth lived with her brother Nathaniel and his family at Concord. Her board money helped his family's finances, and Concord was a place of old friendships for her, with Bronson Alcott the dean of the Concord School close at hand. She wrote to Mary, who was living with George and his wife in Boston: "Indeed, all the lectures are superb and Mr. Alcott says better things than I ever heard him say before . . ."[53] In 1880, William Torrey Harris bought Orchard House in Concord and moved there from St. Louis. When he left St. Louis, there was an impressive enrollment of 7,828 children enrolled in his public school kindergartens.[54]

The new trend that kindergarten education was taking was obvious in the December, 1879, meeting of the American Froebel Union in Dr. Ware's Church in Boston. The principal subject of discussion was the "comparative desireableness of universalizing kindergartens by connecting them with the Public School System, or by Charity Kindergartens."[55] Miss Peabody mentioned the existence of one public kindergarten in Boston and of forty-one in St.

[52] Frank B. Sanborn, *Recollections of Seventy Years,* Vol. II, p. 505.

[53] *Letter,* Elizabeth Peabody to Mary Mann, August, 1879. Robert Lincoln Straker Collection, Antioch College Library.

[54] Susan E. Blow, "History of Kindergarten in the United States," *Outlook,* Vol. 55, April, 1897, p. 934.

[55] *Letter,* Elizabeth P. Peabody to William T. Harris, December 1, 1879. The Harris Papers, Missouri Historical Society.

Louis, and also the charity kindergartens in Boston and New York. She quoted Henry Barnard's preference for charity rather than public school kindergartens because:

Education forgets to be a philanthropy and becomes a business and its progress in the primary stage was most disastrous.[56]

Another new topic was brought to the attention of the members, namely, teaching kindergarten children elements of music by means of colors.[57] Mr. G. Bachellor was the lecturer, and with enthusiasm Miss Peabody dubbed his topic "the only discovery of a harmony of nature available for earliest education since Froebel's."[58]

There was much interest and kindergarten activity in California during this period. Dr. Felix Adler, President of the Society for Ethical Culture, delivered a course of kindergarten lectures in San Francisco. A group of philanthropic citizens, under his guidance and inspiration, formed the San Francisco Public Kindergarten Society on July 23, 1878.[59] Dr. Adler founded the Silver Street Kindergarten, and Kate Douglas Smith became its director. When she was called upon to found the California Kindergarten Training School, she came East to seek the advice of Miss Peabody and other kindergarten leaders. Miss Peabody had invited the young Kate to be her guest. She had written:

You must not go back to San Francisco without seeing Concord. You are a hero-worshiper, and we have heroes of all sizes here just now at our great School of Philosophy.[60]

56 *Ibid.*
57 *Postcard,* Elizabeth P. Peabody, "Our Meeting," December 29, [1879]. The Harris Papers, Missouri Historical Society.
58 *Ibid.*
59 Nora A. Smith, "Kate Douglas Wiggin," in Committee of Nineteen, International Kindergarten Union (eds.), *Pioneers of the Kindergarten in America,* p. 286.
60 Kate Douglas Wiggin, *My Garden of Memory,* p. 146.

Elizabeth Peabody and Kate Smith, both with warm, sympathetic, and dynamic personalities, became friends at
once. Miss Peabody wrote to Mary Mann that Kate was
"equal to Miss M[arwedel] in genius and superior in practice, moral influence and inspiration."[61] After her marriage to Samuel Bradley Wiggin, Kate continued and
expanded her kindergarten activities, traveling to give lectures as Miss Peabody had done in the East. Her letters,
warm and charming, on a topic that was of such deep interest to both, were bright spots in the daily life of Miss
Peabody. An inveterate letter writer herself, she could appreciate their warmth and humor. Wrote the newly-mar-
ried Mrs. Wiggin:

I have just rec'd [sic] a letter from my husband's mother in
which she mentions meeting you at the "Woman's Club" and
says much to my grief that your eyes are troubling you—Never
mind! You can see more with eyes *shut* than anybody else
can with them wide open.[62]

The Story of Patsy, written by Mrs. Wiggin to raise funds
for kindergarten work, far surpassed its author's modest
expectations. It was a potent influence upon the early public acceptance of the kindergarten.

Miss Peabody and her sister were living together again
when Mrs. Mann wrote to Moncure D. Conway:

. . . Elizabeth and I are living in Boston at 54 Bowdoin St.
. . . We are rather dilapidated old ladies, externally, but
E.[lizabeth] is one of those people who are immortally young
in spirit, and circulates freely among her friends whenever she
can get a helping arm, and continues to ply her pen assidu-

---

[61] *Letter*, Elizabeth P. Peabody to Mary Mann, [1880]. Robert Lincoln
Straker Collection, Antioch College Library.
[62] *Letter*, Kate Douglas Wiggin to Elizabeth P. Peabody, November 17,
1882. Horace Mann Collection, Massachusetts Historical Society.

ously. We rejoice greatly in the growth and prosperity of the kindergarten cause here.[63]

From Miss Peabody's active pen came *Last Evening with Allston* and many articles which appeared in the *Kindergarten Messenger* of Syracuse, in *Education*, in *The Index*, in the *Brooklyn Magazine*, and elsewhere. Although she no longer gave her course of lectures, she did attend the Detroit convention of the Friends of Froebel in 1882.

At about this time, Miss Peabody acquired a new interest. She discovered Sarah Winnemucca, a Piute princess who was dedicated to educating the American Indians. Princess Winnemucca opened a school in Nevada for which Miss Peabody tried to raise $100 a month. In March, 1885, Elizabeth journeyed to Washington to lobby for aid to the Indian. In the winter of 1886, she visited President Cleveland, seeking education for her Indian friends.

With resignation she watched her old friends lose their grasp on this life. Susan Blow withdrew from kindergarten work in 1884. Emerson died in 1884, Mary Mann in 1887, and Alcott in 1888. Nevertheless, in 1888 Miss Peabody had the satisfaction of seeing $20,000 included in the budget by the committee of the Boston School Board for the support of the public-school kindergartens.[64] At long last her native city gave evidence of its approval of kindergarten training for all its young children.

Miss Peabody wrote in 1887, "I continue here at 298 Lamartine Street and trust to continue during my natural life—for I am even luxuriously situated."[65] She died on

[63] *Letter*, Mary Mann to Mrs. Moncure D. Conway, January 7, 1883. Horace Mann Collection, Massachusetts Historical Society.

[64] Blow, *op. cit.*, p. 932.

[65] *Letter*, Elizabeth P. Peabody to Eleanor C. Lewis, March 27, [1887]. Robert Lincoln Straker Collection, Antioch College Library.

January 3, 1894, respected and beloved by the younger generation of kindergarten teachers who followed in the path she had made. In April 1896, Elizabeth Peabody House opened in Boston as a settlement house and permanent memorial to the kindergarten pioneer.

In comparing Miss Peabody's publications on the kindergarten with those of the other authors of kindergarten books and articles of the era, it is evident that she outstripped all in quantity and variety. Her interpretation of the spirit and method of the new education reached the lay public as well as educators because of the variety of her means of communication and her determined and constant efforts. Personal appeals, letters, newspaper and magazine articles, lectures, and books awakened interest in the movement and stimulated its growth. Today her works afford much information for historians of the kindergarten movement. Of comparable importance are the inspiration and increased understanding of the kindergarten philosophy which may be derived from her words by modern educators.

VI

Kindergarten Training Schools

IN THE UNITED STATES OF THE NINETEENTH CENTURY, RELI-
gious influences often were reflected in educational reforms. A modern historian of American culture, Frank
Luther Mott, scoffed at the use of religion as an antidote
to the problems of that era by dubbing it the "Home-and-
Jesus formula."[1] In her writings, in her educational theories, and in her daily life, Elizabeth Peabody mirrored the
liberal Unitarianism of her day and gave evidence of the
application of such a formula. Miss Peabody's concern
with religion was not superficial for she had delved deeply
into its intellectual aspects. Her cousin, Moses Coit Tyler,
informed his wife:

I learned the other day some further facts about Miss Peabody. The latter has during her life, amid the activities of a
very wide scholarship, given special attention to two great
branches, theology and history. . . . She was very intimate with
Doctor Channing and imbibed profoundly his ideas upon
theology and has studied deeply all systems of creed.[2]

1 Frank Luther Mott, *Golden Multitudes,* p. 122.
2 Jessica Tyler Austin, *Moses Coit Tyler,* p. 15.

William Henry Channing, Doctor Channing's nephew, explained the nature of Transcendentalism that so motivated its disciples:

Transcendentalism, as viewed by its disciples, was a pilgrimage from the idolatrous world of creeds and rituals to the temple of the living God in the soul. . . . Amidst materialists, zealots, and sceptics, the Transcendentalists believed in perpetual inspiration, the miraculous power of the will, and a birthright to universal good.[3]

The optimistic conception of a religious solution to sociological and educational problems was therefore in accord with her nature and training. She was quick to recognize the religious and moral values of kindergarten training, not only for the child but also for the kindergarten teacher. She said, "To be a kindergartner is the perfect development of womanliness—a working with God at the very fountain of artistic and intellectual power and moral character."[4] It was Miss Peabody's contention that "human influence must embody Divine Providence in order to educate." She held the opinion that Jesus Christ was the one child who had been educated up to the ideal standard. But in order to accomplish an education approaching this for all children, the true kindergartner must possess "Faith" as her first qualification.[5]

There was another aspect to this connection between religion and education in the training of the kindergarten teacher. This was the support given by the ministry to the kindergarten idea and the resultant establishment of church kindergartens and consequent demand for teachers

[3] R. W. Emerson, W. H. Channing, and J. F. Clarke, *Memoirs of Margaret Fuller Ossoli*, Vol. II, p. 13.

[4] Elizabeth P. Peabody, *Lectures in the Training Schools for Kindergartners*, p. 13.

[5] *Ibid.*, p. 15.

to conduct them. Miss Peabody sought such support from many ministers. In answer to his offer, she accepted the assistance of the Reverend Mr. Weiss because she thought that his word with the young mothers of his congregation would be "powerful."[6] In a postcard to the Rev. Mr. Chaney of Leominster, Massachusetts, she asked him to read the *Reminiscences of Froebel* which she had sent him, write a notice of it for the *Christian Register*, and indicate his approval "aloud" to the mothers in his congregation.[7]

A further outgrowth of ministerial support of the new kindergarten education was the sanction it conferred upon this new career for women. Many intelligent women wanted a "wider field of usefulness"[8] for their sex. It was but a step from the mother as teacher to the trained kindergartner. The importance of the mother as teacher was a basic tenet in Froebel's philosophy. Baroness Marenholtz-Bülow claimed that Froebel laid the basis of a true science for mothers which would lead to woman's emancipation. In her opinion:

With the elevation of child-nature, the elevation of woman and her veritable emancipation are closely bound up. The science of the mother initiates her inevitably into a higher branch of knowledge, whereby not mere dry intellectual power, but true sensibility and high spiritual clearsightedness are developed in her. With the knowledge that a divine spark slumbers in the little being on her lap, there must kindle in her a holy zeal and desire to fan this spark into a flame, and to educate for humanity a worthy citizen. With this vocation

6 *Letter,* Elizabeth P. Peabody to Rev. Mr. Weiss, August 20, n.d. Ruth M. Baylor Collection.

7 *Postcard,* Elizabeth P. Peabody to Rev. Mr. Chaney, n.d. Ruth M. Baylor Collection.

8 Sarah Josepha Hale, (ed.), *Woman's Record,* p. 666.

of educator of mankind is bound up everything needful to place woman in possession of the full rights of a worthy humanity.[9]

Amidst the sentimental verbiage of the Baroness's message, the underlying emphasis on the spiritual nature of teaching was evident. The mystical and transcendental thoughts embodied in Froebel's philosophy of education were not new or strange to Elizabeth Peabody. Her association with Emerson, Alcott, and other leaders of New England Transcendentalism made her peculiarly receptive to such ideas. The standards she set for kindergarten teachers were based on a liberal Christian theology. In her *Lectures in the Training Schools for Kindergartners*, she said, "Everything depends on the quality of the first kindergartners we train—their spiritual, moral and intellectual quality—which must be such as to operate in two ways: first, to do for the children the right thing; secondly, to educate the community to require it done as a general thing."[10] She was cognizant of the poor remuneration offered teachers of young children and gave this advice to young women:

I do not say to any particular person, it is your duty to wear yourself out and half starve, for the sake of keeping a kindergarten. It is only you who are sufficiently free from other obligations, to give yourselves the privilege and luxury of working with God, on the paradisaical ground of childhood, who should enter this field.[11]

Although her statement would seem to imply that only financially privileged women were likely to be successful

[9] Marenholtz-Bülow, "Froebel's Educational Views," Barnard (ed.), *Kindergarten and Child Culture*, p. 169.
[10] Peabody, *Lectures in the Training Schools for Kindergartners*, p. 22.
[11] *Ibid.*, p. 19.

kindergartners, it should be interpreted with the attitude of her era toward working women in mind. In Europe, even more than in America, it was unusual for women of culture to work for pecuniary reward. Many of the kindergartners trained by Froebel came from wealthy families. However, in America, we note that the first leaders of the kindergarten movement, Miss Peabody, her sister Mary, Mrs. Matilda Kriege, and her daughter Alma, were, albeit highly cultured, economically poor and self-supporting women. The low status of the educated woman was decried by Lucretia Mott, an American Quaker preacher:

The unequal condition of woman with man also early impressed my mind. Learning, while at school, that the charge for the education of girls was the same as that for boys, and that, when they became teachers, women received only half as much as men for their services, the injustice of this distinction was so apparent, that I resolved to claim for my sex all that an impartial Creator had bestowed, which by custom and a perverted application of the Scriptures, had been wrested from woman.[12]

The *Woman's Record* was the exponent of the rising interest in the education of women and in their participation in careers. Between its covers were found the biographies and achievements of all the successful career women up to the date of the publication of the book in 1872. Mrs. Hale,[13] its editor, noted in her preface that more books had been written by and about women within the era from 1820 to 1870 than all put together in recorded world history. In this world of awakening women, Miss Peabody was an exemplification of the self-dependent, intelligent, philanthropic woman of the group contemptuously designated as old maids.

12 Hale, *op. cit.,* p. 752.
13 *Ibid.,* "Preface," not paginated.

Since the education of children was approved by both ministry and public as woman's natural sphere, Froebel's aim of training teachers, as interpreted and propagated by Elizabeth Peabody, was comparatively well received in America. The pattern for kindergarten training schools was set by Froebel in 1847, in Keilhau, Germany, where he opened The Training School for Children's Nurses and Educators. Its aim was "to train young women who are suited for such work, to tend, develop, and educate the child from its birth up to the time when it is fully prepared to begin its school life, and so up to the beginning of the instruction of the school properly so called."[14] It was interesting to note the status given to the persons so trained. They were not to be known as "nursery maids and nurses" but as "child fosterers and educational helpers." Those who were to be trained to direct whole circles or groups of children were to be known as "directors and educators."[15] Miss Peabody knew of this school by reading and report only, for it was not until 1867, fifteen years after Froebel's death, that she visited the German schools. However, in the interim, other German training schools which followed these plans had been established. With the assistance of the Baroness Marenholtz-Bülow, Froebel established an institution for training kindergartners in the castle of the Duke of Meiningen, Marienthal, at Liebenstein. The Baroness later established another center of kindergarten influence through her training school in Dresden. In 1849, in Hamburg, Froebel and his associate, William Middendorff, were influential in interesting women in becoming kindergartners. Despite the ordinance of August, 1851, forbidding kindergartens and training schools in Prussia, kindergarten training schools

---

[14] Friedrich Froebel, *Education by Development*, p. 229.
[15] *Ibid.*, p. 231.

flourished in Berlin and elsewhere. Baroness Marenholtz-Bülow would have liked to see a faster growth. Said she:

The present want of training schools for Kindergartners in foreign countries makes the quick spread of Kindergartens impossible. Those educated in Germany are rarely sufficiently versed in foreign languages and very unwilling to leave home. The present incapacity of the majority of those who are active abroad destroys very much the good opinion that has been gained of the cause. On the other side, the ignorance of the German languages, as well as the frequent lack of means for distant journeys, prevents the foreign women from using the German training institutions.[16]

Elizabeth Palmer Peabody and her sister, Mrs. Horace Mann, were under no such handicap since they were able translators of both German and French. The Baroness's *Reminiscences of Friedrich Froebel* was translated by Mrs. Mann and published in Boston in 1877. Degerando's *Self-Education* had been translated from the French by Miss Peabody when she was twenty-nine. In 1872, she had translated, from the German, Baroness Marenholtz-Bülow's *The Philosophy and Methods of the Kindergarten*. Elizabeth Peabody's experience with literature in foreign languages and her awareness of books on education in other countries had been increased in the years when she had her bookshop on West Street.

Queen Victoria of England had her own children educated by Froebelian kindergartners and was herself "Lady Patroness" of the training school for kindergartners at 17 Tavistock Square, London.[17] Another important German

16 Louis Walter, *Bertha v. Marenholtz-Bülow in ihrer Bedeutung für das Werk of Fr. Froebel*. Translated and printed as "Bertha Von Marenholtz-Bülow and the Kindergarten," in Barnard (ed.), *Kindergarten and Child Culture*, p. 150.

17 Peabody, "Development of the Kindergarten," Barnard (ed.), *op. cit.*, p. 6.

training school was that founded in Berlin by Froebel's niece and pupil, Madame Henriette Breymann Schrader. It was visited by Mrs. A. Aldrich, the first Director of the kindergarten in Florence, Massachusetts, whose detailed account of what she observed was published in America by Henry Barnard.[18] Of all the European training schools, perhaps the most famous was the one established in Hamburg, in 1854, by Froebel's widow. Mme. Louise Levin Froebel had been Froebel's student teacher before their marriage. She was well-trained to carry on his work.

Miss Peabody's first pilgrimage to Europe in 1867 had as its professed purpose "to see the Kindergartens established and taught by Frobel [sic] himself and his carefully educated pupils . . ." She continues, "I returned in 1868, zealous to abolish my own and all similar mistakes, and establish the *real thing*, on the basis of an adequate training of the kindergartners."[19] Fate assisted Miss Peabody and, as has been noted, the "real thing" was awaiting her upon her return to Boston. Madame Matilda Kriege and her daughter Alma were firmly established in the school Miss Peabody had left in the care of Mrs. Mann and Miss Corliss. Miss Peabody's former school afforded the Krieges the opportunity they sought, and which Miss Peabody also sought, "to bestow the blessing of Froebel's ideas" on America.[20]

An advertisement in the *Boston Transcript* in September, 1868, informed the public of the advent of the Krieges:

[18] Mrs. A. Aldrich, "Notes of Visits to Kindergartens," Barnard (ed.), *op. cit.*, p. 465.

[19] Peabody, "Brief Notice of the Kindergarten in America," Barnard (ed.), *op. cit.*, p. 10.

[20] Caroline D. Aborn, "Matilda H. Kriege," Committee of Nineteen, International Kindergarten Union (eds.), *Pioneers of the Kindergarten in America*, p. 91.

German Kindergarten.—Miss Corliss relinquishes her school, hitherto kept on Pinckney Street, into the hands of Madame Kriege and Miss Alma Kriege, who have been trained at the Kindergarten Seminary of the Baroness Marenholtz, in Berlin. This lady was a personal pupil of Froebel, the founder of the Kindergarten. Madame Kriege has brought with her from Germany the material and apparatus for the kindergarten proper, as taught in German cities. In connection with the school, she proposes to take afternoon and evening classes for the training of kindergarten teachers.[21]

Thus in October, 1868, was established another historic first in the annals of kindergarten education, the first English-speaking Froebelian training school in America. Louise Hall Tharp, in her description of this event, noted the financial sacrifices by the Peabody sisters:

It would look as though the two Peabody sisters had lost a successful school, just as it was showing a consistent profit. But Mary was as altruistic as Elizabeth, though few people realized it. She had the cause of kindergartens just as much at heart; and she knew the German ladies must have a place in which to show what they could do.[22]

Miss Peabody's only regret was that Madame Kriege found the Boston public unprepared for the "true Froebel" because of Miss Peabody's early mistaken attempts to interpret him before she fully understood his practices.[23] Although it has been claimed that it was through Miss Peabody's persuasion that the Krieges came to America,[24] no documentation for such a statement has to date been

---

21 *Ibid.*, p. 92.

22 Louise Hall Tharp, *The Peabody Sisters of Salem*, p. 323.

23 Peabody, "Brief Notice of the Kindergarten in America," Barnard (ed.), *op. cit.*, p. 11.

24 Margaret J. Stannard, "Mary J. Garland," Committee of Nineteen, International Kindergarten Union (eds.), *Pioneers of the Kindergarten in America*, p. 110.

found. It would seem from Miss Peabody's own statement that she had planned to import Fraulein Boelte from Germany to come to Boston and establish a model kindergarten and a training school for kindergartners. Her preference for Fraulein Boelte was because she was "one of the few ladies of position and culture in Germany who, from purely disinterested motives, had become a Kindergartner."[25]

Since there was a dearth of kindergarten literature, Madame Kriege made a great contribution by her book *The Child, Its Nature and Relations*, which was a free rendering of the Baroness Marenholtz-Bülow's *Child and Child Nature*. Lectures from this manuscript formed the basis of the curriculum of this first training school. In 1872, the Krieges went to Germany for a vacation and left their school in the hands of Miss Mary J. Garland, who was their only graduate considered worthy of a certificate of qualification as training teacher as well as kindergarten teacher. In the interim, Miss Peabody, relieved by the Kreiges of the practical details of conducting a kindergarten, devoted her entire time to lecturing and writing about the kindergarten. When Miss Peabody published a magazine, *The Kindergarten Messenger*, in 1873, Madame Kreige contributed letters and articles. After the Krieges returned to America, they became associated with Miss Haine's school in New York where they conducted the training school and kindergarten[26] which had been established by Maria Boelte. Miss Boelte had been reluctant to establish a training school. As she explained:

During my first year's work in America I did not wish to open a regular Training School for Kindergartners, because I had

25 Peabody, *op. cit.,* p. 10.
26 Aborn, *op. cit.,* p. 96.

first to organize my kindergarten and make it a "model" as far as that could be done during one year's work—a thing entirely overlooked in this country.[27]

After the marriage of Maria Boelte and John Kraus, they opened the New York Seminary for Kindergartners where their high scholastic standards were reflected in the course of study. While Madame Kriege's course had been of but twenty-six weeks duration, the New York Seminary required one year's training and a second year of practical work in a kindergarten. Mrs. Kraus said, "A good kindergartner should not only be a kindergartner, but at the same time a good teacher, thus verifying the saying: that a good kindergartner may become any day a teacher—but not vice versa."[28] Mrs. Kraus considered the first year of a kindergarten teacher's work as her test work. "Therefore," said she, "it may seem that to give a Diploma to train others is out of the question where the person has not been tested and testing herself by *years* of faithful work and preparation."[29] The Krauses were very particular in their selection of candidates, choosing only "the best class of cultured women who give their whole time and energy, enabling us to enter into as deep a study as we choose. . . ."[30] Mrs. Kraus considered Kindergartening to be such a practical profession that mere fluency in writing or speaking of Froebel's ideas was insufficient evidence of a trainee's ability. A trainee was required to observe in a kindergarten and by degrees to superintend just one child and gradually larger numbers of children. Professor and Mrs. Kraus published a two volume book entitled *The*

[27] Maria Kraus-Boelte, *The Kindergarten and the Mission of Women*, p. 25.
[28] *Ibid.*, p. 27.
[29] *Ibid.*, p. 28.
[30] *Ibid.*

Friedrich Froebel.

Holograph letter from Friedrich Froebel, Keilhau, July 16, 1848, commending a German kindergartner for her work and asking for a report of her kindergarten to be used to promote the establishment of more kindergartens elsewhere.

und seiner Anstalten nicht nur mit aufrichtigem Beifall ehren,
auch mit ihnen ganz gleiche Rechte und Unterstützung zusichern.

Daß nun solche Theilnahme aus den Wünschen der bessern Zeitgenossen
sich in das Wesen und die Mittel der Kindergärten oder vielleicht
der unterhaltend erziehenden Bildungsbereiche überhaupt hervor,
welchen müßte, lag in der Natur der Sache, und so bildete sich bald
das gemeinsame Entschluß zu einem Zusammentritt mehrerer
— welches sich aber bald zu einer öffentlichen Einladung an
alle deutsche Volksfreunde in Volkslehrer zu einer Versamm-
lung für den genannten Zweck in N° 45 der süddeutschen
Zeitung vom 1 Juli d. J. verweitete.

Einige besondere Abdrücke dieser Einladung erlaube ich mir
Ihnen zu genauerem und die Sache fördernden Gebrauch Ihnen
beizulegen.

Da es jedoch der Wünsch der sich Versammelnden sein muß, eine
so gründliche als umfassende Einsicht in das Wesen und besonders
in die Wirkung der Kindergärten, wie sie bis jetzt in Ausübung
gekommen sind — so weit es immer die Zeit gestattet — zu erlangen,
so drängte sich bald ein anderes Verlangen hervor: auf daß die
bereits schon unterricht bestehenden Kindergärten die Ergebnisse
Ihrer Wirksamkeit mitgetheilt zu sehen, aber auch in dieser
Hinsicht die Erfahrungen aller derer zu hören, welche überzeugt
dem Gegenstand in der Anwendung und in einem gewissen
Verbande mit unsern Bestrebungen ihre prüfende Beachtung
während einer längeren Zeitdauer geschenkt haben und zu
diesem Ende Rundschreiben zur gütigen Einsendung dieser Erfahrungen und Ergebnisse an beide zu erlassen.

Es bleibt mir nun noch übrig von der Sache, daß Ihnen sie
für ein kleines Anzug gefällt, daß wir das durch zwar
natürlich finden, wenn wir besonders von Ihnen Mittheilung
Ihrer Erfahrungen auf diesem Felde wünschen und wenn ich

so erlaube uns Ihnen, verehrter Herr, zur gütigen
Berücksichtigung eine solche Abschrift in der Anlage zu-
zusenden. Ferner würden wir uns, wenn Sie uns gütigst
die oben ausgesprochenen Wünsche erfüllen wollten, und
so uns als die Freude hätte, wiederwärtige Kunde von Ihrem
scheinen und Ihrem brüderischen Wirken zu erhalten.

Genehmigen Sie die Versicherung ausgezeichneter Hochachtung

Ihre
ergebenen
Friedrich Fröbel.

Keilhau
bei Rudolstadt
am 16 Jul 48.

"Patche Kuchen," one of Froebel's Mother Plays, from his book, *Mutter und Kose Lieder* (Blankenburg bei Rudolstadt, 1844).

Silhouettes of family of Dr. Nathaniel Peabody: Mrs. Nathaniel Peabody, age 57; Dr. Nathaniel Peabody, age 61; Elizabeth, age 31; Nathaniel, age 24; George, age 22; Sophia, age 26; Mary, age 29; Wellington, age 20. Profiles done from life, November 8, 1835.

Courtesy of Essex Institute, Salem, Mass.

Portrait of Elizabeth Palmer Peabody accompanying the sonnet in her honor, "Daughter of Memory," by A. Bronson Alcott, in Sonnets and Canzonets (Roberts Brothers, 1882):

Daughter of Memory! who her watch doth keep
O'er dark Oblivion's land of shade and dream,
Peers down into the realm of ancient Sleep,
Where Thought uprises with a sudden gleam
And lights the devious path 'twixt *Be* and *Seem*;
Mythologist! that dost thy legend steep
Plenteously with opiate and anodyne,
Inweaving fact with fable, line with line,
Entangling anecdote and episode,
Mindful of all that all men meant or said,—
We follow, pleased, thy labyrinthine road,
By Ariadne's skein and lesson led:
For thou hast wrought so excellently well,
Thou drop'st more casual truth than sages tell.

Kindergarten class of the West Newton English and Classical School, Washington and Highland Streets, West Newton, Mass., Mrs. Louise Pollock, Kindergartner, Mr. Nathaniel T. Allen, Principal.

The group was daguerreotyped in the fall of 1864. So far as is known, this is the earliest picture taken of a kindergarten class in this country.

C. C. Drew, The Newton Directory, 1868

No.	Froebel's Kindergarten, etc.	Piece.	Gross.

Froebel's Kindergarten, etc.

Continued.

1. STICK-LAYING.

in engaging the attention of the little ones, and keeping them busy, contented, and quiet. But they add to that the far higher service of inculcating manual skill, artistic taste, and the love of study and application, without tears for the pupil or wearisomeness for the instructor.—*The Cultivator and Country Gentleman.*

5/0 assorted sticks, 1, 2, 3, 4 and 5 in. long, respectively, 265 Designs on 12 plates, and instructions, - - - - - - per piece, | 60

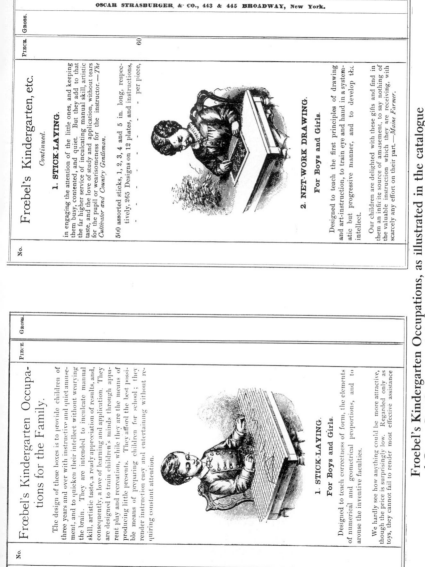

2. NET-WORK DRAWING.

For Boys and Girls.

Designed to teach the first principles of drawing and art-instruction, to train eye and hand in a systematic but progressive manner, and to develop the intellect.

Our children are delighted with these gifts and find in them an infinite source of amusement, to say nothing of the valuable instruction which they are receiving, with scarcely any effort on their part.—*Maine Farmer.*

No.	Froebel's Kindergarten Occupations for the Family.	Piece.	Gross.

Froebel's Kindergarten Occupations for the Family.

The design of these boxes is to provide children of three years and over with instructive and quiet amusement, and to quicken their intellect without wearying the brain. They are intended to inculcate manual skill, artistic taste, a ready appreciation of results, and, consequently, a love of learning and application. They are designed to train children's minds through apparent play and recreation, while they are the means of producing little presents. They afford the best possible means of preparing children for school; they render instruction easy and entertaining without requiring constant attention.

1. STICK-LAYING.

For Boys and Girls.

Designed to teach correctness of form, the elements of numerical and geometrical proportions, and to arouse the inventive faculties.

We hardly see how anything could be more attractive, though the price is surprisingly low. Regarded only as toys, they cannot fail to render most effective assistance

Froebel's Kindergarten Occupations, as illustrated in the catalogue of Oscar Strasburger and Co., 443 and 445 Broadway, New York, 1880.

I. Warshaw Americana Collection, New York City

Froebel's Kindergarten, etc.

Continued.

No.		Piece.	Gross.
2	Perforating-Needles, 1 Perforating-Cushion, 1 package of 10 leaves of paper, ruled in squares on one side, 1 package of 10 leaves of heavy white paper, 93 Designs on 12 plates, and instructions. - - - per piece,	60	

4. WEAVING (BRAIDING OR MAT-PLAITING.)

For Boys and Girls.

Designed to teach neatness and accuracy, and thus to convey a knowledge of the proper combinations of colors. The objects thus made may be preserved and used as bookmarks, and in various other ways.

No.		Piece.	Gross.
1	Steel Weaving-Needle, 20 Mats of assorted colors and widths, with corresponding strips, 75 designs on 12 plates, and instructions, - - per piece,	60	

Froebel's Kindergarten, etc.

Continued.

2. NET-WORK DRAWING.

No.		Piece.	Gross.
1	Slate, 6¼x8½ in., grooved, on one side, in squares (¼ in. wide); with narrow frame, rounded corners, 3 slate pencils, 94 designs on 12 plates, and instructions, - - - per piece,	60	

3. PERFORATING (PRICKING.)

For Boys and Girls.

Designed to advance the child still further in art-instruction, and to create a faculty for free-hand drawing and the production of artistic and beautiful forms. The objects thus made may be used for various purposes in the household.

These occupations are particularly adapted to family use, and are invaluable in directing the early training of the young mind. The price of these Occupations is moderate, but whatever their cost, they will be found to afford a pleasure and instruction to the child which money cannot buy.—*Christian Statesman.*

We know of nothing ever gotten up so simple, and yet so useful, to occupy the attention of little children and keep them amused and out of mischief, as these beautiful boxes.—*The Gospel Banner*

No.	PIECE.	GROSS.

Froebel's Kindergarten, etc.

Continued.

5. EMBROIDERING.

For Girls and Boys.

Designed to teach the elements of fancy-work, to convey correct ideas as to number and form, and to still further educate the eye in the selection and combination of colors. The objects produced, (like those of most of the other occupations, look pretty, and may be used as presents.

Worsted, of 12 different colors, and 3 worsted needles, 1 perforating needle, 10 pieces of Bristol Board, 1 piece of Blotting Paper, 10 leaves of white paper, 136 designs on 12 plates, and instructions. Piece, **60**

No.	PIECE.	GROSS.

Froebel's Kindergarten, etc.

Continued.

6. CORK (or Peas) WORK.

For Boys and Girls.

Designed to instruct in the proportions of geometrical figures and in the production of outlines of solids and of real objects, while teaching also accuracy of measurement and the elements of the perspective, etc.

60 Cork Cubes, 60 pieces of Wire, 1, 2, 3, and 4 inches long, respectively, 1 Piercing Pin, 108 designs on 12 plates, and instructions. - - - - **75**

TOY DEPARTMENT.

Froebel's Kindergarten, etc.
Continued.

No.	PIECE.	GROSS.

8. RING-LAYING.
For Boys and Girls.

Designed to teach the elements of form, as applied to curved and symmetrical figures, and to lead to an artistic developement of the curve—the line of beauty. 10 Rings and 20 Half Rings each, of 2 inches, 1¼ in., ¾ inch diameter. 107 Designs and instructions.
per piece,   60

9. PAPER INTERTWINING.
For Girls and Boys.

Designed to teach the first principles of the art of decoration, the study of angles, and the combination of colors. 100 Strips of Paper, white and colored, 55 Designs, and instructions. - - - per piece,   60

82

TOY DEPARTMENT.

Froebel's Kindergarten, etc.
Continued.

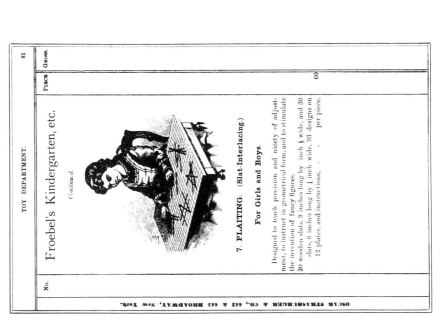

No.	PIECE.	GROSS.
		81

7. PLAITING. (Slat-Interlacing.)
For Girls and Boys.

Designed to teach precision and nicety of adjustment, to instruct in geometrical form, and to stimulate the invention of fancy figures. 30 wooden slats, 9 inches long by ⅓ inch wide, and 30 slats, 6 inches long by ¼ inch wide. 93 designs on 12 plates, and instructions, - - per piece,   60

Holograph postcard from Elizabeth P. Peabody, Boston, to Reverend Mr. Chaney, Leominster, Mass., undated [1877].

Miss Peabody requests Rev. Chaney to write a notice for the *Christian Register* extolling the *Reminiscences of Froebel* so that the attention of mothers would be drawn to it.

Replica of monument to Friedrich Froebel at Schweina, Germany. The sphere, the cylinder, and the cube which form the upper part of the monument are the component parts of Froebel's Second Gift. The card was distributed by Milton Bradley Co., Springfield, Mass., in honor of the founder of the kindergarten, 1882.

Baylor Collection

Mrs. Eudora L. Hailmann's Training School for Kindergartners and Primary Teachers, La Porte, Indiana, 1885-1894.

Baylor Collection

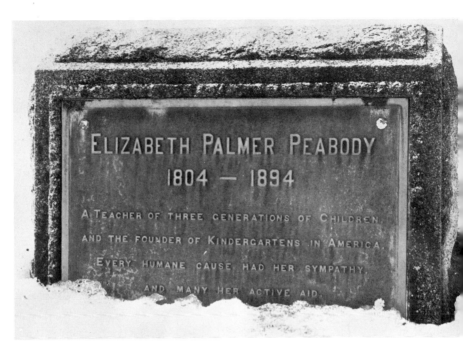

Tombstone of Elizabeth Palmer Peabody in Sleepy Hollow Cemetery, Concord, Mass.

"A teacher of three generations of Children
and the founder of Kindergartens in America.
Every humane cause had her sympathy
And many her active aid."

Kindergarten Guide, which was a most thorough and detailed explanation of Froebel's gifts and occupations and contained illustrations of and suggestions for their use. Miss Peabody wrote in regard to this work:

We like the Manual very much, and my sister [Mrs. Mann] says, "since it is impossible for Mrs. Kraus to teach all the children in the United States herself, the next best thing for her to do is certainly to give these precise and full directions to others." We are indeed delighted with your minuteness, thoroughness, and clearness of direction.[31]

Miss Peabody shared with John Kraus and Marie Kraus-Boelte a determination to permit no shoddy imitations of Froebel nor any quacks seeking to benefit financially from the kindergarten's popularity. In 1890, the model classes were discontinued and Madame Kraus-Boelte gave her full time to training teachers. After Professor Kraus' death in 1896, Maria Kraus-Boelte continued her training school. Over twelve hundred kindergartners were trained by her in her thirty-nine years of work in America.

The third of the German pioneer kindergartners to come to America because of Elizabeth Peabody's persuasions was Emma Jacobina Christiana Marwedel. On Miss Peabody's European tour, it was Miss Marwedel who introduced her to the genuine Froebelian kindergarten in Hamburg and who, admitted Miss Peabody, "inspired me with the courage to make the main object of the remainder of my life to extend the kindergarten over my own country."[32] The dedication of Miss Marwedel's book *Conscious Motherhood* was, in part, to "Miss Elizabeth P. Peabody, Introducer of Froebel's System to America." Miss Peabody

[31] *Steiger's Kindergarten Catalogue,* p. 57, bound with J. Kraus and M. Kraus-Boelte, *The Kindergarten Guide.*
[32] Marwedel, *Conscious Motherhood,* appendix, p. 7.

considered that this book supplemented her own life work. She claimed, "It is in itself a key to the whole of Froebel's philosophy, whose depths she [Miss Marwedel] seems to me to have sounded more thoroughly than any of his disciples."[33]

Emma Marwedel was especially interested in the problem of industrial education for women and in the application of Froebel's methods to the entire system of education. Upon coming to America in 1870, she established, near Brentwood, L. I., a self-supporting school to educate young women as florists and as producers and conservers of fruits and vegetables. The experiment was, unfortunately, not successful. Miss Marwedel's emphasis on manual dexterity was shown in the choice of a title for her book about handwork as a method of filling the gap between the kindergarten and the Manual Labor School. She termed handwork *The Connecting Link*. In her opinion, "The great truth of a natural human development *does not end* with the kindergarten—it rather begins with it."[34] She sought to establish handwork and manual labor as this connecting link between kindergarten, the primary school, and man's labor so that the Froebelian principles would permeate a man's span of life. Miss Marwedel noted the advantages in kindergarten training in America over that offered in Germany. In America, the normal-class pupil entered at the age of eighteen, whereas in Germany the age was fourteen. From 1872 to 1876, in Washington, D. C., Miss Marwedel conducted a kindergarten in connection with her school for Practical and Physical Culture. Thence she went to Los Angeles where a training class of three students and a kindergarten of twenty-five children

33 *Ibid.*
34 Marwedel, *The Connecting Link*, p. 7.

had been set up for her by Mrs. Caroline M. Severance, a follower of Miss Peabody's New Education and a former Boston resident. A famous pupil of this first class was Kate Douglas Wiggin, then Kate Douglas Smith. She wrote of her training:

I am very grateful that my first training came from Miss Marwedel. She was not adapted to all pupils, her English not being perfect and her method not systematic. Her feet never trod the solid earth; she was an idealist, a dreamer, and a visionary, but life is so apt to be crammed with Gradgrinds that I am thankful when I come into intimate contact with a dreamer.[35]

In the curriculum at Miss Marwedel's school, besides the books of manual work made by the students to illustrate the "occupations," there was the study of psychology, history of education, Pestalozzi, Rousseau, and Froebel's Mother Play. There were also classes in games, storytelling, and discussions of metaphysical problems.[36] In reading Mrs. Wiggin's description of her training under Miss Marwedel, any exponent of kindergarten training for young women might well be gratified at the results Mrs. Wiggin acknowledges. "The study and practice of the kindergarten theory of education and of life gave me, while I was still very young, a certain ideal by which to live and work, and it has never faded."[37]

In 1876, Miss Marwedel went to Oakland, California, to carry on a similar type of work. She was the pioneer of the kindergarten movement in the Far West but was dissatis-

---

[35] Kate Douglas Wiggin, *My Garden of Memory,* p. 98.

[36] Earl Barnes, "Emma Marwedel," Committee of Nineteen, International Kindergarten Union (eds.), *Pioneers of the Kindergarten in America,* p. 269.

[37] Wiggin, *op. cit.,* p. 126.

fied with her own accomplishments and often discouraged. In a letter to Miss Peabody in 1882, Mrs. Wiggin said:

If Miss Marwedel gets unhappy again and thinks that we do not appreciate her why I can only say that we *do.* . . . I do admire and believe in her—love to hear her talk—think her full of genius—but she will not do me justice—nor any of my pupils—nor the free K—— work & everybody whom I know has given up the idea of finding any justice in her. Poor Mrs. Cooper who is the essence of love and patience is entirely worn out with her morbid vagaries and has given up in despair.[38]

Will S. Monroe remarked that Miss Marwedel was never wholly understood by others and never adequately understood herself.[39] On her death bed in 1893, she declared to a small group of disciples, "I believe in the power of the kindergarten to reform the world."[40] Despite her belief that her lifework had not been accomplished, she exerted a powerful influence on the growth of training schools for kindergartners by her pioneer effort in establishing the first kindergarten training institution on the Pacific coast and by the effect of her philosophy, of helping humanity, on the work of her followers.

From these three German kindergartners, induced by Miss Peabody to bring Froebel's message to America, stem the myriad training classes and kindergartens which flourished, as Froebel had predicted, on American soil. The kindergarten training school of Miss Mary J. Garland and Miss Rebecca J. Weston in Boston was a successor to that of the Krieges. Miss Garland had been Mrs. Kriege's pupil and Miss Weston had been Miss Garland's pupil. Some of

38 *Letter*, Kate Douglas Wiggin to Elizabeth P. Peabody, November 17, 1882. Horace Mann Collection, Massachusetts Historical Society.

39 Will S. Monroe, "Emma Marwedel and the Kindergarten," *Education*, Vol. 14, February, 1894, p. 341.

40 Fletcher Harper Swift, "Emma Marwedel," *University of California Publications in Education*, Vol. 6, No. 3, 1931, p. 139.

the talented graduates of their school were Laliah B. Pingree, the first supervisor of kindergartens in Boston; Caroline D. Aborn, a later supervisor; Emilie Poulsson, who translated Froebel's *Finger Plays*; Harriet S. Jenks, who compiled the early kindergarten songs; and Lucy H. Symonds, who established a private training school for kindergartners. All these schools and many more had the benefit of the lectures to kindergartners given by Miss Peabody, for she traveled not only to the training schools in Boston but to cities in far off states as well.

The famous graduate of Maria Boelte's first school, Miss Susan E. Blow, expanded Froebel's ideas and demonstrated them in many new ways. Part of her great influence was due to her many books expounding Froebel's theories. She was the author of *Symbolic Education, Letters to a Mother, Mottoes and Commentaries of Froebel's Mother Play, Educational Issues in the Kindergarten,* and other works. Miss Peabody extolled Miss Blow's gratuitous work with the St. Louis Board of Education.[41] After her first two years of work without pay, the Board empowered Miss Blow to select twelve of the kindergartners she had trained and to supervise their work in the St. Louis public schools. Miss Blow possessed private means or she could not have supported the free training school from which hundreds of graduates became volunteer assistants in the public kindergartens. Miss Blow bestowed a diploma upon her students only after a thorough examination on the Froebelian philosophy and after observation of their practice teaching. In 1876, Miss Blow spent the winter with the Baroness Marenholtz-Bülow in Dresden. Her close association in the public school endeavor with Dr. William Torrey Harris resulted in the establishment of

[41] Peabody, "Origin and Growth of the Kindergarten," *Education*, Vol. 2, May, 1882, p. 507.

the first sustained public school kindergarten. Dr. Harris' interest in kindergarten education was revealed in his correspondence with Miss Peabody on the subject. His efforts in conjunction with those of Miss Blow made St. Louis a center of kindergarten development in the 1870's.

Stemming from Miss Marwedel's training school in California was the Silver Street Charity Kindergarten and Training School organized by Kate Douglas Wiggin, one of Miss Marwedel's students. Felix Adler had come to San Francisco from New York in 1878, and raised funds for a free kindergarten in the heart of the San Francisco slums. To this class the students of the San Francisco Normal School were sent for observation of kindergarten activities. With her sister, Nora Archibald Smith, Mrs. Wiggin extended her influence into other training schools by such books as *Kindergarten Practices and Principles, Froebel's Occupations,* and *Froebel's Gifts.* A note to Miss Peabody, signed Kate Wiggin, was on stationery bearing the address of Mrs. Wiggin's California Kindergarten Training School at 1505 Washington Street, San Francisco.[42] Mrs. Wiggin's correspondence with Miss Peabody revealed her deep affection and respect for Miss Peabody's intellect and altruism. In her autobiography she told of collecting from kindergartners a thousand dollars which she sent to Miss Peabody for an eightieth-birthday gift.[43] Miss Peabody was living on very limited funds and the gift was intended to ease her financial problems. To the great shock of the donors, Miss Peabody informed them in her thank-you note that she had contributed $800 of the $1000 to Princess Winnemucca to use in educating the Indians.

The story of the pioneer training schools would not be complete if no mention was made of Dr. William Nicholas

42 *Letter,* Kate Douglas Wiggin to Elizabeth P. Peabody, May 20, 1886. Horace Mann Collection, Massachusetts Historical Society.
43 Kate Douglas Wiggin, *op. cit.,* p. 158.

Hailmann and his wife, Eudora Hailmann. Dr. Hailmann's contribution to kindergarten education in the United States was not influenced in the beginning by Miss Peabody, as were the contributions of other pioneers mentioned. According to a sketch of his life, which he had written, his early training had been undertaken by his mother, a convinced admirer of Pestalozzi. His education continued in private schools in Switzerland, until in 1852, at the age of nineteen, he came to America and began his teaching career.[44] His first interest in the kindergarten arose when on a trip to Europe in 1860 he visited several kindergartens there and was impressed by what he observed.[45] Upon his return to America he became the head of the German-American Academy in Louisville and later of two other similar institutions in the Midwest. With his wife, Eudora Lucas Hailmann, he established a kindergarten in his school in Louisville in 1865 and ten years later opened a kindergarten and training school in connection with the German-American Academy in Milwaukee, Wisconsin. *The Kindergarten Messenger and The New Education*, a magazine which arose from the ashes of Miss Peabody's *Kindergarten Messenger* and Mr. Hailmann's magazine *The New Education*, carried an advertisement of the reopening of Mr. and Mrs. Hailmann's Training Class for Kindergartners in Detroit, on Monday, March 17, 1879.

Dr. Hailmann's contributions to the spread of training classes was intensified by his publications, *Kindergarten Manual*, *Law of Childhood*, and especially by his translation of Froebel's *Education of Man*. Miss Peabody wrote of Dr. Hailmann in 1879, "I do not know any one who

---

[44] Barbara Greenwood, "William Nicholas Hailmann," Committee of Nineteen, International Kindergarten Union (eds.), *Pioneers of the Kindergarten in America*, pp. 249–251.

[45] *Ibid.*, p. 253.

has made such substantial sacrifices to the cause or is doing more for it now."[46]

Although a Daily Normal School was established for elementary teachers in New York in 1856, it was sustained for only three years, when the Saturday Normal School filled its place until its re-establishment in 1869. It was not until 1870, the year of the opening of the Normal College, with Dr. Thomas Hunter as president, that the kindergarten method was taught.[47] Dr. Hunter gave the credit for his information about the kindergarten to Professor Adolph Douai, who taught a German-American school in Hoboken, and to Miss Peabody. Said Dr. Hunter:

My next teacher was a very charming old lady, Miss Elizabeth Peabody, a sister-in-law of Horace Mann. I retain a vivid recollection of the cultivated woman in her refined manner and musical voice. She delivered three or four lectures on the Kindergarten which ratified all that Dr. Douai had taught me, and she captured two of our students who subsequently took private lessons and devoted themselves to this department of teaching. These two young women, Dr. Ida Emily Conant and Dr. Jennie [sic] B. Merrill did a most meritorious work in popularizing the Kindergarten. The latter is at present Superintendent of Kindergartens in New York City, and the former is Associate Professor of Pedagogics in the Normal College.[48]

Dr. Hunter encountered considerable opposition in securing the establishment of a free kindergarten in connection with the Normal College. Not only did certain members of the Board of Education scoff at the idea, but Bernard Smith, president of the Board of Education, exclaimed,

46 Susan E. Blow, "The History of the Kindergarten in the United States," *The Outlook*, Vol. 55, April 3, 1897, p. 934.

47 *Annual Report of the President of the Normal College for the Year 1871*, not paginated. New York: Board of Education, 1871.

48 Anna M. and Jenny Hunter (eds.), *The Autobiography of Dr. Thomas Hunter*, p. 295.

"What! pay money to teach children to play?"[49] Dr. Hunter was obliged to educate some of the leading committee members, just as Dr. Douai and Miss Peabody had educated him. But the training school was not successful "owing to the opposition of the principal of the model school" and because Dr. Hunter was "unable to oversee the work and encourage the professors."[50]

The standard of teacher education in New York in 1869 may be judged by the requirements of admission to the training school for elementary teachers. The applicant was required to be fourteen years old, to pass an examination, and to have spent at least one year in a New York City public school. In 1870, there was a three year course; in 1879, a four year course; in 1888, a five year course. Dr. Hunter claimed that much of the opposition to lengthening the course came from poor parents who wanted their daughters to earn money at an early age, and from wealthy parents who were hostile to granting degrees.[51] Political considerations were also involved, which often nullified the examinations. Dr. Hunter cited an example of a teacher who wrote the word "I" as "i," and when told to capitalize it, wrote "İ." Dr. Hunter commented:

Doubtless she and many others were appointed through political influence; for, it may be said, in passing, that there never has been a time in the educational system when political, religious, or social influence was not powerful in making appointments in the schools.[52]

In contrast, the conscientious and strenuous efforts of the pioneer private kindergarten training schools to establish high standards, not only of scholastic training but of character and fitness for their students must be noted. In

49 *Ibid.*
50 *Ibid.*
51 *Ibid.*, p. 190.
52 *Ibid.*, p. 189.

an article written in 1870 for the *Illinois Teacher*, Elizabeth Peabody said:

I feel some hope that I may be able to place Primary Education in such a light that it will command the enthusiasm and activity of women, if not of men, of the highest class of mind, for only such, I think, should be intrusted with it.[53]

The consecration and devotion of those who established the early training schools was itself an inspiration to the students. Miss Mary J. Garland wrote of her instructor:

But for the singleness of purpose with which Madame Kriege devoted herself to establishing it on a sound basis; but for her fidelity to a high ideal, the history of the Kindergarten in this country might have been very different—less healthy in its growth, less steady in its progress, for in the beginning we have sure prophecy of the end.[54]

The course of kindergarten training in the Garland school was lengthened from six months in 1868, to one year in 1872, to two years in 1892.[55] Miss Peabody endeavored, in the absence of any type of nation-wide examination or control, to give professional acknowledgment to those training schools who taught the "true" Froebelian method. This she did by publishing in the *Kindergarten Messenger* a list of kindergarten training schools, the names of the "genuine" kindergartners, and the names of those by whom they had been trained. Revisions were published as needed.

[53] Peabody, "The Kindergarten, Its Philosophy," *The Illinois Teacher*, Vol. 16, No. 5, May, 1870, p. 152.

[54] Caroline D. Aborn, "Matilda H. Kriege," Committee of Nineteen, International Kindergarten Union (eds.), *Pioneers of the Kindergarten in America*, p. 95.

[55] Margaret J. Stannard, "Mary J. Garland," Committee of Nineteen, International Kindergarten Union (eds.), *Pioneers of the Kindergarten in America*, p. 114.

The *Kindergarten Messenger* of December, 1874, carried this article on the revised list of kindergartners:

Since March 1874, when we gave a list of genuine kindergartners, of whose training in the Method of Froebel we were personally cognizant, there have gone to work many more.[56]

A long list of names and addresses followed. Mrs. Kriege's graduates were indicated by an asterisk, Miss Garland's by a different mark and so forth. In reality, this was a form of accreditation for the Froebelian kindergartners. Not only kindergartners in the United States and Canada were designated, but also missionary kindergartners as follows:

*Mrs. C. B. Thomas, gone to carry Kindergarten to the Karens of Burmah.
*Miss Marston, gone to carry Kindergarten into the Zenani, India.[57]

Miss Peabody did not hesitate to voice her criticism or approval of schools at which she observed, visited, or lectured. She would make some comment, such as this one which referred to Miss Garland's school:

It is of this school that I personally have the most intimate knowledge; having been for six years, lecturer in it upon Religious and Moral Nature.[58]

By such statements, Miss Peabody was a self-appointed, unpaid supervisor of American kindergartners. She gave her approval or expressed her disapproval of kindergarten publications in a column entitled, "What Books Shall We Read?"[59]

[56] Peabody, *Kindergarten Messenger*, Vol. 2, No. 12, December, 1874, p. 20.
[57] *Ibid.*
[58] Peabody, *Kindergarten Messenger*, New Series, Vol. 1, Nos. 1, 2, January and February, 1877, p. 14.
[59] Peabody, *Kindergarten Messenger*, New Series, Vol. 1, Nos. 3, 4, March and April, 1877, pp. 36–44.

Omission from the list of kindergartners was comparable to having one's license revoked or to losing prestige among one's peers. That Miss Peabody's fearless frankness was sometimes resented, and that lack of inclusion on the list was considered a professional insult, was to be seen from Miss Peabody's correspondence. What also was evident from the correspondence was that Miss Peabody, as self-appointed judge and guardian of the Froebelian kindergarten in America, was not to be swayed by pleas, undue influence, or unpleasantness from performing what she, and many of her friends, considered her duty in defense of kindergarten standards. In answer to a query from Superintendent Harris of St. Louis about her refusal to include certain kindergartners, Miss Peabody replied:

I hope you observed that I did not attack the Pollocks at all. I merely did not recommend Mrs. Pollock as a trainer of kindergartners; and I made no personal imputations at any time of Mrs. Coe's or Mrs. Welchman's motives, or discredited their abilities. I only took their own word for it—that they had invented new and better ways, and therefore it was inconsistent in them as well as misleading to the public to advertise themselves as kindergarten teachers.[60]

In answer to Mr. Harris' comment that she should not commend any lady or school because it excited jealousy, Miss Peabody retorted:

But here I must differ. What are the reliable kindergartens and who are the reliable trainers—are the practical questions it is most important to answer—and no fair-minded decent person will be other than nobly stimulated, by just praise bestowed on others. Besides it is the best way of defining the kindergarten to point to good instances of it; and if you knew what lamentations had been written to me of the loss of time

[60] *Letter*, Elizabeth P. Peabody to William T. Harris, January 6, 1877. The Harris Papers, Missouri Historical Society.

and money by poor ladies who had neither to spare who have been cheated and swindled by Mrs. Coe and others—you would agree that it is only just and kind to tell people where to go and get their money's worth.[61]

Thus, the influence of Miss Peabody's zeal in disseminating Froebel's methods and in upholding Froebel's standards was felt by kindergartners throughout the United States and in Canada. Although her magazine *Kindergarten Messenger* never reached its goal of a thousand subscribers, it would be difficult to judge how many students and teachers read it who were not subscribers personally, but whose schools had subscriptions. Miss Peabody directed her words to the literary public as well as to the teaching profession, and by so doing tried to give the kindergarten teacher status in the opinion of the public and of parents. Her lecture on "Childhood" at the Concord School of Philosophy, and the inclusion of "Plea for Froebel's Kindergarten" in *Last Evening with Allston* were efforts in this direction. She explained to the teachers in *The Michigan Teacher*:

When parents shall understand that this is the aim [to develop the child's mind], they will cooperate and assist, at least so far as not to hinder the kindergartner, who ought to follow out her method and compass her ends without being interrupted.[62]

Miss Peabody's constant surveillance of kindergarten teacher-training, her awareness of the abilities as well as of the weaknesses of so many kindergartners, her sincerity, her honesty, and the example of her own efforts at self-improvement brought her the love and respect of the kindergarten profession in America and in Europe. Her

---

[61] *Ibid.*
[62] Elizabeth P. Peabody, "The Kindergarten Attempts in America," *The Michigan Teacher*, Vol. 7, No. 10, October, 1872, p. 340.

correspondence showed that even in her declining years she kept her knowledge of kindergarten activities up-to-date. In 1882, E. Adelaide Manning of London still requested, ". . . I hope you will write when you can and keep me informed of what is going on in America. It will do our Froebel Society good."[63] In 1885, Miss Shirreff, a kindergarten enthusiast, wrote from Luzern, "Your acct. of K.G. work makes me very envious. We have nothing to compare with it."[64] These teachers and many others wrote long letters telling of kindergarten activities in their cities, towns, and countries. They often sent for Miss Peabody's consideration the articles, lectures, and books they had prepared. Miss Peabody, in turn, passed news of them along to where she thought it would do most good. William Hailmann was among the many who frequently sought her advice. He asked her to suggest Froebel Institute officers for the various states and Canadian Provinces, and he consulted her about arrangements for merging *The Kindergarten Messenger and The New Education* into *The Public School*.[65] A letter from a kindergarten associate when Miss Peabody was eighty-one expressed the affectionate concern in which Miss Peabody was held:

You ought not to undertake another such trip, but would best rest on your laurels now, looking back with satisfaction rather upon what you *have accomplished* than trying to accomplish *more*. You have a busy life behind you and require perfect rest now. Don't even write to me ever if you don't very much feel like it. I shall not feel slighted but am content

[63] *Letter,* E. Adelaide Manning to Elizabeth P. Peabody, September 11, 1882. Robert Lincoln Straker Collection, Antioch College Library.

[64] *Letter,* Emily A. E. Shirreff to Elizabeth P. Peabody, August 22, 1885. Robert Lincoln Straker Collection, Antioch College Library.

[65] *Letter,* W. N. Hailmann to Elizabeth P. Peabody, November 2, 1882. Robert Lincoln Straker Collection, Antioch College Library.

to think of you, which you may feel assured, I do every day of my life.[66]

Bronson Alcott expressed the respect, gratitude, and affection felt by her many friends and acquaintances in the sonnet to her which closed with the thought:

> For thou hast wrought so excellently well,
> Thou drops't more casual truth than sages tell.[67]

In conclusion, it may be noted that the successful establishment of the pioneer kindergarten training schools owed much to Miss Peabody's efforts. It was she who encouraged the German kindergartners to open such schools in America. She secured public acceptance of the schools, raised funds for their support, lectured in their classes. She was their initiator, supporter, and guide. Through her example and encouragement, she brought a unity of spirit to the new kindergartners and made them feel as though they were the guardians of something special in education. Froebel's idealistic philosophy attracted high-minded and deep-thinking persons. Miss Peabody's advocacy of the Froebelian ideal of teacher education ensured a high standard in the training schools and a generation of kindergartners who understood the principles upon which the kindergarten practices were founded. This was especially important in an era when educators as well as the public were largely unaware of or uninformed about the new type of education. The establishment of kindergarten training schools was significant as an indication of the progress of the kindergarten movement in America.

---

[66] *Letter,* J. Trautmann to Elizabeth P. Peabody, June 24, 1885. Robert Lincoln Straker Collection, Antioch College Library.

[67] A. Bronson Alcott, "Daughter of Memory," *Sonnets and Canzonets,* p. 103.

VII

Elizabeth Peabody's
Philosophy of Education

AT THE AGE OF SEVENTY, ELIZABETH PEABODY EXPRESSED her conviction "that education must be moral, intellectual and spiritual, as well as physical, from the very beginning of life."[1] This conviction she had held for many years, seeking only the best method of procedure to bring about this all-inclusive education. She and her sisters had begun their education at home under their mother's tutelage, and it was this method which, many years later, she considered ideal for girls from the time they could read, providing, of course, that the mother was cultured and capable.[2] Said she, ". . . the nearest approach to these circumstances, is the ideal of a girl's school."[3]

That she was of a reflective nature as a young girl, and that she pondered deeply upon the purpose of education

[1] Elizabeth P. Peabody, "Preface to the Third Edition," *Record of Mr. Alcott's School*, p. 4.
[2] Elizabeth P. Peabody, "Preface," Second Edition, *Record of a School*, p. xviii.
[3] *Ibid.*

and upon the meaning of life was evidenced by her philosophic utterances to her sister:

It has been my feeling since the time I was as old as you now are [fourteen], that *life* was a serious thing—and that character was of little importance unless the groundwork and foundation was *seriousness,* unless life was pursued with a direct reference to a remote object—as well as with an occasional reference to some immediate one;—unless every action of life, which has been emphatically said to be *"made up of little things,"* was done with the sense of *accountability* full in view . . .[4]

Despite her feeling that life was such a serious affair, her mood and disposition were happy and optimistic rather than gloomy. This she attributed to her experience that "the pleasures of life outweigh by an immense quantity, the *pains* of life."

Lest it be assumed that this optimistic view of life was due to her youth and inexperience, the same thought may be found fifteen years later, when family difficulties clouded the horizon. Then she wrote to Horace Mann concerning her brother George:

Thus we live in a chequered scene. But in George's letters I find some explanation of it. For they evince that vicissitude excites the best thoughts and stimulates the best energies of character.[5]

Of course she was not uniformly cheerful in good times and bad, but she did not despair. Her habit of introspection, her serious view of life's purpose, her loneliness away from home, coupled with "the outward accidents of

[4] *Letter,* Elizabeth P. Peabody to Sophia A. Peabody, June 23, 1822. Berg Collection, New York Public Library.

[5] *Letter,* Elizabeth P. Peabody to Horace Mann, March 7, 1837. Horace Mann Collection, Massachusetts Historical Society.

this disordered system of human things" gave her certain self-doubts.[6] These she confided to Mann:

I have had fifteen years of this intense worry, this feeling that I could not perform *actually* what I was *potentially* capable of in slightly different circumstances, and through it all I have preserved the essential element of hope and joy . . .[7]

She derived satisfaction from helping others, whether they were her family, friends, pupils, or strangers in need of sympathy and assistance. She described the relationship that existed between her and her former pupils:

In my tempestuous voyage I have yet kept a great many little boats in tow and have helped others to guide their barques more steadily than my own. Since I left off keeping school I have received a great many testimonies of what I have done for others. My scholars as they grow up and enter upon the deeper experiences and holier responsibilities of life uniformly turn to me for aid and succor.[8]

The pleasure that she derived from being of service to her fellow-men was consistent with the thought she expressed when she was only eighteen. At that time, she enumerated some of the sources from which pleasure might be derived, "which would at the same time interest and enliven the daily routine of life and contribute towards . . . the perfection of moral character."[9] She identified the pleasures of life as those of the intellect; such as study; those which stemmed from possessing a religious feeling; and those benevolent feelings which developed from love of one's fellow-man. These pleasures were to be

6 *Letter*, Elizabeth P. Peabody to Horace Mann, September 29, 1836. Robert Lincoln Straker Collection, Antioch College Library.

7 *Letter*, Elizabeth P. Peabody to Horace Mann, September 4, 1836. Robert Lincoln Straker Collection, Antioch College Library.

8 *Ibid.*

9 *Letter*, Elizabeth P. Peabody to Sophia A. Peabody, August 22, 1822. Berg Collection, New York Public Library.

attained by study, reading, meditation, by observation of nature, and by service to mankind.[10]

When Elizabeth in 1822 expounded this personal philosophy in which intellectual, spiritual, and moral education were parts of education in its entirety, she had no knowledge of Friedrich Froebel's theory of "Divine Unity." In Froebel's opinion, education became a process for "all-sided unification of life."[11] Hailmann pointed out the agreement between Froebel and Spencer in this fundamental principle.[12] As described by Froebel, this was the two-fold nature of man, in which were united the external (physical) and the internal (spiritual). Alcott, who was not influenced by Froebel, and whom he had not heard of in 1834, aimed at the education of children by contemplation of the "Spirit" in themselves and of the "External" in nature; in that order.[13] Although agreeing with the principle of the unity of the spiritual and material in life, Miss Peabody, after studying Froebel's method of procedure, said that:

Froebel's method of cultivating children through artistic production, in the childish sphere of affection and fancy, is a healthier and more effective way than self-inspection, for at least those years of a child's life before the age of seven.[14]

During Elizabeth Peabody's early years of teaching, before she had heard of either Alcott or Froebel, she used another method to foster the development of character. It was a forerunner of the method of reporting to parents used at the present time in many modern school systems. Its difference was that the report was addressed to the

10 *Ibid.*
11 Friedrich Froebel, *The Education of Man*, p. 2.
12 *Ibid.*, p. 1.
13 Peabody, "Preface," Second Edition, *Record of a School*, p. iv.
14 Peabody, "Preface to the Third Edition," *Record of Mr. Alcott's School*, p. 4.

child rather than to the parent. That it was a novel and unfamiliar method was shown by Miss Peabody's trepidation and misgivings in telling about it:

On parting with my school before the vacation commenced, I ventured upon a fearful experiment. I wrote letters to almost all my scholars—telling them in black and white what I thought of their characters—both in school and out of school. This led me to some disagreeable *truths*—for I was determined I would not mock them by half doing a disagreeable thing. I told some they were unfeminine and indelicate—some that they acted without principle—some that they were vain—some that they were wickedly passionate—in short I did the work thoroughly. I gained the courage to do this from the certainty that I felt a great deal of tender interest for their best welfare and this I expressed freely—and as it was real, I doubted not it would awake a sentiment of corresponding tenderness—and disarm resentment.[15]

Miss Peabody's courage was as great as her frankness, for her school was a private school, and her pupils from wealthy families. She may have lost some pupils. But her thoughts were of the children and not of her own gain:

But I believe never was individual who suffered more from actual mortification than I do from sympathy with that of the young.[16]

There is no evidence of any complaint by student or parent. Perhaps Miss Peabody's letters were worded diplomatically, and thus gave no offense; or perhaps the children recognized her "tender interest," despite the harsh words; or perhaps children in 1825 accepted the criticisms of their teachers with respect. Although this was Miss Peabody's first attempt at reporting to children, it

15 *Letter,* Elizabeth P. Peabody to Sophia A. Peabody, April 23, 1825. Berg Collection, New York Public Library.
16 *Ibid.*

was not uncommon for her to send lengthy reports to their parents. In a letter to Nathan Appleton, the father of Fanny Appleton, who later married Henry Wadsworth Longfellow, Elizabeth gave a long and detailed report of Fanny's activities in school. With characteristic honesty, Miss Peabody mentioned that Fanny was very averse to arithmetic, and fell far behind her class because of inattention. She also complained that Fanny disliked hard study and was too ready to be assisted. When thrown upon her own resources, Fanny would obtain assistance from her schoolfellows.[17]

Did Fanny resent Miss Peabody's unflattering report? Did Mr. Appleton reveal its contents to her? There is no evidence to prove that he rebuked Fanny, although he may have done so. There *is* evidence that Fanny liked Miss Peabody for she wrote to her brother Thomas:

I now go to Miss Peabody's school; and I like Her [sic] very well, though I have to walk in the cold a great way, as it is in Franklin Place . . .[18]

It is questionable whether the use of the capital in "Her" was due to faulty spelling on Fanny's part or was significant as denoting Fanny's esteem for Miss Peabody. It may very well have been the latter, for Fanny's spelling and punctuation are otherwise correct. The friendship between teacher and pupil was a lasting one. In 1855, when Fanny was Mrs. Longfellow and the mother of five children, Miss Peabody recommended a Danish lady as governess who "teaches English branches and speaks Danish, Swedish, German, French and embroidery."[19] Perhaps

[17] *Letter*, Elizabeth P. Peabody to Nathan Appleton, [1827]. Elizabeth Peabody Correspondence, Houghton Library.

[18] *Letter*, Fanny Appleton to Thomas Gold Appleton, February 20, 1827. Elizabeth Peabody Correspondence, Houghton Library.

[19] *Letter*, Elizabeth P. Peabody to Mrs. Longfellow, November 28, 1855. Elizabeth Peabody Correspondence, Houghton Library.

Fanny was sufficiently respectful to ignore her former teacher's lapse in writing of anyone who "speaks . . . embroidery."

Miss Peabody's attitude on discipline was most unusual in an era when strictness and corporal punishment were often accompaniments to learning. For her older pupils she used but one punishment, which was that

when there is neglect and carelessness in school hours—there should be study at home and an extra lesson. This serves as a stimulus to attention and industry.[20]

For kindergarten children she felt that the secret of success was "gradualism" and patience. She made the unqualified statement, "Any child can learn anything, if time and opportunity is given to go step by step."[21] It may be assumed that Miss Peabody meant that any normal child could learn what was commonly taught to children in school. Discipline, as conceived by Elizabeth Peabody, began in infancy when "the soul takes possession of the senses," and the child became aware of the external world.[22] It was through the mother's contact with the child and her wisdom that the child's will was to be guided. This was the beginning of education. "It was the mother, not the child, who was responsible for the perfection of this part of the child's life."[23] Since Miss Peabody contended that the child was a moral person, not born sinful, it was of the greatest importance in his early years that his mother and teacher "kept his [the child's] temper sweet, and his action according to law."[24] This was to be

[20] *Letter*, Elizabeth P. Peabody to Nathan Appleton, [1827]. Elizabeth Peabody Correspondence, Houghton Library.

[21] Peabody, *Moral Culture of Infancy and Kindergarten Guide*, p. 104.

[22] Peabody, "Discipline," *Lectures in the Training Schools for Kindergartners*, p. 53.

[23] *Ibid.*, p. 54.

[24] *Ibid.*

done by gentle rather than by "discordant" action; certainly not by extreme restraint. By the growth of the child's personal affections, the mother was able to present the claims of the sensibilities of others, such as herself, the family, friends, and thus prevent him from concentrating upon himself.[25] Miss Peabody did not believe in "breaking the child's will," but in bringing it into "harmony with God's will through a lower harmony with the will of its loving and loved mother or kindergartner."[26] She considered that the worth and duty of obedience was in ratio with the validity of the command; and that a command was valid only so far as it was inspired by a "disinterested and proper respect for the being who is commanded."[27]

The above principles of discipline were expressed by Elizabeth Peabody in her later years, after she had become familiar with Froebel's system.[28] However, forty years earlier, her principles and practices in her school had been of the same nature. As she explained them in 1836:

On children's confidence I never intruded. Even if they never gave it to me I never asked or implied that I thought I had the least right to it—as indeed I did not think I had. And I always treated my scholars as equals and never with any authority except *what they made for themselves* out of my wishes . . . [29]

A thought requiring exegesis in this statement is that concerning a child's "confidence" or, as Miss Peabody occasionally termed it, his "private conscience." The relative

25 *Ibid.*, p. 55.
26 *Ibid.*, p. 63.
27 *Ibid.*, p. 65.
28 The lecture from which these principles were quoted was published in 1886. It had been delivered to training classes for ten years previously.
29 *Letter*, Elizabeth P. Peabody to Horace Mann, September 4, 1836. Robert Lincoln Straker Collection, Antioch College Library.

importance of the private conscience as compared to a common conscience, at times referred to as a school, social, or universal conscience, was a subject upon which Miss Peabody held emphatic opinions. She claimed:

I think that a private conscience in the young will naturally be highest. Mr. Alcott thinks a common conscience is to be cultivated in a school, and that this will be higher in all, than any one conscience would be, if it were private.[30]

In order to develop the common conscience, Mr. Alcott either punished the class for the misbehavior of one child; or had the miscreant punish the teacher; or discussed the misdeed in front of the entire class; or delegated to scholars, selected for the day, the right of "judgment."[31] Miss Peabody, whose aim was the development of the individual conscience, explained her very different procedure:

All derelictions from duty, I would meet with surprise, as accidental mistakes or indisputable misfortunes, according as the fact might be, and offer my advice, endeavoring to win a confidential exposure of the individual's own moral condition, as it appears to themselves, in order that I might wisely and tenderly give suitable advice. Thus would I establish a separate understanding with each particular scholar, and act the part of a religious friend, with each; while in general assembly, no reference should be made to any moral wrong-doing of any one; but it be courteously and charitably taken for granted; that all mean to act conscientiously and religiously.[32]

Before examining Miss Peabody's theory and methods of teaching language and reading, a consideration of her definition of teaching is fundamental. As she explained:

30 Peabody, "Preface," Second Edition, *Record of a School*, p. xiv.
31 *Ibid.*, p. xviii.
32 *Ibid.*, p. xiv.

Teaching, which in the common sense of the word is the sug
gestion of thoughts by words, is not the kindergartner's special work, but the *a priori* process of drawing out into the
individual consciousness of a child those latent powers whose
free activity gives him conscious relations, first with his kind;
secondly with material nature, including his own body; and
thirdly with God.[33]

These were Froebel's theories; accepted, reworded, and
disseminated by Miss Peabody. The statement contained
the philosophic ideas that formed the basis of his system of
education, namely: teaching by development, rather than
by lecture; self-activity; the threefold unity of the child
with humanity, nature, and God; and the order of procedure in teaching, from the external and objective, to the
spiritual and subjective. Miss Peabody considered Froebel's system worthy because "he found the end in the
means, and never forgot the means in the end."[34] By this
she meant to differentiate between Froebel's aim and
method of accomplishing it and those of previous systems.
The aim of education for moral and spiritual growth was
not new to Miss Peabody, but Froebel's methods of procedure she considered unique and original. Froebel's great
contribution to the "means" of education was his detailed
and organized system of games, songs, symbolic dances,
finger plays, block building, drawing, sewing, pricking,
and nature experiences. Of the use of these in the moral,
intellectual, physical and religious development of children, she heartily approved.[35]

Language and its want of effectiveness as a means of
communication was a topic to which Miss Peabody had

[33] Peabody, "The Use of Language," *Lectures in the Training Schools
for Kindergartners,* p. 89.
[34] Peabody, "The Origin and Growth of the Kindergarten," *Education,*
Vol. 2, May, 1882, p. 508.
[35] *Ibid.,* p. 511.

given serious consideration.[36] She was concerned with the possibility of transforming the current system of language teaching in schools.[37] Words were to be considered not merely by their effect on the ear, but "in the process of their formation by the organs of speech."[38] To this end, she wrote and published *First Nursery Reading Book*. The purpose of the book was

to teach the alphabet by means of English words, whose analysis should give the true sounds that were originally and even now are generally attached to the characters in all languages.[39]

After learning Froebel's system, Miss Peabody advised that the teaching of reading and writing should not begin in kindergarten because:

reading and writing properly belong to a second stage of education, *after* the Kindergarten exercises on the blocks, sticks, peas, etc., are exhausted, or nearly so, and children have become expert in sewing, weaving, pricking and drawing,—arts which shall have taught them to see accurately and discriminate minute differences, and given a certain general cultivation to the mind by habits of observation and classification.[40]

After kindergarten, at about seven years of age, the children should be taught reading and writing simultaneously. Writing would begin with copying the small printed letters. As Miss Peabody further outlined her plan, she proposed teaching reading on a "philosophical method," by which she meant reading for content and interest. She claimed that this method

36 Peabody, "Language," *Aesthetic Papers,* p. 214.
37 *Ibid.,* p. 221.
38 *Ibid.,* p. 220.
39 Peabody, *First Nursery Reading Book,* Title Page.
40 Elizabeth P. Peabody and Mary Mann, "Explanatory Preface," *After Kindergarten—What?,* pp. 1–2.

will make the acquisition an advantage to the mind, instead of the distraction it now is to those whose vernacular is English,—the *pot-pourri* of languages, and whose orthography seems so lawless it should rather by called *kakography* . . .[41]

Obviously, Miss Peabody was aware of the reading difficulties experienced by the children of her era. Her first misconception of Froebel's method, which "confounded and mixed up" the pure kindergarten processes with this second stage of education, had been corrected after she had observed the kindergartens in Germany in 1868.[42] The term "philosophical method" of reading meant that attention was concentrated on the meaning of the subject matter, by question and discussion, rather than on mechanical rote reading, which was the common practice of the era. Miss Peabody criticized the usual procedure of ordinary schools. She said:

There is no greater illusion than the common idea of the method of learning to read, by pronouncing pages of matter, which is not moving the mind or heart of the reader.[43]

She agreed with Mr. Alcott that children should be read to and told stories by their parents and teachers so that their taste for good literature might be patterned after the highest models.[44]

Compatible with her principles of education was her interest in the Utopian communities of her era. Although she never became a member of such a community, and despite the fact that she did not believe in the doctrine of community of goods to the exclusion of individual property, yet certain aspects seemed to her to have educational

41 *Loc. cit.*
42 *Ibid.*, p. 8.
43 Peabody, *Record of a School*, Second Edition, p. 16.
44 *Ibid.*, p. 18.

value.[45] Foremost, believing moral education to be the indispensable foundation of true development, she realized that these communities were seeking a solution to the problem of reconciliation of the social organization with the life of the individual souls who comprised it.[46] Then, too, she approved of the democratic idea of social equality practiced within these communities.[47] Her main objection to this type of community organization was the sacrifice of the sacredness of the family and of personal individuality.[48] It contained, however, the germ of two ideas which Miss Peabody valued and which were incorporated into kindergarten philosophy; manual labor as an educative process, and direct contact with nature. The occupations provided by Froebel's system and the use of nature materials and excursions to seek them were manifestations of these ideas in the kindergarten. Miss Peabody enlarged upon her respect for the artisan as an artist in her preface to Cardinal Wiseman's lecture *The Identification of the Artisan and Artist.* She proposed to reform education from its primary grade so that the workingman could rise to some degree of creativity by a trained intelligence and skilled hands.[49] Art and crafts would be included in the curriculum.

To indicate how she proposed to carry out Cardinal Wiseman's theory, she had published and appended to his lecture her own *Plea for Froebel's Kindergarten as the*

[45] Peabody, "Fourierism," *Last Evening with Allston,* p. 203.

[46] Peabody, "A Glimpse of Christ's Idea of Society," *Dial,* Vol. 2, No. 2, 1841, p. 217.

[47] Peabody, "Plan of the West Roxbury Community," *Dial,* Vol. 2, No. 3, 1841, p. 363.

[48] Peabody, "A Glimpse of Christ's Idea of Society," *Dial,* Vol. 2, No. 2, 1841, p. 223.

[49] Peabody, "Dedication," *The Identification of the Artisan and Artist,* p. 4.

First Grade of Primary Education. She applauded the establishment of a free drawing school in every town of five thousand inhabitants in Massachusetts, but indicated that unless children were prepared for them in the primary department, the drawing classes would be of little use.[50] She explained the nature of the kindergarten training:

Froebel's Kindergarten is a primary art-school; for it employs the prodigious but originally blind activity and easily trained hand of childhood, from the age of three years, in intelligent production of things within the childish sphere of affection and fancy; giving thereby a harmonious play of heart and mind in actively educating—without straining the brain—even to the point of developing invention, while it keeps the temper sweet and spirits joyous with the pleasure of success.[51]

Miss Peabody considered art education as religious, because "art is the image in man of God's creativeness."[52] She thought that art and science balanced one another in education since the method used in science was analysis of matter while the method of art was expression.[53] Speaking of the method of teaching art in order to develop originality, Miss Peabody pointed out that no mechanical imitation and no patterns were permitted, but that the children "were led on to act from their own thoughts," with only suggestions from the teacher.[54]

Her approval of industrial education for those children who had to earn a livelihood early was based on the inference that without such training they would be unskilled laborers, without self-respect or social position. She warned against pseudo-kindergartens as primary art

---

[50] Peabody, "A Plea for Froebel's Kindergarten," *ibid.*, p. 43.
[51] *Ibid.*
[52] *Ibid.*, p. 45.
[53] *Ibid.*
[54] *Ibid.*, p. 46.

schools, since these were "mere alteration of the old routine with plays and imitative working by patterns . . ." The reform of fundamental education by competent, trained kindergartners was her suggested solution to the "demoralizing" influence of the public schools as organized in the nineteenth century.[55]

Today Miss Peabody's theories and practices seem very advanced, not only in comparison with the educational practices of her era, but also in relation to current practices. She believed that the aim of education was for moral and spiritual growth as well as for intellectual growth. In modern parlance, this is what is meant by educating the "whole" child. Her detailed written reports on a child's progress have much in common with the teachers' reports to parents which are required in progressive schools today. Her advocacy of gentle discipline, nature study, and creativity in art would do credit to an educator of the twentieth century. Many modern educators are in accord with Miss Peabody's contention that reading and writing should be taught in the second stage of the child's education, not in kindergarten. Her principles, enunciated more than one hundred years ago, are valid today. Since much that is now known about psychology was not available to Miss Peabody, it may be assumed that Miss Peabody was able to perceive intuitively that which has been established today by experiments, tests, and measurements. That she was able to evolve, recognize, appreciate, and apply such advanced theories is a measure of her courage as well as of her intellect.

[55] *Ibid.*, p. 47.

VIII

Influence on American Education

ELIZABETH PALMER PEABODY PARTICIPATED IN MANY INTEL-
lectual and social movements of her era, but she gained a
permanent niche in history as champion of the kindergarten in America. Her enthusiasm and energy pierced public apathy and aroused Bostonians to an appreciation of
Froebel's kindergarten system. Through her early home
training and through the influence of Dr. William Ellery
Channing, she was imbued with a serious, spiritual view
of the purpose of life. Yet, though serious, she was optimistic, and though spiritual, she was a person who translated ideals into deeds. She was one of that Transcendental
group which included Ralph Waldo Emerson, Henry
Thoreau, George Ripley, A. Bronson Alcott, and Margaret Fuller. The influence of the Transcendental movement upon the intellectual and social life of New England
was notable. Austin said that the "literary flowering of the
1860's would have been impossible—or at least very differ-

ent—without its influence."[1] She helped in perpetuating and extending its literary influence by her contributions to and publication of the second volume of the *Dial*.

Elizabeth Peabody, a serious scholar of theology and history, was considered by her contemporaries "a woman of prodigious learning"[2] and a "feminine pundit."[3] Nevertheless, she was not an originator, although she was an initiator. She put into practice with great understanding, enthusiasm and foresight, the ideas conceived by others. Theodore Parker said of her:

> She is a woman of most astonishing powers, has a many-sidedness and a largeness of soul quite unusual; rare qualities of head and heart. I never before knew just with what class to place her; now I see she is a Boswell. Her office is to inquire and answer, "What did they say?" "What are the facts?" A good analyst of character, a free spirit, kind, generous, noble.[4]

It was in this Boswellian attitude that she was amanuensis to Channing, recorder for Alcott, apostle of Froebel. She sought genius in others and assisted it in its flowering with no other than the most altruistic motives. Jones Very, Margaret Fuller, and Nathaniel Hawthorne benefited from her concern for their interests. She brought to the attention of her community the plight of the Poles, the Hungarians, the Negro, and the Indian. Sanborn said:

> Like her sister, Mrs. Mann, Miss Peabody was a true lover of the poor and seldom have I known persons to whom, as by instinct, there gravitated whatever was defeated or unfortunate, more certainly than to these sisters.[5]

1 James C. Austin, *Fields of the Atlantic Monthly*, p. 300.
2 Frank P. Stearns, *The Life and Genius of Nathaniel Hawthorne*, p. 39.
3 *Ibid.*, p. 117.
4 Frank B. Sanborn, *Recollections of Seventy Years*, Vol. II, p. 548.
5 *Ibid.*, p. 561.

Her aim was ever to benefit humanity, sometimes by one method, sometimes by another. Her lectures on history were given with the purpose of helping to recreate mankind by the knowledge of the successes and failures of the past. Her acceptance of Froebel's theories stemmed from a similar source, the desire to improve humanity by the moral, intellectual, spiritual, and physical education of the child from his infancy.

Because her own reputation as a teacher was so well established among the first families of Boston, she was an accepted herald of the "New Education." She was loved and respected by pupils, parents, and associates. Mrs. Porter, a friend, told this anecdote:

Not many years ago, at a time when I had charge of some tableaux in aid of some good worth . . . Mrs. Howe, and her daughters, Maud and Julia, and several well-known young people took part, and we persuaded Miss Peabody to be dressed to represent "the Grandmother of Boston," and I think from that night it was our pet name for her. . . . What a jolly night of fun it was! and dear Miss Peabody as the Grandmother of Boston bore off the honors.[6]

Her initial efforts in the education of young children in the school she established in 1860 prepared the Boston public to receive the trained German kindergartners when they arrived. Her lectures throughout a large section of the country broadcast the knowledge of Froebel's system. Her publications in book form and as articles in magazines and newspapers brought the kindergarten before the eyes of the public. Through the *Kindergarten Messenger* she disseminated to teachers much needed information about the practical problems which arose in connection

[6] Maria Porter, "Elizabeth Palmer Peabody," *Bostonian*, Vol. 3, No. 4, January, 1896, p. 350.

with the establishment of kindergartens. She kept the standards high, united the far-flung kindergarten teachers, encouraged, admonished, and acted in the capacity of supervisor, confidante, and, if need be, fund-raiser. As president of the American Froebel Union, which she organized, she encouraged the publication of translations and original works on kindergarten and assisted in the establishment of new kindergartens. Her correspondence was addressed to parents, educators, politicians, and publishers. Kate Douglas Wiggin said:

Every night that I spent in Concord was enriched by the conversation of that noble and venerable woman, Elizabeth Peabody, the revered and eminent champion of childhood, who had been instrumental in inspiring a greater number of mothers and educators than any woman of her day. Her mind was a complete storehouse of fascinating and varied knowledge and her memory endless.[7]

She realized the importance of the kindergarten demonstration and exhibit at the Philadelphia Exhibition in 1876 and assisted in the arrangements. A rapid growth of kindergartens resulted from this Centennial Exhibition.

As Froebel's disciple in America, she clarified his vague terms, interpreted his mystical philosophy, explained his symbolism, and enunciated the definite concepts which he intended to convey. She was the forerunner of progressive education in the United States. In the various aspects of the modern educational program are found methods and subject matter which were initiated by Elizabeth Peabody and recommended by her in lectures and publications in the nineteenth century.

Parker claimed that Froebel was one of the leaders in

[7] Kate Douglas Wiggin, *My Garden of Memory*, p. 154.

the manual training movement and that his influence was
so strong because "the establishment of kindergartens
tended to carry with it the idea of manual training for
even older children."[8] Not only the motor processes, but
the social experiences in school were emphasized by Froebel as educative practices. According to Parker:

These factors have found practical application in the kindergarten, and their application in other parts of the elementary
school is now being considered and tested.[9]

Miss Peabody lectured to kindergartners in her effort to
perpetuate the social nature of the kindergarten. She said:

The kindergarten must, then, succeed by complementing the
nursery; and the child begin to take his place in the company
of his equals, to learn his place in their companionship, and
still later to learn wider social relations and their involved
duties.[10]

Miss Peabody made a special effort to impress upon kindergarten teachers that teaching children to read in kindergarten was unprofitable. She quoted Professor Agassiz,
who termed it *the American insanity* of teaching children to read before they have learned the things signified
by words."[11]

The importance of Miss Peabody's efforts to stimulate
the manufacture of Froebel's kindergarten materials was
appreciated by the early kindergarten teachers. Before the
advent of kindergartens, schoolroom equipment had consisted mainly of books, slates, chalk, pens, desks, and

[8] Samuel C. Parker, *A Textbook in the History of Modern Elementary
Education,* p. 426.
[9] *Ibid.,* p. 488.
[10] Elizabeth P. Peabody, *Lectures in the Training Schools for Kindergartners,* p. 66 .
[11] *Ibid.,* p. 145.

benches. Except for a few enlightened educators, such as Bronson Alcott and his cousin William, teachers did not attempt to make the classroom attractive to children. The introduction of manual activities, singing, games, dancing, and play into the program of the kindergarten created the demand by the teachers for suitable materials. E. Steiger and Company responded to Miss Peabody's urging. The firm supplied kindergarten materials until 1944. Milton Bradley and Company were also persuaded by Miss Peabody to manufacture equipment for kindergartens. They supplied kindergarten furniture as well as the *gifts* and *occupations*, which were the materials designed by Froebel such as blocks, sticks, metal rings, tablets and sewing cards. In the Midwest, it was Carl H. Doerflinger who undertook the speculative business of making equipment for the few kindergartens in existence.

Although in today's kindergartens many of Froebel's gifts and occupations have been discarded, the movable furniture, the sand table, balls, blocks, drawing materials, and nature equipment may still be found. And this equipment has invaded, as well, the first and second grades.

In the long, informative letters to parents, by which Miss Peabody reported the progress of her pupils, the interest Miss Peabody took in each child is revealed. Her attitude toward reporting exemplified the difference, often discussed at the present time,[12] between a positive attitude, and the negative attitude of some teachers who saw reporting as a dreary clerical task when it could and can be an opportunity for a challenging study of each child.

Miss Peabody's publications have preserved for posterity the early experiments, psychological in nature, which

[12] John W. M. Rothney, *Evaluating and Reporting Pupil Progress,* pp. 29–30.

preceded Dewey, Hall, and Gesell. Her detailed psychological observation of little Foster Haven, and her analysis of the processes followed by Mr. Alcott in the Temple School were the instinctive beginnings of a scientific approach. Miss Peabody was a humanist while John Dewey was a pragmatist, yet he too realized the ability of Froebel to translate the vague idea of natural development into daily classroom practice.[13] Dewey's own philosophy was based upon the spirit of Froebel's teachings. He said:

The efforts to return to Froebel's spirit . . . have tried to keep the best in his contributions. His emphasis upon play, dramatization, songs and story telling, which involve the constructive use of material, his deep sense of the importance of social relations among the children—these things are permanent contributions which they [the teachers] retain.[14]

Dewey's problem in relation to the use of Froebelian aims was not the problem faced by Elizabeth Peabody in the generation preceding Dewey. To her vigilance and outspoken courage was due the credit for the establishment of the "genuine" kindergarten, based upon Froebel's principles, rather than a play school for the pecuniary gain of the owners, who had never studied Froebel's methods. If Miss Peabody had not preserved during the period of its establishment the fundamental principles, the pure spirit, and the standards of Froebel, the kindergarten might not have achieved the foothold it did in American education. It was important for every kindergartner to know what Froebel intended before she could win converts to his method or put it into practice in a satisfactory manner. In later years, kindergartners were divided into two schools of thought, one keeping to the traditional materials of the

13 J. and E. Dewey, *Schools of Tomorrow,* p. 61.
14 *Ibid.,* p. 106.

nineteenth-century kindergarten, and the other utilizing the newer knowledge of psychology and child study. However, this was after kindergartens had become rooted as an American educational institution. Therefore, these differences of opinion among trained personnel caused none of the chaos, disintegration, and distrust of the system that would have resulted in the lay mind before kindergartens had achieved acceptance. Had she been alive at the time of these modifications, which came thirty years after the acceptance of kindergartens, she might have been one of the leaders in the restatement of Froebel's principles in the light of recent contributions of biology, sociology, and modern psychology to the science of education.[15] Miss Peabody was a seeker for truth and was the first to admit error, accept a new doctrine, or apply new knowledge.

Miss Peabody's emphasis on the quality of training for kindergarten teachers and her own example of dedicated service was of importance to later developments. During the early years of the movement, the brevity of the course was dictated by the demand for kindergartners, yet it was not as meager as the training of grade teachers at the time.[16] Since music, drawing, and nature study had not become a part of general education, the primary teacher received no instruction similar to that of the kindergartner in these areas.[17] It was in their participation and training for work with the parent and the community that Miss Peabody and the pioneers of the early private training schools for kindergartners rendered particular service. Nina Vandewalker pointed out that in this direction they

[15] For a report on the formulation of contemporary kindergarten thought see Committee of Nineteen, *The Kindergarten,* authorized by the International Kindergarten Union, 1913.

[16] Nina C. Vandewalker, "Training in Retrospect and Prospect," *Kindergarten Training Schools,* p. 5.

[17] *Ibid.,* p. 6.

have set standards that few public training schools have been able to reach.[18] Miss Vandewalker felt that the study of kindergarten statistics alone could give but little insight into the spirit that has made the kindergarten and kindergarten training the force that these have become in American education.[19] That Miss Peabody's spirit, energy, and vitality played an important part in the inspiration and dedication of the pioneer workers was attested to in a report by a committee of the International Kindergarten Union. The report indicated that

to develop insight and impart vitality, now that the pioneer days are over, is the greatest task of the modern [kindergarten] training school.[20]

Elizabeth Peabody's appreciation of the importance of the mother in the education of the child has been reciprocated by the esteem in which the mothers, even in recent years, have held the kindergarten. When, in 1939, in New York City, kindergartens were cut out of the city budget, an organization was formed by mothers of kindergarten children to make kindergartens mandatory by New York State law.[21] The movement, which crystallized into the United Kindergarten Mothers' Association, grew "like Jack's beanstalk,"[22] to represent the demand of forty thousand mothers that kindergartens be reinstated.[23] Thus it was demonstrated that kindergartens had come far indeed

[18] *Ibid.*, p. 8.

[19] *Ibid.*, p. 9.

[20] Committee of Nineteen, "Ideals in Kindergarten Training," *Kindergarten Training Schools*, p. 57.

[21] Anne Petersen, "Women Wage Fight to Revive Kindergartens," *The New York Times*, December 10, 1939.

[22] Violet J. Brown, "Calling Eighty Thousand Parents," *Brooklyn Eagle*, November 24, 1939.

[23] Helen R. Touvim, "New York Mothers Fight Closing of Public School Kindergarten," *The New York Sun*, November 24, 1939.

from the day when, single-handed, Elizabeth Peabody initiated the kindergarten into nineteenth-century Boston, to the day when forty thousand mothers of kindergarten children in the public schools of New York City would, by their actions in defense of the institution which she established, rise up and call her work blessed. The spirit that vitalized the pioneer kindergarten was not dead, it had been well established by Miss Peabody, disseminated by her disciples, and it reappeared multiplied a thousand-fold in the public consciousness when the continued existence of the kindergarten was threatened.

What, then, from the findings of this study, is the place of Elizabeth Palmer Peabody in the history of American culture and education? What is her relationship to the modern kindergarten? What is her reputation in modern kindergarten theory?

Elizabeth Peabody stands as an early example of the modern woman, who by her own efforts, courage, energy, and intelligence carved a worthy niche in American society. Miss Peabody engaged in many activities to educate mankind spiritually as well as intellectually. In Froebel's system she found that combination of the social, moral, spiritual, aesthetic and intellectual in education for which she had been seeking. Her unchallenged status today among historians and educators is as the person who successfully transplanted the kindergarten from Germany to America. The growth of kindergartens in America and their acceptance by the American public stem in large part from her pioneer efforts. The kindergarten movement, which she initiated, showed progress in her day and has continued expanding to the present.

Although the modern kindergarten has discarded the formalism and much of the early materials, yet it has kept the principles enunciated by Froebel, accepted by Elizabeth Peabody, and established by her in America. The principles of learning through play, of the importance of early childhood education, of the place of the mother in education are accepted by modern educators. Although they do not bear her name, yet, as this study has shown, these and others mentioned may be traced to her pioneer efforts in kindergarten education in America. Her work was found worthy in the past and her theories are valid in the present:

> What shall we give to thee, O princely heart?
> That nothing for thyself didst seek apart?
> God, in that liberal vein, enriched thee so
> That little's left for Friendship to bestow.[24]

[24] *Ms.*, Julia Ward Howe to Elizabeth Palmer Peabody on her eightieth birthday. Horace Mann Collection, Massachusetts Historical Society.

Appendix A

List of Books from Miss Peabody's Library and Bookshop

The Concord Free Public Library is the repository of the remnants of Miss Peabody's extensive personal library, and of her stock of books from her bookshop at 13 West Street, Boston. Many of these books were given to the library by Miss Peabody in 1878, as their bookplates attest. For many years, they were a part of the library's regular circulating collection. However, interest in Elizabeth Peabody in recent years was sufficient to cause the library to place the books in a special Peabody Collection, as a service to scholars.

According to *The Chicago University Press Manual of Style*, Eleventh Edition, 1949, p. 40, great latitude is allowed in capitalization of foreign titles. The author's copies have been followed in preparing this list.

A Gentleman Who Was a Swede [author], *An History of the Late Revolution in Sweden*. Edinburgh: Printed for the Author, 1776.

Theory of Teaching with a Few Practical Illustrations, by a Teacher [Elizabeth P. Peabody]. Boston: E. P. Peabody, 1841.

Charles Dickens, *Household Words*, Vol. II, No. 27, Saturday, September 28, 1850. Whitefriars, London: Bradbury and Evans, 1850.

Fabre D'Olivet, *De l'Etat Social de l'Homme ou Vues Philosophiques sur l'Histoire du Genre Humain.* Paris, France: J. L. J. Briere, 1822.

Cornelius C. Felton, *Classical Studies: Essays on Ancient Literature and Art.* Boston: Gould, Kendall and Lincoln, 1843.

Gunderode. Boston: E. P. Peabody, 109 Washington Street, 1842.

Heinrich Laube, *Die Krieger.* Mannheim: Verlag von Heinrich Hoff, 1837.

Wolfgang Menzel, *Die deutsche Literature.* Stuttgart: Gebrüder Frandh, 1828.

August Graf von Platen-Hallermunde, *Gesammelte Werke.* Stuttgart: Cotta, 1848.

Rev. Enoch Pratt, *A Comprehensive History, Ecclesiastical and Civil, of Eastham, Wellfleet and Orleans, County of Barnstable, Massachusetts, from 1644 to 1844.* Yarmouth: W. S. Fisher & Co., 1844.

D. G. Rossetti, translator, *The Early Italian Poets.* London: Smith, Elder and Co., 1861.

Leonardo Ventunini, *Rime Scelte di Poeti Illustri de Nostri Tempi.* Lucca, 1770.

Appendix B

Ruth M. Baylor Collection of Holograph Material Relevant to This Study

The letters are kept at the owner's residence.

Elizabeth Peabody Correspondence

Sophia Peabody, postmarked Salem, Massachusetts, to Elizabeth P. Peabody, care of Rev. Theodore Parker, West Roxbury, August 8, [1837].

Sophia [Peabody] to Miss Elizabeth P. Peabody, care of Rev. R. Waldo Emerson, Concord, Massachusetts, August 8, 1838.

William Ellery Channing, Boston, to Miss Peabody, December 11, 1838.

Sophy [Sophia Peabody] to Lizzie [Elizabeth Peabody], Tuesday, November 19, 1839.

Elizabeth P. Peabody, Eagleswood, Perth Amboy, New Jersey, to Mr. Weiss, February 24, 1856.

William D. O'Connor, Philadelphia, to Miss Peabody, May 9, 1858.

William D. O'Connor, Philadelphia, to Miss Peabody, June 27, 1858.

Sophia Hawthorne, Rome, to Elizabeth Peabody, January 8, 1859.

Sophia Hawthorne, 46B, 3rd etage, Bautzner Strasse, Dresden, to Elizabeth P. Peabody, December 4, 1868.

Elizabeth P. Peabody, 298 Lamartine Street, Jamaica Plain, Massachusetts, to Dear Sir [a publisher], April 10, 1887.

E. P. Peabody, 142 East 19 Street, New York, to Mr. Holmes [editor of *The Sunday Herald,* Washington Street, Boston], Friday, n.d.

Sophia Peabody to Miss Elizabeth P. Peabody, care of Mr. S. F. Haven, Lowell, Massachusetts, postmarked Boston, September 16, n.d.

Elizabeth P. Peabody, Concord, Massachusetts, to Mr. Weiss, Milton, Massachusetts, August 20, n.d.

Elizabeth P. Peabody, postmarked Boston, Massachusetts, July, 11 a.m., to Rev. Mr. Chaney, c/o Hollis Thiel Chant, Boston, forwarded to Leominister, Massachusetts. Postcard.

Sophia Hawthorne, Leamington, to Elizabeth Peabody, November 1, n.d.

[Sophia Hawthorne] to Elizabeth Peabody, Sunday, n.d.

Fragment, concerning religion, in Elizabeth Peabody's handwriting, unsigned, n.d.

Friedrich Froebel Correspondence

Friedrich Froebel, Keilhau near Rudolstadt, to Dear Madam, [a kindergarten teacher], July 16, 1848.

Friedrich Froebel, Bad Liebenstein, to Mrs. Pastor Winkler, Reichenbach, May 28, 1849.

Appendix C

Chronology of the Development of Kindergartens in America

1836	Caroline L. Frankenberg, who had studied with Froebel in Germany, opened a German-speaking school in Columbus, Ohio, based on Froebel's Thesis.
1851	Prof. John Kraus settled in San Antonio, Texas. He contributed articles upon Froebel-Pestalozzian methods to *The Army and Navy Gazette*.
1854	Henry Barnard visited the kindergarten exhibit at the Education Exhibition in London. He reported favorably on the kindergarten to the Governor of Connecticut.
1855	Henry Barnard established the *American Jour- of Education*.
	Charles Dickens wrote an article on "Infant Gardens" in *Household Words*.
1856	Barnard published "Froebel's System of Infant Gardens" in the *American Journal of Education*.
	Mrs. Carl Schurz established a private kindergarten in Watertown, Wisconsin, for her children and those of relatives and neighbors.
1858	Caroline L. Frankenberg returned to Ohio and opened a German-speaking kindergarten.

1859 Elizabeth Peabody heard of Froebel and the kindergarten as a result of a meeting with Mrs. Schurz. Mrs. Schurz then sent her the preface to Froebel's *Education of Man*.

Miss Anna Q. T. Parsons and Mrs. Ednah D. Cheney reviewed Jacob's Manual, "Le Jardin des Enfans [sic]" and its preface by Mme. Marenholtz-Bülow in *The Christian Examiner*. The book had been sent to America by Miss Macdaniel, who had attended the Baroness's lectures at the Louvre.

1860 Miss Peabody opened an English-speaking kindergarten in Boston at 15 Pinckney Street.

1861 Dr. Adolph Douai introduced the kindergarten into the German-English school in Newark, New Jersey.

Dr. E. A. Sheldon opened a department for training teachers in Pestalozzian principles in Oswego, N. Y., where he was superintendent of schools.

1862 Miss Peabody published "Kindergarten—What Is It?" in the *Atlantic Monthly*.

Her kindergarten was at 24½ Winter Street, Boston.

Miss Peabody distributed a *Report and New Prospectus of Kindergarten* in Boston.

1863 Mrs. Horace Mann and Elizabeth Peabody published *Moral Culture of Infancy and Kindergarten Guide*.

Oswego Training Department became a State Normal School. Its Pestalozzian principles paved the way for the acceptance of kindergarten.

1864 Mrs. Louise Pollock opened a kindergarten in West Newton, Massachusetts.

Mrs. Pollock translated a German kindergarten manual and wrote a series of articles for *The Friend of Progress*.

Miss Peabody's kindergarten was situated at 15 Pinckney Street once more. Miss Margaret Corliss was her assistant.

1865 William N. Hailmann opened a kindergarten in his German-American school in Louisville, Kentucky.

1867   Henry Barnard became first Commissioner of Education for the United States. He organized the National Bureau of Education.

1867   Dr. Barnard invited Prof. John Kraus to become a member of the staff of the Bureau of Education.

Miss Peabody went to Europe to study kindergartens. Her expenses were covered by the history lectures given during the winter. She visited all of the important kindergartens abroad. Mrs. Matilda Kriege and Miss Alma Kriege came to New York to teach kindergarten methods.

1868   At Mrs. Mann's invitation, the Krieges established a training class and kindergarten in Miss Peabody's school in Boston.

The *Boston Evening Transcript* carried an advertisement of a kindergarten to be conducted by Mrs. S. J. Crockett at 28 Clarendon Street.

The *Boston Evening Transcript* carried an advertisement of a German Kindergarten School to be conducted by Madame Kriege and Miss Alma Kriege at 127 Charles Street.

At request of Henry Barnard, U. S. Commissioner of Education, John Kraus prepared a report of the history of the rise and progress of kindergartens.

1869   Milton Bradley was inspired by Miss Peabody to manufacture kindergarten materials and to publish kindergarten literature.

A kindergarten was established in the German-English Academy of Detroit.

Edward Wiebe prepared *Paradise of Childhood*.

1870   Miss Peabody read "Kindergarten Schools" to a Sub-Committee of the Boston School Board.

Elizabeth published "The Kindergarten. Its Philosophy" in *The Illinois Teacher*.

"Object Teaching" appeared in the magazine.

"Kindergarten" appeared in the same magazine.

1870   First American public-school kindergarten was established in Boston. It lasted for seven years.

Miss Susan Pollock opened a kindergarten at D and 7th Streets in Washington, D. C.

The Society of Superintendents and Principals

of Chicago invited Miss Peabody to address them on "Genuine Kindergartens Versus Ignorant Attempts at It."

Miss Peabody lectured on "Kindergartens" at the Teachers' Convention in Watertown, Wisconsin, and in private parlors in the midwest.

1870–71 Prof. John Kraus translated a pamphlet by Baroness Marenholtz-Bülow and made a report upon the kindergarten for the "Report of the Commissioner of Education."

Miss Peabody wrote "Kindergarten Culture" for the Annual Report for 1870 of the National Commissioner of Education.

Emma Marwedel established an industrial school in Washington, D. C.

A charity kindergarten in New York in the village of College Point was the first of its kind.

1871 Miss Peabody spent ten weeks in Washington assisting in the establishment of a kindergarten there and working in the Bureau of Education, Department of the Interior.

At General Eaton's request, Miss Peabody returned to Washington.

There was a kindergarten in Detroit and one in Lansing, Michigan.

Miss Peabody traveled to Rome to meet Baroness Marenholtz-Bülow.

She met Maria Boelte in London.

1871 Charlotte Cushman gave $1000 for the normal class and model kindergarten in Boston. Miss Peabody's "begging" had supported it the three previous years.

1871–72 Miss Mary J. Garland studied with Mrs. Kriege.

1872 The first kindergarten in a public school in Wisconsin was a German kindergarten, opened in 1872 in the First Ward School in Milwaukee.

The Michigan Teacher published a series of articles by Miss Peabody on "The Kindergarten in America."

May 16 Miss Rebecca J. Weston and other kindergartners celebrated Miss Peabody's sixty-eighth birthday with her at 29 Follen Street, Cambridge, where she lived with Mary Mann.

John Philbrick, Superintendent of Schools in Boston, established a kindergarten in the Somerset Street School for two years.

The National Education Association was organized. At its first meeting, in Boston, a committee was appointed to report on kindergartens. Prof. Hailmann of Louisville presented a paper entitled "The Adaptation of Froebel's System of Education to American Institutions."

Mme. Kriege published *The Child, Its Nature and Relations,* a free rendering of the German of Baroness Marenholtz-Bülow.

Emma Marwedel established a kindergarten training school in Washington, D. C.

Maria Boelte came to America. She taught kindergarten in Henrietta D. Haines' private school in New York. Miss Blow became her first teacher-trainee.

The Krieges returned to Germany to rest. They left the kindergarten and normal training class at 98 Chestnut Street to Miss Mary J. Garland, their "ablest pupil."

1872   Miss Rebecca J. Weston was a member of Miss Garland's first training class.

Miss Peabody solicited funds for the support of Miss Garland's school.

1873   Frau Bertha Semlex, a pupil of Froebel, established a private kindergarten for one year in California.

Maria Boelte married John Kraus. They founded the New York Normal Training School for Kindergarten Teachers, Kindergarten, and Adjoining Classes.

Maria Kraus-Boelte read a paper before the National Education Association on kindergartens.

The committee of the National Education Association reported favorably on kindergartens. On the committee were Prof. John Kraus, Dr. Adolph Douai, William T. Harris, J. W. Dickenson, William N. Hailmann, George A. Baker, John Hancock.

Miss Weston became Miss Garland's assistant, then associate. (1873–1895)

Miss Peabody established the *Kindergarten Messenger* [1873–1875].

William T. Harris and Susan E. Blow opened a public school kindergarten in St. Louis as an experiment. The work was approved by the School Board. The kindergarten was in the Des Peres School in Carondelet, where Miss Blow then resided.

1873–75   Miss Peabody lectured on kindergartens in Chicago, Milwaukee, Cleveland.

1874   Upon their return from Germany, Mme. Kriege and her daughter conducted the kindergarten and training class at Miss Haines' school in New York.

1874   Emma Marwedel opened a training school at 800 - 18 Street, Washington, D. C. She was assisted by Prof. Hiehle, a pupil of Froebel.

Two more experimental kindergartens were opened in the St. Louis public schools. One was conducted by Miss C. P. Dozier.

The National Education Association met in Detroit. Miss Peabody attended.

Mrs. Alice H. Putnam opened a kindergarten in Chicago. A class to study Froebel developed into a kindergarten association of two hundred members.

Miss Peabody gave a lecture in the Cosmean hall of Florence, Massachusetts, on the kindergarten.

The *New York State Educational Journal* published a letter from Miss Peabody.

1874–75   Mr. S. H. Hill of Florence, Massachusetts, contributed funds to open a charity kindergarten and later placed in trust a sum sufficient to sustain and extend the work.

Dr. Thomas Hunter established a kindergarten in connection with the model school of the normal college in New York.

1876   Emma Marwedel opened a kindergarten and training class in Los Angeles. Kate Douglas Smith [Wiggin] studied with her.

The Philadelphia Centennial Exposition stimulated the interest in kindergartens. Miss Peabody was active in the arrangements for the kindergarten exhibit. Miss Ruth Burritt was the kindergartner who gave the demonstration, upon the recommendation of the Froebel Society of Boston.

At the Centennial Convention of the N.E.A. in Baltimore, Mme. Kraus-Boelte lectured on and exhibited kindergarten work. It was sent to the Centennial Exhibition in Philadelphia later in the same year.

1876   *Kindergarten Messenger* became a department of *The New England Journal of Education.*

1877   Mary Mann translated Baroness Marenholtz-Bülow's *Reminiscences of Froebel.*

The first free kindergarten in New York was at Ethical Culture School.

Miss Peabody organized The American Froebel Union. Its founding-members were: Maria Kraus-Boelte, Elizabeth Corry Agassiz, Pauline Agassiz Shaw, Ida Agassiz Higginson, Mary Mann, Mrs. Asa Grau, Kate Gannet Wells, Mary J. Garland, Rebecca J. Weston, William T. Harris, John Kraus, Henry Barnard, and Elizabeth Peabody.

Prof. Kraus and Mrs. Kraus prepared the *Kindergarten Guide.*

Miss Peabody urged Josephine Jarvis to publish a translation of Froebel's *Mutter-Spiel und Kose-Lieder* and made all arrangements with Fanny E. Dwight for music, and Lee and Shepard for publication. It appeared in 1879.

Trinity Church, Toledo, Ohio, established a kindergarten as a part of its parish work.

Miss Peabody resumed publication of the *Kindergarten Messenger.*

Meeting of the American Froebel Union in Boston.

At a meeting of the American Froebel Union at 4 Park Street, Boston, Miss Peabody requested to be on the committee to have the society change its organ from the *Kindergarten*

Messenger to the *New Education* and to incorporate.

Mrs. Pauline Agassiz Shaw of Boston, daughter of Louis Agassiz opened two free kindergartens, one in Jamaica Plain, one in Brookline.

1878
January

The first issue of the *Kindergarten Messenger and the New Education* appeared. It was edited by W. H. Hailmann. It took the place of the former *Kindergarten Messenger* as the organ of the American Froebel Union. It lasted six years.

At the meeting of the American Froebel Union, Miss Peabody was elected as acting president, representing the Baroness Marenholtz-Bülow.

Miss Peabody gave a course of six lectures in Miss Garland's Training School, in Mrs. Gardner's Training School, in Mrs. Aldrich's Training School, in Miss Burritt's Training School, in Mrs. Van Kirk's Training School.

A Summer Kindergarten Institute opened at Sandusky, Ohio. Its object was to give teachers and mothers an insight into the character and claims of kindergarten training with specific reference to the home and the school. There were two daily lectures and demonstration and practice, for ten dollars, for the four week course.

Dr. Felix Adler founded the Silver Street Kindergarten in San Francisco. Kate Douglas Smith [Wiggin] became its director.

The San Francisco Public Kindergarten Society was founded by a group of philanthropic citizens inspired by Dr. Adler.

1879

Mrs. Sarah B. Cooper, through the members of her Bible class, undertook the support and direction of a free kindergarten in San Francisco, connected with the Howard Presbyterian Church.

The Golden Gate Kindergarten Association was organized by Mrs. Cooper as a philanthropic association for the extension of the kindergarten.

In Detroit, a Western Kindergarten Association

was organized, the meetings of which were held in Chicago and Detroit alternately.

1879
November 8   At Berkeley, California, Miss Marwedel at a meeting of kindergartners, formed a California Kindergarten Union. She was president, Kate D. Smith, vice-president.

1880   Kate Douglas Smith [Wiggin] founded the California Kindergarten Training School and the California Froebel Society. Until 1892 this school trained all the directors and student assistants of the Golden Gate Association.

Dr. William Torrey Harris left St. Louis. There was an enrollment of 7,828 children in the public school kindergartens in St. Louis at the time.

Elizabeth Peabody arranged the convention of the American Froebel Union in Newton, Mass.

The Oshkosh, Wisconsin, Normal School opened a kindergarten, the first one to be officially and directly connected with any state normal school in the United States.

1881   Henry Barnard published *Kindergarten and Child Culture Papers,* a reprint of articles that had appeared in the *Journal.*

Miss Peabody solicited funds to publish the thirty-one volumes of *American Journal of Education.*

Miss Peabody gave her course of lectures for the last time before the training class conducted by Miss Garland and Miss Weston in Boston. She was seventy-seven years old.

Although her sight was very bad, Miss Peabody went to Philadelphia to speak in behalf of colored kindergartners. Miss Angelina Brooks read her lectures for her to the group.

Chatauqua added a kindergarten department to its summer school for teachers.

1882   Miss Peabody attended the Kindergarten Convention at Detroit.

1882   Kate Douglas Wiggin wrote *The Story of Patsy,* had it privately printed, and sold it for twenty-five cents a copy for the benefit of the kindergarten cause.

On the recommendation of Elizabeth Peabody and Ruth Burritt, Eliza A. Blaker was asked to go to the Hadley Roberts Academy in Indianapolis, Indiana, to organize a kindergarten.

William N. Hailmann collected $800 for the charity kindergartens of Detroit.

Clara A. Burr operated two kindergarten classes at Oswego State Normal School.

Kate Douglas Wiggin sent two kindergartners to Oregon and one to New Tacoma, Washington Territory in May.

She sent a kindergartner to a school in Portland, Oregon in September.

Kate Douglas Wiggin spoke on kindergarten education at three Oregon meetings, held under the auspices of the Unitarian Church.

1883   The Woman's Christian Temperance Union established and maintained kindergartens. Bethel Mission in Chicago was the first of their projects.

The New Education merged with *The Public School of Boston.*

The kindergarten movement was left without representation in the field of educational journalism until 1888.

Mrs. Shaw supported thirty-one kindergartens in Boston, Cambridge, and Brookline.

1884   Kate Douglas Wiggin raised among kindergartners a thanks offering of $1000 for Elizabeth Peabody's eightieth birthday. Elizabeth sent $800 of it to help Sarah Winnemucca in her work for the Indians.

Miss Peabody was elected president of the Froebel Union in Boston.

Free Kindergarten Society was incorporated in Indiana for "the education and moral training of the children of the poor."

Eliza A. Blaker was superintendent of their kindergartens.

Susan E. Blow withdrew from kindergarten work.

Mothers' clubs were formed in the kindergartens of Indiana. They were among the very first parent-teacher organizations of the United States.

1885   New Orleans Exposition had a kindergarten conducted by Mrs. Anna J. Ogden and Miss Mary Crosby of Washington.

The American Froebel Union became the Kindergarten Department of the National Education Association.

1886   Miss Peabody published *"Lectures to Kindergartners,"* a series of lectures which for nine or ten years she had delivered before the kindergarten training classes in Boston and other cities.

Kate Douglas Wiggin wrote *The Birds' Christmas Carol* for the benefit of the Kindergarten Association in California.

1887   Thirty-two kindergartens were transferred by the Sub-Primary School Society to public support in Boston.

1887   Emma Marwedel wrote *Conscious Motherhood,* an application of Froebel's doctrine to the development of childhood.

Anna E. Bryan opened a training school for kindergarten teachers in Louisville, Kentucky. The Louisville Kindergarten Association was formed.

1888   Committee of Boston School Board included $20,000 for support of kindergartens by the city. Laliah H. Pingree was the first director. Her salary was paid by Mrs. Pauline Agassiz Shaw. The Kindergarten Magazine was founded in Chicago by Mrs. Alice B. Stockham and Miss Cora L. Stockham.

1889   Saturday classes in domestic training were organized, in connection with the kindergartens in Indiana, for older girls. There was also a class for training nursery maids.

These ventures were the pioneer efforts at domestic training in the Middle West.

Mrs. Shaw gave Boston Normal School the salary for a teacher in kindergarten theory and practice.

1891   At a convention of the NEA held in Toronto,

Ontario, Dr. A. S. Draper proposed a resolution, unanimously carried: that the kindergarten should be recommended as a part of all school systems.

1892   The International Kindergarten Union was organized at the National Education Conference at Saratoga. It was to act in sympathy and harmony with the NEA, only extending the field of work more widely. Mrs. Sarah B. Cooper was elected president.

Bibliography

I. Unpublished Letters and Journals
Listed alphabetically according to the institution or private collection in which located.

Antioch College Library, Yellow Spring, Ohio.
Hawthorne Collection
Benjamin Pickman Mann Collection
Robert Lincoln Straker Collection
Copies of many of the documents in these collections were in the private collection of Mr. Robert Lincoln Straker in New York. Mr. Straker was largely responsible for building up this extensive collection which concerns Horace Mann directly and Elizabeth Peabody indirectly.

Ruth M. Baylor Collection, New York, New York.
This small private collection contains, in addition to many original published works and kindergarten periodicals of the era, holograph material as listed in Appendix B.

Boston Public Library, Boston, Massachusetts.
Field's Correspondence
These letters relate to Mrs. Hawthorne's financial difficulties with her publisher.

Miscellaneous Manuscripts

Impressions and recollections of Miss Peabody, written for the Memorial Meeting in 1894, form the bulk of this collection.

Hawthorne Collection

These letters do not relate to Miss Peabody's kindergarten activities.

Concord Free Public Library, Concord, Massachusetts.

Alcott Letters and Journals

Special permission must be obtained for the student's use of this collection. The *Journals* give detailed information about Miss Peabody and about the Temple School.

Peabody Collection

There are letters from Miss Peabody to William Torrey Harris in this collection as well as a postcard-photograph of Elizabeth Peabody in 1887, inscribed and signed.

Garland Junior College, Boston, Massachusetts.

A record of school finances and activities kept by Miss Mary Garland in 1872, and a similar school record for 1882, kept by Miss Rebecca Weston, are interesting and informative. There is an inscribed photograph of Miss Peabody and photographs of early kindergartens in this collection.

Houghton Library, Harvard University, Cambridge, Massachusetts

Elizabeth Peabody Correspondence

There are about sixty letters from Elizabeth Peabody to other persons and seven letters addressed to her. Few relate directly to kindergarten education.

Library of Congress: Manuscript Division, Washington, D. C.

Included are two letters from Miss Peabody and a group of papers of Mrs. Horace Mann concerned with educational problems in South America.

Massachusetts Historical Society, Boston, Massachusetts.

Horace Mann Collection

Caroline H. Dall Collection

Among the many letters of Mary and Horace Mann there are few significant references to Miss Peabody. This collection is uncatalogued. There are letters written by Miss Peabody to her family. Letters from Kate Douglas Wiggin to Miss Peabody are also in these files.

Missouri Historical Society, St. Louis, Missouri.
The Harris Papers
This is a most valuable collection for purposes of research into kindergarten education. It includes about one hundred letters of William Torrey Harris. The correspondence between Harris and Miss Susan E. Blow contains mention of Miss Peabody. Both Dr. Harris's and Miss Blow's letters directly concern kindergarten education.

New York Public Library, New York, New York.
The Henry W. and Albert A. Berg Collection
Despite the large size of this collection, it is of limited value in the study of Miss Peabody's kindergarten activities. It is an excellently catalogued literary collection.
Duyckinck Collection
This is a small collection of letters which relate to Miss Peabody's lectures and publications.
Bryant-Godwin Collection
Only a few letters are contained in this file. Their value to this study lies only in their indications of Miss Peabody's efforts to publish her educational writings.

The Pierpont Morgan Library, New York, New York.
Hawthorne Collection
The catalogue of this collection indicates its literary emphasis on Hawthorne and reveals no items significant to Miss Peabody's kindergarten activities.

Radcliffe College: The Women's Archives, Cambridge, Massachusetts.
These files of manuscript material about Miss Peabody have been of great help in locating sources. However, there is only one postcard by Elizabeth Peabody in the collection at present.

St. Louis Public Library, St. Louis, Missouri.
Letters of Miss Susan Blow to Mrs. Henry Hitchcock, 1879–1912, and forty-four handwritten essays by Miss Blow on Froebel and child training comprise this collection.

Syracuse University Library, Syracuse, New York.
Gerrit Smith Miller Collection
There are twelve letters from Elizabeth Peabody to Gerrit Smith in this collection. They range in date from 1855 to 1872.

Washington Square Library, New York University, New York, New York.
Will S. Monroe Collection of Henry Barnard Manuscripts
This collection has been useful in documenting educational activities concurrent with kindergarten education and in noting trends and influences of the era. It is uncatalogued. The letters are arranged chronologically.

Wheelock College Library, Boston, Massachusetts.
Lucy Wheelock Collection
Uncatalogued pamphlets, undated newspaper clippings, and Miss Wheelock's manuscript notes are the bulk of this collection.

II. Miss Elizabeth Palmer Peabody's Publications:

Author, Editor, Publisher, Reviewer, Translator.

A. Author:

American Kindergarten. In *Moral Culture in Infancy, and Kindergarten Guide,* by Mary Mann. Boston: T. O. H. P. Burnham, 1863.

"An Address to the Graduates of Mrs. Van Kirk's Training Class of 1879." *Kindergarten Tract No. 20.* E. Steiger, N. Y.

"After Kindergarten—What?" *Kindergarten Messenger,* January–February, 1874.

After Kindergarten—What? A Primer of Reading and Writing for the Intermediate Class and Primary Schools Generally. By Mary Mann and Elizabeth P. Peabody. Three Parts. N. Y.: E. Steiger & Co., 1878.

"The American Froebel Society." *Kindergarten Messenger,* January–February, 1877.

"The Americanizing of Froebel's Kindergarten." *Kindergarten Messenger,* January–February, 1877.

"The Atheism of Yesterday." Previously published in *The Christian Examiner*. In *Last Evening with Allston and Other Papers*, pp. 226–239, 1886.

"The Being of God." *Christian Examiner*, LXV; 5th Series, III, September, 1868.

"Bem's Charts." *Free Presbyterian* (Yellow Springs, Ohio), IV, No. 23, No. 179, April 4, 1855, p. 2, col. 1–3.

"Bem's Method of History. An Appeal to Teachers and Boards of Education." *American Journal of Education and College Review* (New York), I, No. 3, March 1856, pp. 269–278. Reprinted, Perth Amboy.

"The Birthday Blessing." Poem. *Boston Observer* (1834).

Blank Centuries Accompanying the Manual of the Polish-American System of Chronology. Boston: E. P. Peabody, 1850.

Blank Centuries for Monographs of History, Noted According to Zaba's Method for Organizing the Memory. Cambridge: John Wilson & Sons, 1870.

"Mr. Burnet's Will." *The Religious Magazine*, 1858. In *Last Evening with Allston and Other Papers*, pp. 217–226, 1886.

"Verses to G. C. on his Twelfth Birthday." 1830. For George Cabot. In *Last Evening with Allston and Other Papers*, pp. 343–344, 1886.

"Charity Kindergartens in the United States." *Barnard's American Journal of Education*, XXX, 1880, pp. 846–848.

"Childhood." Read in Concord, August 2, 1882. In R. L. Bridgman (ed.): *Concord Lectures on Philosophy*. Cambridge, Mass.: King, 1883, pp. 119–123.

"Christmas in Kindergartens." *Kindergarten Messenger*, January–March, 1875.

Chronological History of the United States, Arranged with Plates on Bem's Principle. New York: Sheldon, Blakeman & Co., 1856.

Conversations with Children on the Gospels. Two volumes. Recorded by Elizabeth P. Peabody; edited by A. Bronson Alcott. Boston: Monroe & Co., 1836, 1837.

"Command of Language to be Gained in Kindergarten." *Kindergarten Messenger*, November, 1873.

"Crawford's Orpheus." In *Aesthetic Papers*, pp. 110–111, 1849. Also in *Last Evening with Allston and Other Papers*, pp. 136–137, 1886.

"Development of the Kindergarten." *Barnard's American Journal of Education*, XXX, 1880, pp. 5–16.

"Discipline." In *Education in the Home, the Kindergarten, and the Primary School*. London, 1887, pp. 53–73.

"The Dorian Measure." Pamphlet, July 1848. In *Aesthetic Papers*, 1849, pp. 64–110. Also in *Last Evening with Allston and Other Papers*, 1886, pp. 73–135.

"Drawing and Kindergarten; a Letter to a Member of the Boston School Committee." Cambridge, Mass., May 19, 1871. *The Massachusetts Teacher*, XXIV, No. 10, October, 1871, pp. 351–361.

Education in the Home, the Kindergarten, and the Primary School. With an Introduction by E. Adelaide Manning. London: Swan, Sonnenschein, Lowrey & Co., 1887.

Edward's First Lesson in Grammar, by the Author of The Theory of Teaching. Boston: Thomas H. Webb & Co., 1843.

"Ego-theism, the Atheism of Today." *Monthly Religious Magazine*, XIX, No. 3, March, 1859, pp. 165–174. Also in *Last Evening with Allston and Other Papers*, 1886, pp. 240–252.

"Emerson as Preacher." Read in Concord, August 1884. In F. B. Sanborn (ed.), *Genius and Character of Emerson*. Boston: James R. Osgood, 1885, pp. 146–172.

"Essay on the Earliest Ages." Appendix to *Polish-American Chronology*, 1850, pp. 109–118.

"Exhibition of Allston's Paintings in Boston in 1839." *Dial*, I, No. 1, July, 1840. In *Last Evening with Allston and Other Papers*, 1886, pp. 30–61.

"Explanatory Note." In Mary Mann: *Juanita, a Romance of Real Life in Cuba Fifty Years Ago*. Boston: D. Lothrop Co., 1887, pp. 435–436.

"The Favorite." Poem. In *Aesthetic Papers*, 1849, pp. 247–248.

"Female Education in Massachusetts; Reminiscences of Subjects and Methods of Teaching. With a letter from the author, relating to her mother, Mrs. Elizabeth P. Peabody, and reminiscences of school life and teaching by Mary T. Mann." *Barnard's American Journal of Education*, XXX, July, 1880, pp. 289–320. Reprinted, Hartford, Conn., 1884, pp. 289–320.

"The Festival of Froebel's Birthday." *Kindergarten Messenger*, May–June, 1877, pp. 68–71.

First Lessons in Grammar on the Plan of Pestalozzi. By a Teacher in Boston. Boston: Carter & Hendee, 1830.

First Nursery Reading Book, Intended to Teach the Alphabet by Means of English Words, Whose Analysis Should Give the True Sounds that were Originally and even now are Generally Attached to the Characters in all Languages. Boston: E. P. Peabody, 13 West Street, 1849. New York: G. P. Putnam, 1849.

"Fourierism." *Dial,* IV, No. 4, April, 1844, pp. 473–483. Also in *Last Evening with Allston and Other Papers,* 1886, pp. 204–216.

"Froebel's Principles and Methods in the Nursery." *Barnard's American Journal of Education,* XXX, July, 1880, pp. 499–512.

"The Genius of Nathaniel Hawthorne." *Atlantic Monthly,* XXII, September, 1868.

"Genuine Kindergartens." *Kindergarten Messenger,* July, 1873.

"Genuine Kindergartens." *Kindergarten Messenger,* May, 1874.

"A Glimpse of Christ's Idea of Society." *Dial,* II, No. 2, October, 1841, pp. 214–228. Reprinted as "Brook Farm Interpretation of Christ's Idea of Society," in *Last Evening with Allston and Other Papers,* 1886, pp. 181–201.

"Glimpses of Psychology." *Kindergarten Messenger,* January–June, 1874.

"Glimpses of Psychology. Spirituality, Understanding, Moral Sentiment, Individual Freedom of Will, Conscience." In *Education in the Home, the Kindergarten, and the Primary School.* London, 1887, pp. 189–213.

"Guide to Recitation; from the Manual and Chart of History on Bem's Principle." Supplement to 1852 edition of *Polish-American System of Chronology.* New York: G. P. Putnam, 1852.

"Hazard and Froebel." *Boston Daily Advertiser,* April 23, 1870.

"The History of Goodness for a Little Child." *The Family School,* I, No. 1, September 1, 1836.

"The History of Goodness, No. II. Comment on the History of Goodness." *The Family School,* I, No. 2, November 1, 1836.

"How to Begin a Kindergarten." *Kindergarten Messenger,* June, 1875.

"Hymn to a Spirit Shrouded." Poem. *Aesthetic Papers,* 1849.

"Independency of Kindergartens." *Kindergarten Messenger,* August, 1874.

"Industrial Schools for Women." *Harpers Magazine,* XL, May, 1870.

"Introduction—The Word 'Aesthetic.' " *Aesthetic Papers,* 1849, pp. 1–4.

"Invention in Kindergartens." *Kindergarten Messenger,* November–December, 1877.

"Is Children's Play Trifling?" *Kindergarten Messenger,* March–April, 1877, pp. 54–59.

Key to History (series title):
  First Steps to the Study of History. Being Part First of a Key to History. Boston: Hillard, Gray & Co., 1832.
  Part II: *The Hebrews.* Boston: Marsh, Capen & Lyon, 1833.
  Part III: *The Greeks. Being Exercises on Homer, Hesiod, Herodotus, Thucydides, Xenophon, Plutarch; on the History of Sculpture, Architecture, Painting, Poetry, and Philosophy; and on Heeren's, Gillies', and Mitford's Histories; with Original Matter.* Boston: Marsh, Capen & Lyon, 1833.

"Kindergarten—A Letter." *Illinois Teacher* (Peoria), XVI, No. 11, November, 1870, pp. 363–365.

"The Kindergarten." In *Education in the Home, the Kindergarten, and the Primary School.* London, 1887, pp. 1–23, 75–88.

"The Kindergarten—Attempts in America." *The Michigan Teacher,* VII, No. 10, October, 1872, pp. 339–341.

"The Kindergarten: Its Philosophy." *Illinois Teacher* (Peoria), XVI, No. 5, May, 1870, pp. 150–152.

"Kindergarten Culture." Reprinted from the *Annual Report for 1870 of the National Commissioner of Education.* Washington: J. H. Holmes, 1870.

"A Kindergarten Festival, in Honor of the Birthday of Frederick Froebel." *Kindergarten Messenger,* March–April, 1877, p. 33.

"Kindergarten in Italy. Being an Introduction to the Instructions of Baroness Marenholtz-Bülow, for the Teachers of Kindergarten in Italy." Translation with Introduction by Elizabeth P. Peabody. *Circular of Information of the Bureau of Education,* for July, 1872.

The Kindergarten. Washington: Government Printing Office, 1872, pp. 9–13, September 13, 1872.

"Kindergarten Literature." *Kindergarten Messenger*, July, 1873.

"The Kindergartens of Germany." *Christian Examiner*, XVII, 5th Series, V, November, 1859.

"Kindergarten Schools." *The Massachusetts Teacher*, XXIII, 3rd Series, V, No. 7, July, 1870, pp. 233–241.

"The Kindergarten Schools of Germany." *The Herald of Health and Journal of Physical Culture*, XLIV, New Series, II, No. 6, June, July, 1868, pp. 257–263.

"The Kindergarten System." *Cambridge Chronicle*, XXV, No. 17, April 23, 1870, p. 1, col. 7.

"Kindergarten—What Is It?" *Atlantic Monthly*, November, 1862. Reprinted from the *Atlantic Monthly*, November, 1862.

"Kindergartens—The need for their establishment and support; an appeal to the citizens of Boston." Broadside. *Boston Herald*.

"Kindergartens." *Christian Union*, August, 1879.

"Kindergartens in the Orient." *Kindergarten Messenger*, June, 1875.

"Language." In *Aesthetic Papers*, 1849, pp. 214–224. Also in *Last Evening with Allston and Other Papers*, 1886, pp. 138–152.

"Language." In *Education in the Home, the Kindergarten, and the Primary School*. London, 1887, pp. 89–105.

"Language in Children." *Kindergarten Messenger*, June, 1875.

Last Evening with Allston and Other Papers. Boston: D. Lothrop & Co., 1886.

"Last Evening with Allston." *Emerson's Magazine*, V, October, 1857. In *Last Evening with Allston and Other Papers*, 1886, pp. 1–20.

Lectures in the Training School for Kindergartners. Boston: D. C. Heath & Co., 1886.

Lectures on the Nursery and Kindergarten (series title):
"No. 1: The Education of the Kindergartner." Pittsburgh: Benj. Singerly, 1874. Philadelphia: H. N. Kinney & Co., 1874. Second Edition. Pittsburgh: Joseph S. Travelli, 1875.
"No. 2: The Nursery." Pittsburgh: Joseph S. Travelli. Second Edition, 1875.

"A Letter from a Veteran Kindergartner." *The School Moderator,* Vol. 7, No. 18. Lansing, Michigan, May 19, 1887, pp. 431–432.

"A Letter from Miss Peabody." *The New York State Educational Journal,* II, No. 6, April, 1874, pp. 264–268.

"Letter from Miss Peabody." *Barnard's American Journal of Education,* V, 1880, pp. 584–587.

"Letter from Rome." *The Herald of Health and Journal of Physical Culture,* August, 1868.

"Letter to a Mother: An Extract." *The Family School,* I, No. 2, November 1, 1836.

"Life and Genius of Allston." Published some years previously; from an essay first published in the *American New Monthly Magazine,* I. In *Last Evening with Allston and Other Papers,* 1886, pp. 21–29.

"Meditations of a Widow." Poem. In *Aesthetic Papers,* 1849, pp. 212–213.

"Memorial of Madame Susanne Kossuth Meszlonyi." Written in 1850; published in pamphlet form, December, 1855. In *Last Evening with Allston and Other Papers,* 1886, pp. 253–292; 345–350.

"Memorial to Dr. William Wesselhöft. To which is added his last address to the Homeopathic Association." Boston: Nathaniel C. Peabody, 1859.

"Method of Spiritual Culture," an explanatory preface to the Second Edition of *Record of a School.* Boston, 1836.

Moral Culture of Infancy and Kindergarten Guide, with music for the plays. In *Moral Culture in Infancy, and Kindergarten Guide,* by Mary Mann. Boston: T. O. H. P. Burnham, 1864. Cambridge, Mass., 1869. Fourth Edition, New York: J. W. Schemerhorn and Co., 1870.

"The Motive in Kindergarten." *Kindergarten Messenger,* May, 1875.

"Music in Kindergartens." *Kindergarten Messenger,* December, 1874.

"The Name—Kindergarten." *Kindergarten Messenger,* August, 1875.

"The Necessity of Kindergarten Culture." Annual Report of the Commissioner of Education, 1870. *Barnard's American Journal of Education,* XXX, September, 1880, pp. 584–587.

"New Bookstore and Foreign Library." Boston, August, 1840.

"New Manual for Bem's Charts of Universal History." *American Journal of Education and College Review,* III, No. 4, April, 1857, pp. 345–349.

"A New Movement for Integrated Education." *Kindergarten Messenger,* October, 1874.

"A Note Upon the Concord School of Philosophy." *Christian Register,* LIX, No. 42, October 16, 1880.

"The Nursery." No. 2: The Nursery, in "Lectures on the Nursery and Kindergarten," Second Edition, Pittsburgh: Joseph S. Travelli, 1875. In *Education in the Home, the Kindergarten, and the Primary School.* London, 1887, pp. 25–51.

"Object Teaching." *Illinois Teacher* (Peoria), XVI, No. 7, July, 1870, pp. 231–232.

"On Mother's Unions." *Kindergarten Messenger,* March–April, 1877.

"Order of Development in Children." *Kindergarten Messenger,* October, 1875.

"The Origin of the Kindergarten." *Kindergarten Messenger,* May, 1873.

"Origin and Growth of Kindergartens." *Education,* II, No. 5, May–June, 1882, pp. 507–527.

"Our Boy." *Kindergarten Messenger,* July, 1875.

"Personal Training." *Kindergarten Messenger,* March–April, 1877.

"Phenomena of Child Life." *Kindergarten Messenger* (Syracuse), December, 1881; January, 1882.

The Piutes. Second Report of the Model School of Sarah Winnemucca. Cambridge: John Wilson & Son, 1887.

"Plan of the West Roxbury Community." *Dial,* II, No. 3, January, 1842, pp. 361–372. Reprinted as "Brook Farm Interpretation of Christ's Idea of Society," in *Last Evening with Allston and Other Papers,* 1886, pp. 181–201.

"A Plea for Froebel's Kindergarten as the First Grade of Primary Education," in *The Identification of the Artisan and Artist.* Boston: Adams & Co., Lee & Shepard, 1869, pp. 42–48. Also in *Barnard's American Journal of Education,* XXX, July, 1880. Also in *Last Evening with Allston and Other Papers,* 1886, pp. 331–342.

"A Point with Respect to Drawing." *Kindergarten Messenger,* October, 1875.

The Polish-American System of Chronology, Reproduced, with some Modifications, from General Bem's Franco-Polish Method. Boston: G. P. Putnam, 1850. Boston: G. P. Putnam, 1851. New York: G. P. Putnam, 1852. In same volume: "Guide to Recitation. From the Manual and Chart of History, on Bem's Principle." 48 pp. Accompanying Tables.

"Postscript to Prospectus." *The Family School,* I, No. 2, November 1, 1836.

"Primeval Man." Written in 1854. *Journal of Speculative Philosophy,* XVII, No. 1, January, 1881, pp. 70–89. In *Last Evening with Allston and Other Papers,* 1886, pp. 153–180.

"Prospectus." *Aesthetic Papers,* 1849, pp. iii–iv.

"Prospectus." *The Family School,* I, No. 1, September 1, 1836.

"A Psychological Observation." Memoir of Foster Haven. Written late 1837 or early 1838. In portfolio, July, 1865. In *Lectures in the Training Schools for Kindergartners,* 1897, pp. 107–156. Also in *Education in the Home, the Kindergarten, and the Primary School.* London: 1887, pp. 107–156.

"Purpose of Human Life." *The Family School,* I, No. 2, November 1, 1836.

"Recollections of the Most Beautiful Hours in Life for the Last Hour." Comment on a tale by J. P. Richter. *The Family School,* I, No. 2, November 1, 1836.

"Endorsement" in Hall, Mary L., *Our World or First Lessons in Geography.* Boston: Ginn Bros., 1873.

Record of a School, Exemplifying the General Principles of Spiritual Culture. Boston: James Munroe & Co., 1835. New York: Leavitt, Lord & Co., 1835. Philadelphia: Henry Perkins. Second Edition, with an Explanatory Preface and other Revisions, Boston: Russell, Shattuck & Co., 1836. New York: Leavitt, Lord & Co., 1836.

Record of Mr. Alcott's School, Exemplifying the Principles and Methods of Moral Culture. Preface signed by E. P. Peabody. Third Edition, Revised. Boston: Roberts Brothers, 1874.

"The Relations between the Kindergarten and Quakerism." *Kindergarten Messenger,* September, 1873.

"The Relations between the Kindergarten and the So-

Called Positive Philosophy." *Kindergarten Messenger*, August, 1873.

"The Relations of the Kindergarten and the Catholic Church." *Kindergarten Messenger*, August, 1873.

"The Relations of Judaism and the Kindergarten." *Kindergarten Messenger*, August, 1873.

"Religious Nurture." In *Education in the Home, the Kindergarten, and the Primary School*, 1887, pp. 157–186.

"Remarks" (of E. P. Peabody). Proceedings of the convention of friends of Froebel. Held at Detroit, Michigan, June 21, 22, and 23, 1882. *Kindergarten Messenger* (Syracuse), VI, No. 7, July, 1882, pp. 99–106.

Reminiscences of Rev. Wm. Ellery Channing, D.D. Boston: Roberts Brothers, 1880.

Report and New Prospectus of Kindergarten. April, 1862.

"The School in the Woods." *Kindergarten Messenger*, January–March, 1875.

"Some Effects of the Kindergarten upon Adults." *Kindergarten Messenger* (Syracuse), VI, No. 7, July, 1882, pp. 98–99.

"Spirit of the Hebrew Scriptures."

"The Creation." *Christian Examiner*, XVI, May, 1834.

"Temptation, Sin, and Punishment." *Christian Examiner*, XVI, July, 1834.

"Public Worship; Social Crime and Retribution." *Christian Examiner*, XVII, September, 1834.

"A Spirit's Reply." Poem. In *Aesthetic Papers*, 1849, p. 111.

"A Story." "A little raindrop from the skies . . ." Poem. Anonymous. *The Family School*, I, No. 2, November 1, 1836.

"Story Versus History for Kindergartens." *Kindergarten Messenger*, January, 1874.

"Sunday School Studies—An introduction to a Series of Readings, with a Sunday School Class, on the Gospel of St. John." *The Family School*, I, No. 2, November 1, 1836.

To Fathers and Mothers, a Letter in the Form of a Broadside. Boston, 1873.

"To Kindergartners and Members of the American Froebel Union." 1880. Page 1, notice of meeting of American Froebel Union on March 31 and April 1, 1880.

"Training Kindergartners." *Kindergarten Messenger,* November–December, 1877.

"Training of Kindergartners." *Kindergarten Messenger,* October, 1875.

"The Twofold Being." Poem. In *Aesthetic Papers,* 1849, pp. 245–246.

Universal History, Arranged to Illustrate Bem's Charts of Chronology. New York: Sheldon & Co., 1859, 1875.

The Way for a Child to be Saved, by the Author of "Record of a School." Boston: Crocker, Crocker & Brewster, 1835. New York: Leavitt, Lord & Co., 1835.

"What Was Froebel's Discovery?" *Kindergarten Messenger,* May–June, 1877.

"When Should Children Be Taught to Read? Sham Kindergarten Culture." *Herald of Health and Journal of Physical Culture,* No. 2, August, 1871, pp. 58–61.

"Who Is the True Kindergartner?" *Kindergarten Messenger,* January–March, 1875.

"The World's Need of Women." *Christian Examiner,* LXIX, November, 1860.

B. Editor:

Aesthetic Papers. Edited by Elizabeth Palmer Peabody. Boston: Published by the Editor, 1849. New York: G. P. Putnam, 1849.

The Casket. 1828. Contained a free rendering of Fouquet's *Undine* for children.

Crimes of the House of Austria against Mankind. Proved by Extracts from the Histories of Coxe, Schiller, Robertson, Grattan, and Sismondi, with Mrs. M. L. Putnam's History of the Constitution of Hungary, and its Relations with Austria. Edited by E. P. Peabody. May, 1850. Privately Published.

Second Edition. Copyrighted by Rodolphe Garrique. New York: G. P. Putnam, 1852.

The Family School.

I, No. 1, September 1, 1836. Boston: Marsh, Capen & Lyon.

I, No. 2, November 1, 1836. Salem Observer Press.

Froebel, F. W. A.: *Mother-Play, and Nursery Songs.* Illustrated by fifty engravings. With notes to Mothers. Translated from the German. Edited by Elizabeth Palmer Peabody; songs translated by Fanny E. Dwight;

text by Josephine Jarvis. New York: Charles T. Dillingham, 1878. Boston: Lee & Shepard, 1879. Boston: Lee & Shepard, 1896.

Mother-Play and Nursery Songs; Poetry, music, and pictures for the noble culture of child life, with notes to mothers. Translated from the German by Fanny E. Dwight and Josephine Jarvis, edited by Elizabeth Palmer Peabody. Containing all the original music and finger exercises with facsimiles of over fifty engravings from the author's edition. Original American Edition. Boston: Lee & Shepard, 1906.

Hazard, Rowland Gibson, *Essays on Language and Other Papers.* Edited by Elizabeth P. Peabody. Boston: Phillips, Simpson & Co., 1857.

Kindergarten Messenger. Edited by Elizabeth P. Peabody from May, 1873 to December, 1875, and from January to December, 1877. Merged with the *New England Journal of Education.*

Shirreff, Emily A. E. *The Kindergarten: Principles of Froebel's System and their Bearing on the Education of Women. Remarks on the Higher Education of Women.* American Edition. Edited by Elizabeth P. Peabody. Syracuse: C. W. Bardeen, 1889.

Wiseman, Nicholas, Cardinal. *The Identification of the Artisan and Artist the Proper Object of American Education. Illustrated by a Lecture of Cardinal Wiseman, on the Relation of the Arts of Design with the Arts of Education. Addressed to American Workingmen and Educators, with an Essay on Froebel's Reform of Primary Education,* by Elizabeth P. Peabody. Boston: Adams & Co.; Lee & Shepard; Patrick Donahoe. New York: Wood & Holbrook; J. W. Schermerhorn, 1869.

C. Publisher:

Aesthetic Papers. Edited by Elizabeth Palmer Peabody. Boston: Published by the Editor, 1849.

Channing, Wm. E. *Emancipation.* Boston: E. P. Peabody, 13 West Street, 1840.

Confessions of St. Augustine. Edited by Elizabeth P. Peabody. Preface by Elizabeth P. Peabody. Boston: E. P. Peabody, 1842.

The Dial. Elizabeth P. Peabody became publisher with

the issue of January, 1842, and continued to April, 1843.

Fowle, W. B. *A Method of Teaching Linear Drawing Adapted to the Public Schools*, by the Author of "Easy Lessons in Perspective." Boston: E. P. Peabody, 1841.

Günderode. Boston: E. P. Peabody, 109 Washington Street, 1842.

Hawthorne, Nathaniel. *Grandfather's Chair.* 1840.

The Liberty Tree. 1841.

Famous Old People. 1841.

Lowell, Anna C. *The Theory of Teaching, with a few practical illustrations.* Boston: E. P. Peabody, 1841.

Peabody, E. P. *Blank Centuries Accompanying the Manual of the Polish-American System of Chronology.* Boston: E. P. Peabody, 1850.

Peabody, E. P. *First Nursery Reading Book,* intended to teach the alphabet by means of English words, whose analysis should give the true sounds that were originally and even now are generally attached to the characters in all languages. Boston: 13 West Street, 1849. New York: G. P. Putnam, 1849.

Schmid, Peter. *The Common-School Drawing-Master. Part I: Containing Schmid's Practical Perspective.* Translated by Mary T. Peabody. Boston: E. P. Peabody, 13 West Street, 1846.

D. Reviewer:

"Harriet Martineau. *Five Years of Youth.*" Review. *The Family School.* I, No. 2, November 1, 1836.

"Hawthorne. *The Blithedale Romance.*" Review. *North American Review,* LXXVI, p. 228, 1853.

"Hawthorne's *The Marble Faun.*" Review. *Atlantic Monthly,* September, 1868. In *Last Evening with Allston and Other Papers,* 1886, pp. 293–330.

"Heine's *Letters on German Literature.*" Review. *The Family School,* I, No. 1, September 1, 1836.

"Nature—A Prose Poem." Review of Emerson. *Nature. Atlantic Monthly,* Unidentified; February, 1838, pp. 319–326.

E. Translator:

"Angelica Sleeps." From the Italian of Berni. *Dial,* I, No. 2, October, 1840, p. 172.

De Gerando, [sic] Joseph Marie, le Baron: *The Visitor to the Poor*. Translated from the French, by a Lady of Boston. Introduction by Joseph Tuckerman. Boston: Hillard, Gray, Little & Wilkins, 1832.

Gerando, [sic] Joseph Marie, Le Baron de. *Self-Education, or the Means and Art of Moral Progress*. Translated from the French, Anonymous. Boston: Carter & Hendee, 1830. Boston: Carter & Hendee, 1832, Preface by Elizabeth P. Peabody. Boston: Marsh, Capen & Lyon, 1833.

Self-Education; or the Means and Art of Moral Progress. Translated from the French of M. le Baron Degerando [sic]. By Elizabeth P. Peabody. Third Edition, with Additions. Boston: T. O. H. P. Burnham, 1860.

III. General References

Arranged alphabetically according to author's name.

Alexander, Carter. *How to Locate Educational Information and Data*. New York: Bureau of Publications, Teachers College, Columbia University, 1950.

Boas, Louise S. *Women's Education Begins: The Rise of Women's Colleges*. Norton, Mass.: Wheaton College Press, 1935.

Boone, Richard G. *Education in the United States*. New York: D. Appleton and Company, 1893.

Borrowman, Merle L. *The Liberal and Technical in Teacher Education*. New York: Bureau of Publications, Columbia University, 1956.

Brickman, William W. *Guide to Research in Educational History*. New York: New York University Bookstore, 1949.

Brockhaus, Eberhard (pub.). *Der Grosse Brockhaus*. Wiesbaden, 1953.

Brubacher, John S. *A History of the Problems of Education*. New York: McGraw-Hill, 1947.

Butler, J. Donald. *Four Philosophies and Their Practice in Education and Religion*. New York: Harper and Bros., 1957.

Butts, R. Freeman and Cremin, Lawrence A. *A History of Education in American Culture*. New York: Holt, 1953.

Carman, Harry J. and McKee, Samuel, Jr. *A History of the United States*. Boston: D. C. Heath and Co., 1931.

Curti, Merle. *The Social Ideas of American Educators*. New York: Charles Scribner's Sons, 1959.

Davis, Sheldon E. *Educational Periodicals during the Nineteenth Century*. U. S. Bureau of Education. Bulletin No. 20. Washington, D. C.: Government Printing Office, 1919.

Dexter, Edward G. *A History of Education in the United States*. New York: The Macmillan Company, 1904.

Duggan, Stephen. *A Student's Textbook in the History of Education*. Third Edition. New York: Appleton-Century-Crofts, 1940.

Good, Carter V. (ed.). *Dictionary of Education*. New York: McGraw-Hill, Second Edition, 1959.

Goodsell, Willystine. *Education of Women, Its Social Background and Problems*. New York: Macmillan, 1923.

Graves, Frank P. *A History of Education in Modern Times*. New York: Macmillan, 1913.

——. *Great Educators of Three Centuries*. New York: Macmillan, 1912.

——. *A Student's History of Education*. New York: Macmillan, 1916.

Gregory, Winifred. *Union Serial List of Publications*. New York: H. W. Wilson Company, 1943.

Guggenheimer, Aimee. "Froebel and the Kindergarten," in *New York State Library, Bulletin 60*, May, 1901, Bibliography 26.

Harris, Chester W. (ed.). *Encyclopedia of Educational Research*. Third Edition. New York: Macmillan, 1960.

Hastings, James (ed.). *Encyclopaedia of Religion and Ethics*. Revised Edition. New York: Peter Smith, 1930.

Kiddle, Henry and Alexander J. Schem (eds.). *The Cyclopedia of Education*. New York: Steiger, 1876.

Knight, Edgar W. *Education in the United States*. New York: Ginn and Co., 1951.

Martin, George H. *Evolution of the Massachusetts Public School System*. New York: D. Appleton and Company, 1902.

Mead, G. H. *Movements of Thought in the Nineteenth Century*. Chicago: University of Chicago Press, 1936.

Meyer, Adolphe E. *An Educational History of the American People*. New York: McGraw-Hill, 1957.

Monroe, Paul (ed.). *A Cyclopedia of Education.* New York: Macmillan, 1913.
———. *A Textbook in the History of Education.* New York: Macmillan, 1905.
Montessori, Maria. *The Montessori Method.* London: William Heinemann, 1912.
Moore, Ernest Carroll. *Fifty Years of American Education.* New York: Ginn and Co., 1917.
Noble, Stuart G. *History of American Education.* New York: Rinehart, 1954.
Parker, Samuel C. *A Textbook in the History of Modern Elementary Education.* Boston: Ginn and Company, 1912.
Pochmann, Henry A. *German Culture in America.* Madison: The University of Wisconsin Press, 1957.
Runes, Dagobert D. (ed.). *The Dictionary of Philosophy.* New York: Philosophical Library, 1942.
Ulich, Robert. *History of Educational Thought.* New York: American Book Company, 1945.

IV. Secondary References

Arranged alphabetically according to author's name.

A. Books, Pamphlets, Articles in Books and Theses:

Alcott, Amos Bronson. *Concord Days.* Boston: Roberts Brothers, 1862.
———. *Sonnets and Canzonets.* Boston: Roberts Brothers, 1888.
Almy, Dr. Millie. *Pre-School Education.* Prepared by Dr. M. Almy and the World Organization for Early Childhood Education. Paris, France: UNESCO, 1960. (January, 1960, Vol. XII, No. 1.)
Alstetter, Mabel Flick. "The Life and Work of Elizabeth Palmer Peabody." Unpublished Master's thesis. George Peabody College for Teachers, Nashville, 1935.
Anniversary Committee for the Boston Kindergarten Association. Fiftieth Anniversary of the Establishment of Kindergartens, Boston, Mass., 1928.
Association for Childhood Education, Kindergarten Centennial Committee. *A Brief Historical Outline of Early Childhood Education.* Washington, D. C.: A. C. E., 1937.
———. *This Is What Happened.* Kindergarten Portfolio, Section 7. Washington, D. C.: A. C. E., 1944.

——. Kindergarten Centennial Committee. *The Kindergarten Centennial 1837–1937.* Washington, D. C.: A. C. E., 1937.

Austen, Jessica Tyler (ed.). *Moses Coit Tyler, 1835–1900, Selections from his Letters and Diaries.* New York: Doubleday, Page and Company, 1911.

Austin, James C. *Fields of the Atlantic Monthly.* San Marino, California: The Huntington Library, 1953.

Bailey, Sarah L. *Historical Sketches of Andover.* Boston: Houghton, Mifflin and Co., 1880.

Barnard, Henry (ed.). *Kindergarten and Child Culture Papers.* Republished from *The American Journal of Education.* Hartford: Office of Barnard's *American Journal of Education,* 1890.

——. Special Report of the Commissioner of Education on the Condition and Improvement of Public Schools in the District of Columbia, June, 1868. Washington, D. C.: Government Printing Office, 1871.

Bell, Margaret. *Margaret Fuller.* New York: Albert and Charles Boni, 1930.

Bilbo, Queenie M. *Elizabeth Palmer Peabody, Transcendentalist.* Unpublished Ph.D. thesis, New York University, New York, 1932.

Billington, Ray Allen. *The Journal of Charlotte L. Forten.* New York: The Dryden Press, 1953.

Blow, Susan E. *Educational Issues in the Kindergarten.* New York: D. Appleton and Company, 1900.

——. *Symbolic Education.* New York: Appleton, 1895.

—— and Eliot, Henrietta R. (translators), *The Mottoes and Commentaries of Friedrich Froebel's Mother Play.* New York: D. Appleton and Company, 1898.

Booth, John Nicholls. *Introducing Unitarianism.* Boston: American Unitarian Association, 1951.

Boston Public School Kindergarten Department. *History of the Kindergarten Department.* Unpublished, 1956.

Bradley, Milton. *The Kindergarten and the School.* Springfield, Mass.: Milton Bradley and Co., 1886.

Brooklyn Kindergarten Association. *Reports Nos. 1–13.* Brooklyn, 1891–1904.

Brooks, Van Wyck. *The Flowering of New England.* New York: E. P. Dutton and Company, 1955.

Bülow-Wendhausen, Bertha Von. *Greeting to America.* New York: W. B. Harrison, 1900.

———. *The Life of the Baroness Von Marenholtz-Bulow* by her niece. New York: W. B. Harrison, 1901.

Butler, Vera M. *Education as Revealed by New England Newspapers Prior to 1850*. Ed.D. dissertation, Temple University. Philadelphia: The Author, 1935.

Carlyle, Thomas. *Sartor Resartus: The Life and Opinions of Herr Teufelsdrockh*. Boston: Fraser's Magazine, 1833, 1834. London: Chapman and Hall, 1872.

Carpenter, J. E. "Unitarianism," in James Hastings (ed.). *Encyclopaedia of Religion and Ethics*. Vol. XII, pp. 519–527. New York: Charles Scribner's Sons, 1928.

Cheney, Ednah Dow. *Reminiscences of Ednah Dow Cheney*. Boston: Lee and Shepard, 1902.

Committee of Nineteen, International Kindergarten Union. *The Kindergarten*. Boston: Houghton Mifflin Co., 1913.

——— (eds.). *Pioneers of the Kindergarten in America*. New York: The Century Co., 1924.

Conway, Moncure D. *Autobiography, Memories and Experiences*. Boston: Houghton Mifflin Company, 1904.

———. *Life of Nathaniel Hawthorne*. New York: A. Lovell and Company, 1890.

Cooke, George Willis. *An Historical and Biographical Introduction to the Reprint of the Dial, Vols. I and II*. Cleveland: The Rowfant Club, 1902.

Crawford, Mary C. *Old Boston Days and Ways*. Boston: Little, Brown and Company, 1909.

———. *Romantic Days in Old Boston*. Boston: Little, Brown and Company, 1910.

Dall, Caroline H. *Margaret and Her Friends*. Boston: Roberts Brothers, 1895.

Davis, Sheldon E. *Educational Periodicals during the Nineteenth Century*. U. S. Bureau of Education. Bulletin No. 28. Washington, D. C.: Government Printing Office, 1919.

Dewey, John. *The School and Society*. Chicago: University of Chicago Press, 1900.

Dewey, John and Evelyn. *Schools of To-Morrow*. New York: E. P. Dutton and Co., 1915.

Documents of the City of Boston for 1860. Boston: George C. Rand and Avery, City Printers, 1861.

Easum, Chester Verne. *The Americanization of Carl Schurz*. Chicago: University of Chicago Press, 1929.

Eby, Frederick. *The Reconstruction of the Kindergarten.* Published dissertation for Ph.D., Clark University, Worcester, Mass., reprinted from *The Pedagogical Seminary,* Vol. VII, July, 1900.

Endicott, C. M., revised by William S. Peabody. *A Genealogy of the Peabody Family.* Boston: David Clapp and Son, 1867.

Farmer, Lydia Hoyt (ed.). The National Exposition Souvenir. *What America Owes to Woman.* Buffalo, N. Y., Chicago: Charles Wells Moulton, 1893.

Faust, Clarence Henry. *Relationship of A. Bronson Alcott to the Educational Movements of His Time.* Unpublished Master's thesis, University of Chicago. Chicago, 1929.

Fenner, M. S. and Fishburn, E. C. *Pioneer American Educators.* Washington, D. C.: National Education Association, 1944.

Fields, James T. *Yesterdays with Authors.* Boston: n.p., 1883.

Forest, Ilse. *Preschool Education.* New York: The Macmillan Company, 1927.

Froebel, Friedrich. *Education by Development.* Translated by Josephine Jarvis. New York: D. Appleton and Company, 1909.

———. *The Education of Man.* Translated by W. N. Hailmann. New York: D. Appleton and Company, 1909.

———. *Mothers' Songs, Games and Stories.* Translated by Frances and Emily Lord. London: William Rice, 1920.

Frothingham, Octavius Brooks. *Memoir of William Henry Channing.* Boston: Houghton, Mifflin, 1886.

Fuller, Sarah Margaret. *Memoirs of Margaret Fuller Ossoli.* Boston: Phillips, Sampson and Company, 1882.

Gallaudet, T. H. *Plan of a Seminary for the Education of Instructors of Youth.* Boston: n.p., 1825.

Garland, Mary J. *A Sketch of the Life of Elizabeth Palmer Peabody.* Written for the Elizabeth Peabody House Association. Boston: T. Todd, n.d.

———. *Elizabeth P. Peabody, May 16, 1804–January 3, 1894.* Massachusetts Teachers' Association, Report of the Committee on Necrology, Boston, n.p., 1894.

Gates, Arthur I. *Teaching Reading.* Washington, D. C.: National Education Association, 1953.

Goddard, H. G. *Studies in New England Transcendentalism.* New York: Columbia University Press, 1908.

Gohdes, Clarence. *The Periodicals of American Transcendentalism.* Durham: The Duke University Press, 1931.

Graves, Rev. Charles. *What Unitarians Believe.* Pamphlet, n.d., n.p.

Gross, Doris Lane. "Three Portraits: Women of Transcendental New England." Unpublished Master's thesis, University of Maine, Orono, 1935.

Haefner, George E. *A Critical Estimate of the Educational Theories and Practices of A. Bronson Alcott.* New York: Author, 1937.

Hailmann, William N. "Adaptation of Froebel's System of Education to American Institutions," in The Addresses and Journal of the National Education Association, *Proceedings.* Peoria, Illinois: National Education Association, 1873.

———. *Kindergarten Culture in the Family and Kindergarten.* New York, n.p., 1873.

———. *Law of Childhood and Other Papers.* Chicago: A. B. Stockham and Company, 1891.

———. *Four Lectures on Early Child-Culture.* Milwaukee, Wisconsin: Carl Doerflinger, 1880.

Hale, Edward Everett. *A New England Boyhood.* Boston: Little, Brown & Co., 1900.

Hale, Sarah Josepha. *Woman's Record.* New York: Harper and Brothers, 1872.

Hall, G. Stanley. *Aspects of Child Life and Education.* New York: Ginn and Company, 1907.

Hanaford, Phoebe A. *Women of the Century.* Augusta: True and Company, 1882.

Harper, Ida Husted. *Life and Work of Susan B. Anthony.* Indianapolis: The Hollenbeck Press, 1898.

Harrison, Elizabeth. *A Study of Child Nature.* Copyright, 1890. New York: Macmillan, 1931.

Hawthorne, Julian. *Nathaniel Hawthorne and His Wife.* Boston: Ticknor and Company, 1884.

———. *Hawthorne and His Circle.* New York: Harper Brothers, 1903.

Hayes, Cecil B. *The American Lyceum.* U. S. Office of Education, *Bulletin, 1932, No. 12.* Washington, D. C.: U. S. Government Printing Office, 1932.

Hazard, Rowland G. *Freedom of Mind in Willing.* New York: D. Appleton and Company, 1864.

Higginson, Thomas Wentworth. *Atlantic Essays.* London: n.p., 1872.

——. *Carlyle's Laugh and Other Surprises.* Boston: Houghton Mifflin, 1899.

——. *Cheerful Yesterdays.* Boston: Houghton Mifflin, 1898.

Hill, Patty Smith. "Kindergarten." A reprint from *The American Educator Encyclopedia.* Chicago: The United Educators, Inc., 1942.

Hughes, James. *The Kindergarten, Its Place and Purpose.* New York, n.p., 1877.

Hunter, Anna M. and Jenny, (eds.). *The Autobiography of Dr. Thomas Hunter.* New York: The Knickerbocker Press, 1931.

Hunter, Thomas. *Annual Report of the President of the Normal College for the Year 1871.* New York: Board of Education, 1872.

——. *Dedication of the New York Normal College Edifice.* October 29, 1873. New York: Board of Education, 1873.

——. *Report of the President of the Normal College for the Term ending May 14, 1870, submitted to the Board of Education May 18, 1870.* New York: Board of Education, 1871.

Hymes, James L., Jr. *Discipline.* New York: Bureau of Publications, Teachers College, Columbia University, 1951.

Imhoff, Myrtle M. *Early Elementary Education.* New York: Appleton-Century-Crofts, 1959.

James, William. *Letters of William James.* Boston: The Atlantic Press, 1920.

Kilpatrick, William Heard. *Froebel's Kindergarten Principles Critically Examined.* New York: The Macmillan Co., 1916.

Kindergarten Engrafted on the American Public-School System. Extracts from Official Reports on the Public Kindergartens Established by the Board of Public Schools of the City. St. Louis, Missouri, 1877.

King, Caroline Howard. *When I Lived in Salem: 1822–1866.* Brattelboro: Stephen Daye Press, 1937.

Kornmann, Elisa. *Steiger's Elementary Sewing Designs on Practice-Cloth with Directions and Suggestions.* New York: E. Steiger and Co., 1897.

Kraus, John. *The Kindergarten, Its Use and Abuse, in America.* Bound with Kraus-Boelte, Maria. *The Kinder-*

garten and the Mission of Women. Louisville, Ky.: NEΛ, 1877.

Kraus-Boelte, Maria and Kraus, John. *The Kindergarten Guide.* Vol. 1: The Gifts, Vol. 2: The Occupations. New York: E. Steiger, 1882, 1891, 1892.

Kraus-Boelte, Maria. *The Kindergarten and the Mission of Women.* Bound with Kraus, John. *The Kindergarten in America.* Louisville, Ky.: NEA, 1877.

Kraus-Boelte, Maria. Mme. *Kraus' Preliminary Sewing Without a Needle.* n.p., c. 1899.

Kriege, Matilda H. *The Child, Its Nature and Relations.* A free rendering of the German of the Baroness Marenholtz-Bülow. New York: E. Steiger, 1872.

———. *Friedrich Froebel, A Biographical Sketch.* New York: E. Steiger, 1876.

Lathrop, Rose Hawthorne. *Memories of Hawthorne.* Boston: Houghton Mifflin, 1897.

Lubbock, Percy. *The Letters of Henry James.* New York: Charles Scribner's Sons, 1920.

MacKenzie, D. "Transcendentalism," in James Hastings, editor. *Encyclopaedia of Religion and Ethics.* Revised Edition, pp. 419–425. New York: Peter Smith, 1930.

MacVannel, John Angus. *Kindergarten Problems.* New York: Columbia University Press, 1909.

Marenholtz-Bülow, Bertha Maria Von. *Child and Child Nature.* Translated by Alice M. Christie. London: S. Sonnenschein, 1879.

———. *The New Education by Work According to Froebel's Method.* Translated by Mrs. Horace Mann with the assistance of Professor Leopold Noa. Camden, New Jersey: Philotechnic Institute, 1876.

———. *Reminiscences of Friedrich Froebel.* Translated by Mrs. Horace Mann. Boston: Lee and Shepard, 1877.

———. *The School Workshop.* Translated by Miss Susan E. Blow. Syracuse, New York: C. W. Bardeen, 1882.

Martineau, Harriet. *Society in America. Vols. I and II.* New York: Saunders and Otley, 1837.

Marwedel, Emma. *Conscious Motherhood or the Earliest Unfolding of the Child.* Boston: Interstate Publishing Company, 1887.

———. *The Connecting Link to Continue the Three-fold Development of the Child from the Kindergarten to the Manual Labor School.* San Francisco: n.p., 1890.

McCart, Doris Louise. "Elizabeth Peabody, A Biographical Study." Unpublished Master's thesis, University of Chicago, 1918.

McCuskey, Dorothy. *Bronson Alcott, Teacher.* Boston: Macmillan, 1940.

Mead, G. H. *Movements of Thought in the Nineteenth Century.* Chicago: University of Chicago Press, 1936.

Miller, Perry (ed.). *The American Transcendentalists.* New York: Doubleday and Co., 1957.

Monroe, Will S. *History of the Pestalozzian Movement in the United States.* Syracuse, New York: C. W. Bardeen, 1907.

——. "Lyceum Movement in the United States," in Paul Monroe (ed.). *A Cyclopedia of Education,* Vol. IX, p. 101. New York: Macmillan, 1913.

——. "Marwedel, Emma (1817–1893)," in Paul Monroe (ed.). *A Cyclopedia of Education,* Vol. IX, pp. 338–341. New York: Macmillan, 1913.

——. "Peabody, Elizabeth Palmer (1804–1894)," in Paul Monroe (ed.). *A Cyclopedia of Education,* Vol. IX, p. 610. New York: Macmillan, 1913.

Mott, Frank Luther. *A History of American Magazines.* 1865–1885. Vol. III. Cambridge, Mass.: Harvard University Press, 1938.

——. *Golden Multitudes.* New York: Macmillan, 1947.

National Education Association. *The Addresses and Journal of Proceedings of the National Education Association at Boston, 1872.* Peoria, Ill.: The Association, 1873.

National Kindergarten Association. Florence J. Ovens, editor. *The Kindergarten in the United States.* New York: National Kindergarten Association, 1937.

New York City Board of Education. *Fifty-third Annual Report of the Board of Education of the City of New York for the Year Ending December 31, 1894.* New York: Hall of the Board of Education, 1895.

——. *Journal of the Board of Education of the City of New York, 1870.* New York: The New York Printing Co., 1870.

——. *Journal of the Board of Education of the City of New York, 1892.* New York: The New York Printing Co., 1892.

——. *Journal of the Board of Education of the City of*

New York, 1897. New York: The New York Printing Co., 1897.

――――. *Minutes of the Board of Education of the City of New York, 1896.* New York: Board of Education, 1897.

Norris, Lloyd. *The Rebellious Puritan.* New York: Harcourt, Brace and Company, 1927.

Owen, Robert. *The Life of Robert Owen: Written by Himself.* London: G. Bell and Sons, Ltd., 1920.

Payne, Joseph. *Science and the Art of Education.* New York: E. Steiger, 1876.

Peabody, Mrs. Elizabeth Palmer. *Sabbath Lessons.* Salem: Cushing, 1813.

――――. *Holiness* or *The Legend of St. George: A Tale from Spencer's [sic] Faerie Queene.* By a mother. Boston: E. R. Broaders, 1836.

Peabody, Mary Tyler (Mrs. Horace Mann). *Flower People.* Boston: Ticknor and Fields, 1862.

Peabody, Selim H. *Peabody Genealogy,* Boston, 1909.

Pestalozzi, J. H. *How Gertrude Teaches Her Children.* London: Swan Sonnenschein and Company, Ltd., 1907.

――――. *Leonard and Gertrude.* London: D. C. Heath and Company, 1885.

Pochmann, Henry A. *German Culture in America.* Madison: The University of Wisconsin Press, 1957.

Quick, Robert H. *Essays on Educational Reformers.* New York: D. Appleton and Company, 1890.

Raymont, Thomas. *A History of the Education of Young Children.* London: Longmans, Green and Company, 1937.

Roberts, Josephine Elizabeth. *Elizabeth Palmer Peabody.* Ph.D. thesis: Western Reserve University. Cleveland, Ohio, 1937.

Robinson, Harriet H. *Massachusetts in the Woman Suffrage Movement.* Boston: Roberts Brothers, 1881.

Ronge, Johannes and Bertha. *A Practical Guide to the English Kindergarten.* Second Edition. London: 22 Portugal Street, 1858.

Rothney, John W. M. *Evaluating and Reporting Pupil Progress.* Washington, D. C.: National Education Association, 1955.

Rusk, Ralph L. *The Life of Ralph Waldo Emerson.* New York: Columbia University Press, 1949.

Rusk, Robert R. *A History of Infant Education*. London: University of London Press, 1933.

Salmon, David and Winifred Hindshaw. *Infant Schools: Their History and Theory*. London: Longmans, Green and Company, 1904.

Sanborn, Frank B. *Bronson Alcott at Alcott House, England and Fruitlands, New England (1842–1844)*. Cedar Rapids, Iowa: The Torch Press, 1908.

——— (ed.). *The Genius and Character of Emerson*. Boston: James R. Osgood and Co., 1885.

———. *The Life and Genius of Goethe*. Boston: Ticknor and Co., 1886.

———. *Recollections of Seventy Years*. Boston: Roberts Brothers, 1909.

Sanborn, Frank B. and William T. Harris. *A. Bronson Alcott: His Life and Philosophy*. Boston: Roberts Brothers, 1893.

Schlesinger, Arthur M., Jr. *Orestes A. Brownson, A Pilgrim's Progress*. Boston: Little, Brown, 1939.

Schurz, Carl. *Intimate Letters 1841–1869*. Translated and edited by Joseph Schafer. Madison: State Historical Society of Wisconsin, 1928.

Seeley, Levi. *The Common-School System of Germany and Its Lessons to America*. New York and Chicago: E. L. Kellogg and Co., 1896.

Shepard, Odell (ed.). *The Journals of Bronson Alcott*. Boston: Little, Brown and Co., 1938.

———. *Pedlar's Progress, The Life of Bronson Alcott*. Boston: Little, Brown and Co., 1937.

Shirreff, Emily. *A Short Sketch of the Life of Friedrich Froebel*. London: Chapman and Hall, Ltd., 1887.

———. *The Kinder-garten*. Syracuse, New York: C. W. Bardeen, 1889. London: Swan Sonnenschein, 1889.

Smith, Ira L. *Half a Century of Progress*. Washington, D. C.: The Association for Childhood Education, 1942.

Stearns, Frank Preston. *The Life and Genius of Nathaniel Hawthorne*. Philadelphia: J. B. Lippincott Co., 1906.

Stearns, John William (ed.). *The Columbian History of Education in Wisconsin*. Madison, Wisconsin: State Committee on Educational Exhibit for Wisconsin, 1893.

Stebbins, Emma (ed.). *Charlotte Cushman, Her Letters and Memories of Her Life*. Boston: Houghton, Osgood, 1878.

Steiger, Ernst. *German and French Kindergarten Method, Globes, etc.* New York: E. Steiger, 1878.

——. *Illustrated Catalogue of Kindergarten Gifts and Occupations Material.* New York: E. Steiger, 1876.

——. *Kindergarten Literature.* New York: E. Steiger, 1876.

——. *What Is the Effect of Kindergarten Education?* New York: E. Steiger, 1876.

——. *Der Kindergarten in Amerika.* New York: E. Steiger, 1872.

——, publisher. Kindergarten Tracts; Nos. 1 through 23. New York: E. Steiger, 1872 and thereafter, n.d.

Stern, Madeleine B. *Louisa May Alcott.* Norman, Okla.: University of Oklahoma Press, 1950.

——. *Imprints on History.* Bloomington: Indiana University Press, 1956.

Straker, Robert L. *Horace Mann and Others.* Yellow Springs, Ohio: The Antioch Press, 1963.

Suhl, Yuri. *Ernestine Rose 1810–1892.* New York: Reynal and Co., 1959.

Swift, Fletcher H. *Emma Marwedel, 1818–1893, Pioneer of the Kindergarten in California.* University of California Publications in Education, Vol. 6, No. 3. Berkeley, California: University of California Press, 1931.

Swift, Lindsay. *Brook Farm, Its Members, Scholars and Visitors.* New York: Macmillan Co., 1900.

Temple, Josiah Howard. *History of Framingham, Massachusetts.* Framingham: Published by the town of Framingham, 1887.

Tharp, Louise Hall. *Until Victory.* Boston: Little, Brown and Co., 1951, 1953.

——. *The Peabody Sisters of Salem.* Boston: Little, Brown and Company, 1950.

Thornbrough, Emma Lou. *Eliza A. Blaker, Her Life and Work.* The Eliza A. Blaker Club, Inc. and The Indiana Historical Society. Indianapolis: 1956.

Thursfield, Richard Emmons. *Henry Barnard's "American Journal of Education."* Baltimore: Johns Hopkins Press, 1945.

Tyler, Mary Hunt. *Grandmother Tyler's Book.* New York: Putnam, 1925.

Vandewalker, Nina C. "The Kindergarten," in Paul Monroe (ed.). *A Cyclopedia of Education,* Vol. III, pp. 598–606. New York: Macmillan, 1913.

———. *The Kindergarten in American Education.* New York: Macmillan, 1908.

———. *Kindergarten Training Schools.* United States Bureau of Education. *Bulletin, 1916, No. 5.* Washington, D. C.: Government Printing Office, 1916.

Wagenknecht, Edward. *Mrs. Longfellow: Selected Letters and Journals of Fanny Appleton Longfellow.* New York: Longmans, Green & Co., 1956.

Walz, John A. *German Influence on American Education and Culture.* Philadelphia: Carl Schurz Memorial Foundation, 1936.

Wesley, Edgar B. *NEA: The First Hundred Years.* New York: Harper and Brothers, 1957.

Wiebe, Edward. *The Paradise of Childhood.* Quarter Century Edition. Springfield, Massachusetts: Milton Bradley Company, 1896.

Wiggin, Kate Douglas and Nora Archibald Smith. *Froebel's Gifts.* Boston and New York: Houghton Mifflin, 1900.

———. *Froebel's Occupations.* Boston and New York: Houghton Mifflin, 1900.

———. *Kindergarten Principles and Practice.* Boston and New York: Houghton Mifflin, 1900.

Wiggin, Kate Douglas. *The Relation of the Kindergarten to the Public School.* San Francisco: C. A. Murdock and Company, 1891.

———. *My Garden of Memory.* Boston: Houghton Mifflin, 1923.

———. *Children's Rights, A Book of Nursery Logic.* Boston: Houghton, Mifflin & Co., 1892.

———. *The Story of Patsy.* Boston: Houghton Mifflin Co., 1889.

Wilderspin, Samuel. *Infant Education.* London: W. Simpkin and R. Marshall, 1824.

Worthington, Marjorie. *Miss Alcott of Concord.* New York: Doubleday & Co., 1958.

B. Newspapers and Periodicals:

Abt, Isaac A., M.D. "An Inquiry Into the Status of the Kindergarten," *Archives of Pediatrics,* Vol. XXVI, April, 1909.

Adler, Felix. "The Workingman's School and Free Kindergarten," *Society for Ethical Culture, United Relief Works Reports.* New York: Society for Ethical Culture, 1881.

The American-German Review. Carl Schurz Issue. Vol. XVIII, August, 1952.

Anagnos, Michael. "Horace Mann and Elizabeth Peabody," *Kindergarten News,* Vol. IV, No. 26, February, 1894.

B——. "Miss Elizabeth Palmer Peabody—Personal," *Phrenological Journal,* Vol. XCVII, March, 1894.

Blow, Susan E. "The History of the Kindergarten in the United States," *Outlook,* April 3, 1897.

——. "The Kindergarten," *Kindergarten Messenger,* Vol. III, December, 1875.

Bond, Mrs. E. Powell. "The Relation of Kindergartening to Motherhood," *Kindergarten Messenger and the New Education,* Vol. II, April, 1878.

Boone, Mary Stanley. "The Kindergarten from a Mother's Point of View," *Education,* Vol. XXV, November, 1904.

Bradley, Milton. "A Reminiscence of Miss Peabody," *Kindergarten News,* Vol. IV, February, 1894.

Brown, Violet J. "Calling Eighty Thousand Parents," *Brooklyn Eagle,* November 24, 1939.

Bryan, Anna. "The Letter Killeth." *Proceedings* National Education Association, 1890.

By a Bostonian. "A Few Reminiscences of Miss Elizabeth Palmer Peabody," *Kindergarten Review,* May, 1890.

Cheney, Ednah Dow. "Elizabeth Palmer Peabody," *Kindergarten Review,* Vol. XIV, May, 1904.

Cheney, S. and F. Sanborn. "The Funeral Service; Remarks by Mrs. Cheney and Mr. Sanborn," *Kindergarten News,* Vol. IV, February, 1894.

The Connecticut Common School Journal, published under the direction of the Board of Commissioners of Common Schools. Vol. I, Hartford: Printed by Case, Tiffany and Co., 1838–9. Vol. II, 1839–40.

Davis, M. D. "A Century of the Kindergarten," *School Life,* Vol. XXII, 1936.

Devereaux, Anna W. "The True Place of the Kindergarten," *Education,* Vol. XXV, April, 1905.

Garland, Mary J. "Elizabeth Palmer Peabody," *Kindergarten News,* Vol. IV, February, 1894.

Hailmann, W. N. "Hailmann's Kindergarten Training

School," *Kindergarten Messenger and the New Education,* Vol. II, August, 1878.

——. "Kindergarten Training," *Kindergarten Messenger and the New Education,* Vol. II, May, 1878.

Higginson, Thomas Wentworth. "Pre-Collegiate Women," *Harper's Bazaar,* Vol. XXVII, January 27, 1894.

Hocker, Edward W. "The First American Kindergarten Teacher," *The American-German Review,* Vol. VIII, February, 1942.

Jarvis, Josephine. "Miss Peabody and Early Translations of Froebel's Works," *Kindergarten Review,* Vol. XIV, May, 1904.

Jenkins, Elizabeth. "How the Kindergarten Found Its Way to America." *The Wisconsin Magazine of History,* Vol. XIX, September, 1930.

Kraus-Boelte, Maria. "A Tribute to My Old Friend, Elizabeth P. Peabody," *Kindergarten Review,* Vol. XIV, May, 1904.

L——, E. H. "Recollections of a Pupil of Miss Peabody's Kindergarten," *Kindergarten Review,* Vol. XIV, May, 1904.

Lawson, Douglas E. "Corrective Note on the Early History of the American Kindergarten," *Educational Administration and Supervision,* Vol. XXV, December, 1939.

Leidecker, Kurt F. "The 101st Year of the Kindergarten," *The American-German Review,* Vol. VII, June, 1941.

McDaniel, Fanny L. and Anna Q. T. Parsons. "The Seedtime of Kindergarten Thought in America," *Kindergarten Review,* Vol. XIV, May, 1904.

Monroe, Will S. "Emma Marwedel and the Kindergarten," *Education,* Vol. XIV, February, 1894.

"Obituary of Miss Elizabeth Palmer Peabody." *Springfield Republican,* January 5, 1894.

Ogden, Anna B. "Popular Errors in Kindergartening," *Kindergarten Messenger and New Education,* Vol. II, March, 1878.

Owen, Grace. "Study of Original Kindergartens," *Elementary School Teacher,* Vol. VII, December, 1906.

Parker, Jane Marsh. "Elizabeth Peabody, A Reminiscence," *Outlook,* Vol. XLIX, February 3, 1894.

Parsons, Anna Q. T. "Reminiscences of Miss Peabody," *Kindergarten Review,* Vol. XIV, May, 1904.

Peabody, Dr. Nathaniel. "Advertisement," *Salem Gazette,* September 10, 1830.

Pearson, Norman Holmes. "Elizabeth Peabody on Hawthorne," *Essex Institute Historical Collections.* Special Issue, Vol. XCIV, July, 1958.

Petersen, Anne. "Women Wage Fight to Revive Kindergartens," *The New York Times,* December 10, 1939.

Porter, Maria S. "Elizabeth Palmer Peabody," *The Bostonian,* Vol. III, January, 1896.

Ripley, Grace, "Degerando on Self-Education," *Christian Examiner,* Vol. IX, September, 1830.

Roberts, Josephine E. "Horace Mann and the Peabody Sisters," *New England Quarterly,* Vol. XVIII, 1945.

———. "Elizabeth Peabody and the Temple School," *New England Quarterly,* Vol. XVI, 1942.

Rogers, Rachel L. "Professor John Kraus and Mrs. Marie Kraus-Boelte and Their United Work." *Kindergarten News,* Vol. VII, September, 1896.

Sanborn, F. B. "Memoir of A. Bronson Alcott," *Barnard's American Journal of Education,* Vol. XXVII, 1877.

Schriftgiesser, Karl. "Boston Kindergartens to Celebrate Their Fiftieth Anniversary," *Boston Evening Transcript,* Wednesday, January 18, 1928.

Schroeder, Henrietta. "Girlhood Days at Keilhau," *Kindergarten Magazine,* Vol. VII, October, 1895.

Seguin, E. "Report on Education. Chapter III. The Kindergarten," *Kindergarten Messenger and the New Education,* Vol. II, March, 1878.

Sheldon, William E. "Memorial Addresses—Report of Committees on Necrology," National Education Association, *Proceedings,* 1894.

Shute, M. C. "One Hundred Years of the Kindergarten," *National Education Association Journal,* Vol. XXVI, 1937.

Smith, I. L. "Half a Century of Progress," Association for Childhood Education, *Proceedings,* 1942.

Touvim, Helen R. "New York Mothers Fight Closing of Public School Kindergarten," *The New York Sun,* November 24, 1939.

University of the State of New York. "One Hundredth Anniversary of Kindergarten," *Bulletin to the Schools,* Vol. XXIII, No. 12, March 1, 1937.

Weston, R. J. "A Birthday Visit," *Kindergarten News,* Vol. IV, February, 1894.

Wheelock, Lucy. "Miss Peabody and the Kindergarten," *Education,* Vol. XV, September, 1894.

———. "Kindergarten Idea Is A Century Old," *New York Times,* April 18, 1937.

Williams, Talcott. "The Kindergarten Movement," *The Century,* Vol. XLV, January, 1893.

Wilson, John B. "A Transcendental Minority Report," *The New England Quarterly,* Vol. XXIX, June, 1956.

Index

Aborn, Caroline D., 137
Adler, Felix, 118, 138
Alcott, Amos Bronson: contacts
    with Elizabeth Palmer Pea-
    body, 49, 58, 59, 60, 61, 62, 64,
    78, 84, 89, 90, 114, 117, 125,
    147, 156, 159, 164, 169; pro-
    gressive theories, 80, 81, 151,
    168; death of, 120
Alcott, Louisa May, 89, 90
Aldrich, Mrs. A., 129
Allen, Professor N.T., 88, 89
Allston, Washington, 63, 73, 81
American Froebel Union, 113
Association for Childhood Edu-
    cation International, 40

Bancroft, George, 30
Barnard, Henry, 23, 31, 34, 37,
    108, 114, 116, 118, 129
Barop, Johannes, 25
Bellows, Henry Whitney, 52
Blake, Henry W., 24, 26
Blow, Susan, 105, 120, 137
Boelte, Amèly, 104
Bookshop, West Street, 30, 76,
    81, 82, 128

Bormann, School-Counsellor, 27,
    28
Boston German-English School,
    37
Boston Transcript, 129
Bradley, Milton, 95, 96
Brook Farm, 82
Burritt, Ruth, 114

Carlyle, Thomas, 82
Channing, Mary, 54
Channing, William Ellery, 49,
    51, 52, 53, 54, 57, 60, 64, 65, 71,
    81, 122
Channing, William Henry, 123
Chaney, George L., 124
Cheney, Ednah Dow, 37
Children's Gardens, 34
Church: Catholic opposition to
    Froebel, 25; Christianity in
    America, 30, 35, 59, 61, 80, 82;
    Unitarianism, 51, 52, 53, 54,
    128; ministerial support for
    kindergartens, 86, 88, 123, 124;
    Catholic support for kinder-
    gartens, 100; Judaism, 54, 94
Civil War, 34, 52, 90

Combe, George, 66
Concord School of Philosophy, 49, 102, 116, 117, 118
Conway, Moncure Daniel, 120
Corliss, Margaret, 129
Cushman, Charlotte Saunders, 106

Degerando, M. le Baron, 68, 83
Dickens, Charles, 35, 77
Diesterweg, Friedrich Adolph Wilhelm, 27
Discipline; in kindergarten, 153, 154, 155, 156
Dix, Dorothea Lynde, 52
Doerflinger, Carl H., 111
Douai, Adolph, 99, 114

Elizabeth Peabody Settlement House, 39, 121
Emerson, Ralph Waldo, 49, 62, 82, 120
Everett, Edward, 30, 49

Folsom, Charles, 69
Fourier, Charles, 82
Frankenberg, Adolf, 32
Frankenberg, Caroline Louise, 32, 33, 38
Franklin Academy, 41
Froebel, Friedrich: early life, 23, 24; establishment of the kindergarten, 25, 26, 27, 28; Froebelian influence, 29, 31, 32, 36, 40, 54, 63, 73, 84, 89, 91, 94, 99, 102, 104, 127, 134, 137, 139, 145, 147, 151, 155, 157, 158, 160, 161, 163, 164, 166, 167, 168, 169, 172, 173; interest in phrenology, 66, 67
Froebel, Karl, 28
Froebel, Louise Levin, 94, 95, 104, 129
Froebel Union, 105, 114, 116, 117
Fuller, Margaret, 52, 62, 78

Gall, F.J., 66
Garland, Mary J., 107, 113

German influence on American education, 29, 30, 31, 33, 34, 36, 37, 84, 94, 147, 159
Godwin, Parke, 74, 92
Goethe, Johann Wolfgang von, 82, 102
Göttingen University, 24, 30, 33
Graves, Charles, 52

Hailmann, Eudora Lucas, 139
Hailmann, William Nicholas, 100, 110, 111, 113, 139
Haines, Henrietta B., 104, 131
Hale, John P., 66
Hale, Sara Josepha, 50, 126
Harris, William Torrey, 73, 95, 97, 105, 107, 112, 113, 117, 138
Harvard College, 30, 43, 55, 76, 79
Haven, Foster, 91
Haven, Lydia, 55, 91
Hawthorne, Julian, 70, 71, 92, 103
Hawthorne, Nathaniel, 48, 62, 75, 92, 103
Hawthorne, Rose Lathrop, 103, 115
Hawthorne, Sophia Peabody, 44, 48, 56, 65, 67, 92, 103
Hawthorne, Una, 103, 104
Hedge, Frederick H., 71
Heine, Heinrich, 74
Higginson, Thomas Wentworth, 81
Hoffman, Charles, 91
Home and Colonial Infant School Society, 31
Howe, Samuel Gridley, 49, 52, 115
Hunter College, 99
Hunter, Thomas, 99

Indian education, 120
Industrial Education, 99, 134
Infant Garden, 34
Infant schools, 31

Institution for the Culture of Occupational Inclinations of Children and Youth, 32

James, Henry, Sr., 71
Jenks, Harriet S., 137

Kindergarten exhibitions, 34, 91, 109, 114, 120
Kindergarten: origin, 25; German-speaking in America, 32, 33, 35, 38, 84; symbolism, 73; English-speaking in America, 39, 40, 84, 85, 88, 89, 94, 105, 106, 107, 108, 139; public, 96, 100, 117, 118; charity, 98, 118; supervision of, 113, 142, 143, 144, 145; missionary, 143; advertisement, 129
Kindergarten curriculum: physical activity, 80, 81, 85, 112; nature study, 72; music, 80, 81, 118; art, 80, 81, 85, 160, 161; foreign language, 85; deletion of reading, 115, 158, 159, 162, 167; language arts, 157, 158; social relations, 167; reporting on pupil progress, 151, 152, 153, 162, 168; deletion of writing, 115, 158, 162
Kindergarten materials and equipment: 94, 111, 112, 168; gifts and occupations, 54
Kindergarten training schools: 91, 94, 98, 107, 111, 115, 127, 128, 129, 130, 131, 132, 133, 135, 136, 137, 138, 139, 140, 141; demand for teachers, 123, 125; supervision of, 142
Kraitsir, Dr., 69
Kraus-Boelte, Maria, 98, 104, 112, 113, 114, 131, 132
Kraus, John, 33, 98, 99, 114, 132, 133
Kriege, Alma, 38, 40, 94, 107, 126, 129
Kriege, Matilde, 40, 94, 107, 108, 126, 129, 131

Lane Theological Seminary, 30
Lange, Wichard, 25, 32
Langethal, Henry, 24
Longfellow, Fanny Appleton, 88
Longfellow, Henry Wadsworth, 88
Lowell, Anna C., 98
Lutheran Orphanage, 33
Lynn Academy, 44

Mann, Charlotte, 56
Mann, George Combe, 66, 105, 117
Mann, Horace, 30, 49, 52, 56, 57, 58, 66, 71, 75, 92
Mann, Horace Jr., 91
Mann, Maria, 116
Mann, Mary Peabody, 44, 48, 56, 67, 78, 86, 91, 92, 114, 115, 117, 119, 120
Martineau, Harriet, 49, 61, 62, 68, 69, 74, 75
Marwedel, Emma Jacobina, 99, 107, 119, 133, 134, 135, 136
Mazzini, Guiseppe, 94
Meyer, Adolf, 34
Middendorff, William, 24, 25, 29, 32, 127
Moore, Rebecca, 37, 38
Moral values: of education, 148, 150, 154, 157, 160, 162, 165; Miss Peabody's lectures on, 143; values and standards, 72, 73, 74, 76, 78, 80, 82, 83, 92, 100, 123, 125
Mott, Frank Luther, 122

National Education Association, 113
Negro, 90
North Andover Academy, 41

Parsons, Anna Q.T., 37
Palmer, Joseph, 42
Palmer, Joseph Pearse, 43
Parker, Theodore, 72

Peabody, Elizabeth Palmer (Mrs. Nathaniel), 41, 42, 43, 44, 45, 46, 47, 48, 55
Peabody, George, 44, 55, 56
Peabody, Nathaniel Cranch, 44, 55, 56, 76, 117
Peabody, Dr. Nathaniel, 41, 43, 44, 47, 48
Peabody, Wellington, 44, 55, 56
Perkins Institute for the Blind, 52, 115
Periodicals: carried news of kindergartens, 31, 32, 37, 57, 74, 86, 87, 88, 94, 97, 105, 108, 109, 110, 111, 131, 139, 142, 143, 145, 146
Pestalozzi, Johann Heinrich, 23, 27, 31, 34, 37, 51, 53
Phillips Andover Academy, 41
Phrenology, 66, 67
Pingree, Laliah B., 137
Pollock, Louise, 88
Pollock, Susan, 96, 105, 108
Porter, Maria, 50, 82
Poulsson, Emilie, 137

Ripley, George, 68, 82
Robinson, Harriet H., 72
Ronge, Bertha Meyer, 34, 37, 89, 104
Ronge, Johannes, 34
Rousseau, Jean Jacques, 74
Royal Seminary at Berlin, 27
Russell, William, 82

Salem Latin School, 48
Sanborn, Frank B., 49
San Francisco Public Kindergarten Society, 118
Saturday Club Women, 36
Schewe, Dr., 66
Schrader, Henriette Breymann, 129
Schurz, Agathe, 35, 36
Schurz, Carl, 34, 35
Schurz, Margarethe Meyer, 34, 35, 36, 37, 38
Severance, Mrs. Caroline, 135

Shaw, Pauline Agassis, 108, 112
Sheldon, E.A., 87
Smith, Nora Archibald, 138
Spring, Marcus, 37, 38
Spring, Mrs. Marcus, 37
Spurzheim, Johann Gasper, 67
State Normal School, Trenton, N.J., 30
Stearns, Frank Preston, 75
Steiger, Ernst, 109, 111, 112
Stowe, Calvin E., 30
Sumner, Charles, 49
Symonds, Lucy H., 137

Temple School, 58, 85
Ticknor, George, 30, 71
Training School for Nurses and Educators, 127
Transcendentalism, 63, 81, 82, 123, 125, 163
Tyler, Moses Coit, 72

United Kindergarten Mothers' Association, 171
United States Office of Education, 40
United States Sanitary Commission, 52

Vaughan, Benjamin, 76
Very, Jones, 62
Victoria, Queen, 128
Voltaire, 74
Von Marenholtz-Bülow, Baroness Bertha, 26, 27, 28, 29, 37, 66, 93, 99, 104, 113, 124, 127, 128, 137
Von Raumer, Minister, 28
Von Wydenbrugh, Minister, 27

Ward, Anna Hazard, 69
Ward, Samuel, 76
Weiss, John, 88, 124
Weld, Theodore, 37, 38, 55
Weld, Mrs. Theodore, 37
Wiebe, Edward, 24, 94, 102
Wiggin, Kate Douglas Smith, 102, 118, 119, 135, 136, 138
Winnemucca, Sarah, 120